SAVING FACE

Saving Face

Disfigurement and the Politics of Appearance

Heather Laine Talley

NEW YORK UNIVERSITY PRESS
New York and London

NEW YORK UNIVERSITY PRESS
New York and London
www.nyupress.org

References to Internet websites (URLs) were accurate at the time of writing.
Neither the author nor New York University Press is responsible for URLs that
may have expired or changed since the manuscript was prepared.

LIBRARY OF CONGRESS CATALOGING-IN-PUBLICATION DATA

Talley, Heather Laine.
  Saving face : disfigurement and the politics of appearance / Heather Laine Talley.
    pages cm
  Includes bibliographical references and index.
  ISBN 978-0-8147-8410-5 (hardback) -- ISBN 978-0-8147-8411-2 (pb)
  1. Aesthetics--Social aspects. 2. Disfigured persons. 3. Face--Social aspects. 4. Physical-
appearance-based bias. 5. Surgery, Plastic--Social aspects. I. Title.
  HQ1219.T35 2014
  305.9'08--dc23
                          2014009793

New York University Press books are printed on acid-free paper,
and their binding materials are chosen for strength and durability.
We strive to use environmentally responsible suppliers and materials
to the greatest extent possible in publishing our books.

Manufactured in the United States of America
10 9 8 7 6 5 4 3 2 1

Also available as an ebook

CONTENTS

ACKNOWLEDGMENTS

Faces are singular. No two are exactly the same. Yet faces often resemble one another, and in this way, they indicate our lineage or whom we come from. Likewise, this book is a sole project, but it reflects the contributions of a great many.

As a truly adventurous thinker, Monica J. Casper blends imagination and an appreciation for unique data with a steady infusion of classic sociology and emergent theory. Monica models how thinking and writing are inextricable processes. She has been a mentor and guide from the embryonic stages of this project through the final moments of book writing. I am most grateful for her steady support.

Laura Carpenter has proved to be a savvy sociological tour guide, offering priceless guidance about navigating the discipline. Steven J. Tepper has been generous in collaboration, and I have learned much about creativity, intellectual and otherwise. Jeff Bishop asked hard questions of this project that pointed me in new directions. Over the years, I have encountered incredible teachers who have fundamentally changed the way I think as well. Their imprint is on these pages. I am especially appreciative to Jane Simmons, Karin Peterson, Heidi Kelley, Ken Betsalel, Dee James, Karen Campbell, Ronnie Steinberg, Peggy Thoits, George Becker, and Richard Pitt.

Confidentiality limits my ability to thank all those who generously agreed to be interviewed and who proffered access to key materials, but the completion of this book depended on their participation and openness to the critique of the social scientist, which demonstrates a sincere commitment to ever-enhanced patient care. Special thanks to Allen Furr for establishing a key point of entry and for several significant conversations regarding the profession of sociology. In describing his work as a burn unit physical therapist, Tonas Kalil planted the seeds for this project many years ago. The counselors and children I met at burn camp generously shared their stories and fortified my dedication to engaged scholarship. Maureen Kalil shared stories collected over many years working alongside burn communities; her cooking nourished me at several points throughout this project, too. I also benefited from the work of Mona Frederick, Gayln Martin, and Sarah Nobles, who created a support structure for emerging scholars through the Robert Penn Warren Center Dissertation Fellows Program at Vanderbilt University. Throughout the process of writing this book, my students reminded me of what is most compelling about academia—teaching and learning. Special thanks to Sebastian Pope, Shana McClain, Mikayla Mann, Tatjana Moffitt, Devan Lalas, Nicholas Weitzel, and Zuleyka Hamilton, who invigorated me with their intellectual curiosity; to Kit Sudol for her sharp insight; and to Ted Coyle for book writing advice. The editorial guidance of Ilene Kalish and the comments of anonymous reviewers at NYU provided a framework through which I could reimagine my work. Their questions and suggestions have proved vital.

Conversations with scholar-teacher friends including Matt Whitt, Kate Zubco, Soma Chaudhuri, Sammy Shaw, Sarah Hanson, and Nicole Seymour have shaped my thinking and buoyed my spirit. Erin Rehel generously offered ideas about several chapters. Dan Morrison read every word, gently extended suggestions, and most importantly said: Keep going. Colleagues at the *Feminist Wire* and *Feminist Teacher* approach scholarship, activism, and teaching as synergistic, transformative practices. Through our efforts to do "the work," vibrant feminist communities have emerged. I am most inspired by and grateful to Stephanie Gilmore, Aishah Shadiah Simmons, Tamura Lomax, and Darnell Moore for our collaborations (a.k.a. life-giving feminist troublemaking). Lisa Jean Moore has offered equal parts reassurance and professional real talk.

In the beginning years of this project, several friends offered indispensable support including Gayle Parrott and Sarah Beth McLellan. Lyndi Hewitt provided critical insight and encouragement. Verba Roberson Holton served as an unparalleled idea collaborator. In recent years Vijay Das, Alex Fisher, Marcie Owenby, Alicia Randolph, and Marcia Ghidina interjected moments of pure delight. Kia Asberg, Brenda Clark, Carol McCrory, and Cathy Williams embodied unconditional support. E. V. VonSeldeneck and Aicha Xavier Mahr readied me for the next great thing. Sarah Jane Glynn emerged as firebrand friend and ally. Vali Forrister dispensed kindhearted dares. Ana-Helena Rodriguez Allen, Sarah Hutchinson Spalvins, and Millie Bryant were travel mates, from place to place and through life. This motley crew of friends has morphed into a gorgeous chosen family.

Chief among friend-family are Elizabeth Eve and Kathryn Cartledge, whose steady stream of love has changed me for the better. Keith Bramlett has thoroughly infused my thinking and my teaching with passion, self-reflexivity, and critical praxis, but more importantly in knowing him I found a model for living: Remain hopeful about what is possible. Work for a better world. Make life simply beautiful in the meantime. Bramlett and Phil Weast have fortified me from the very beginning. For the serendipity that has brought each of you into my world, I am most grateful.

Cullen Talley, Travis Talley, Christopher Flow, Lauren Talley, and Heather Hayes have offered treasured forms of support over the years—from house-painting help to sensible (much needed) advice—first things first. Sami, Marki, and Riley Reed sustained my joy. Morris Talley believed in my capacity to accomplish anything. And Pamela Flow instilled tenacity for keeping on and belief in endless possibilities. Each of you is deeply lodged in my heart.

Lee Crayton deserves special acknowledgment for wrangling technology and the pup. In our years together, we have intellectually journeyed alongside one another, ventured to change our corner of the world, and made home together. But more importantly, you have made me curious and hopeful about what's next. Let's.

Introduction

It's like if you're not pretty, you're not even a human.
—14-year-old girl in a personal conversation, 2007

In the summer of 1990, my tween friends and I invented a game. The rules were simply this: One girl posed a question, and everyone in the room had to answer . . . honestly. Our game worked differently from Truth or Dare, the ubiquitous slumber party game in which adolescents, most often girls, ask each other revealing personal questions or challenge fellow players to embarrassing tasks. In our version, players were faced with telling the "real truth" about *another* player. These questions had tricky answers. The game, tinged with all kinds of girlhood sadism, always ended with someone in tears. Most often that someone was me.

Some questions were fairly benign, such as "Who is the most fun to spend the night with?" There were moderately hurtful questions, like "If you had to choose one best friend in the room who would it be?" Of course, you hoped you were the one, but not every girl could be every other girl's best friend. So there was a sheepish camaraderie that arose amongst those of us not picked. But there were also questions that resulted in the articulation of a clearly delineated hierarchy. Sometimes, one girl would ask each girl to rank everyone in the room from smartest to stupidest. I was rarely the smartest, but I was never the stupidest, and so I don't know what the girl who was crowned "most stupid" really felt like. I can tell you that she shrugged and laughed and, well, said something stupid. Being perceived as dumb was (and still is) a viable role for a girl, and one that you could manage with humor in order to shake off any stigma that might remain from having failed the second grade.

Without exception, the game culminated in a question of the highest stakes: "Rank everybody in this room. 10 is beautiful, and 1 is ugly." Unlike being dumb, being ugly was simply untenable. During the 1980s and 1990s in my Southern Louisiana, there was no feminist consciousness around beauty culture. As a girl, I understood very clearly that any future worth having was contingent on being beautiful. My childhood dream was twofold. I wished to be very thin and very blonde. It seemed to me that if these two things were true, then everything else—a loving family, a beautiful house, a good job, interesting friends, and invitations to glamorous social events—was possible.

I knew of no other avenue for being happy.

Being asked to rank each girl in the room was a dangerous dare. If you were too generous, you would be lying. This was, of course, against the rules, but if you were honest, you could never take it back. Everyone would know what you really thought, but perhaps more terrifyingly, you would know what everyone else thought. I don't know what it felt like to be told that I was unintelligent, but I do remember what it felt like to be called ugly—not explicitly, of course, but numbers don't lie.

This was not the first time that the thought had occurred to me that I might be ugly. As a child, I always had a sense that my family was exceptionally beautiful. I feared I was not. In comparison to my blue-eyed, tow-headed blond brothers and my blonde mother, who was more glamazon than suburban mom, I had dirty blonde (emphasis on dirty) hair, gapped teeth that were not only crooked but as an oral surgeon explained later "entirely too small for your head," a decidedly pointy chin that appeared to me almost witchy, a forehead that seemed to take up almost half of my face, and gluttonously round cheeks. In family pictures throughout my childhood, I am often sullen. Sometimes, though, I'm protesting, sneering at the camera. I discovered that anger and sarcasm could trump sad. Sneering was a way to avoid crying. It seemed unfortunate that such beautiful people would have their picture tainted with my face, but it seemed cruel that I had to take the picture at all. I imagined that our neighbors upon receiving our Christmas card remarked, "They're really a beautiful family. It's such a shame about Heather."

When I look at childhood photographs, what I see is shaped by a vantage point that my ten-year-old self could never have imagined. I left Louisiana. I pierced my nose. I dyed my dishwater hair chestnut brown. And I am struck by how not ugly I was. I was not a beautiful child, but I was not especially unsightly either. The truth is that this is where most of us live: in the space between what is perceived to be attractive and what is designated as ugly. Regardless of where we find ourselves on the appearance spectrum, aesthetic intervention contours all of our lives.

Beauty culture—the shared set of language, meanings, norms, and practices focused on the cultivation of attractiveness—has received inordinate amounts of scholarly attention in the last thirty years, and for good reason.[1] In anthropologist Michael Taussig's recent examination of body beautification, he asks: "Have we not become blind to the force of the aesthetic, of beauty, if you will, coursing through everyday life? Surely beauty is as much infrastructure as are highways and bridges, storytelling and the Internet, rainfall and global warming."[2] Not only have rates of cosmetic surgery exploded, but other methods for optimizing appearance have proliferated, too. Skin whitening, cosmetic dentistry, Botox injections alongside other facial fillers, and laser skin resurfacing are on the rise, rapidly shifting our bodily (and cultural) infrastructure. Correspondingly, the desire to be intervened upon has solidified as a widely shared cultural longing, contingent on social class and access to resources. Research indicates that most of us would pursue cosmetic surgery if we were not financially constrained.[3] Cultural critics have crafted nuanced accounts describing the ways gender norms, makeover culture, heightened consumerism, credit availability, and global travel coalesce to make the production of beautiful bodies not only more accessible, but also more desirable. The irony, of course, is that cosmetic intervention is characterized as "elective" surgery. Studies of beauty culture seem to suggest the contrary—beauty feels essential or requisite in this day and age. Yet attractiveness is not the only longing that results in aesthetic intervention, and cosmetic surgery is only one method of managing bodily appearance.

This book is largely about surgical work that is labeled "reconstructive" and is overwhelmingly understood as necessary, not elective. As opposed to crafting bodies that more closely approximate cultural ideals, reconstructive surgery is aimed at repairing those facial features deemed untenable and even disfiguring. Such surgery is often more technically complicated, and it typically produces far less glamorous effects. When we consider so-called necessary reconstructive surgery alongside elective cosmetic surgery, we can see how appearance writ large, and not simply beauty, motivates medical interventions.

Compared to the prevailing appearance ideals, which in the United States prize whiteness, symmetry, prominent bone structure, and flawless, unblemished skin, I have an unremarkable face. It is not beautiful, but neither does it bear evidence of congenital difference or disease or trauma. Yet I have routinely purchased astoundingly expensive facial cleanser to ward off adult acne. I have bleached my teeth in place of regular dental care in the years of gaping insurance coverage, and I've undergone (and paid for) minor surgeries to remove embarrassing cysts. I have *not* done these things to be more beautiful, but rather so that I remain visually "normal." As someone who studies aesthetic surgery, I have a mental checklist of what procedures might produce an attractive effect. So far I have resisted the lure of cosmetic surgery, but I have invested financial resources, time, and energy to manage the other end of the appearance spectrum.

As a child, the fear that I was ugly was consuming. I am not unique. Research indicates that girls as young as six identify their appearance as their most pressing concern.[4] Girls dream of being beautiful—but perhaps equally important, girls fear being ugly. While the intense desire to be beautiful certainly generates insidious consequences, anxieties around ugliness can be taxing too. Moreover, race, ethnicity, and class amplify girls' aesthetic worries. When beauty standards are racialized and classed, girls who are nonwhite or who do not have access to basic health care (regularly dentistry, for example) must contend with the social devaluation of their appearances.[5] My own experience suggests that fearing ugliness is, at core, a fear about the future—as if a good life is exclusively determined by what we look like. While I fervently reject such conclusions now, my sociological imagination suggests that such sensibilities abound, and not only for growing girls. This anxiety persists into adulthood and becomes a motivating impetus to monitor and alter one's appearance throughout life. Bodily features outside the norm from birthmarks to acne to scars are routinely medically treated, pharmaceutically medicated, or surgically fixed. So much seems to depend on appearing normal.

Reconstructive surgeries often facilitate vital physiological processes such as eating, and in this way, the practice is unlike cosmetic intervention. Yet the most commonly cited difference between the specialties is that cosmetic surgery is elective while reconstructive surgery is needed. The cases described throughout this book—the surgeries featured on the reality television show *Extreme Makeover*, facial feminization surgery marketed to trans women, the medical mission work of Operation Smile (an international nonprofit), and facial transplantation (an emerging technology)—are not all immediately intelligible as forms of *reconstructive* surgery. Some cases explored here have been characterized elsewhere as cosmetic, while others more immediately register as reconstructive. For example, *Extreme Makeover* was promoted as entertainment prominently featuring cosmetic surgery. By contrast, face transplantation is generally regarded as the most extreme form of facial reconstructive surgery. Some might contest that these are analogous cases. Yet these practices share much in common besides a technical history. While this book describes four very different kinds of techniques aimed at four distinct patient populations, the explanations offered for why one would undergo surgery and the benefits promised of such intervention are remarkably similar across each case. Each approaches its work as a *necessary* intervention, signaling that the very distinction between optimization and repair, cosmetic and reconstructive, seems to be eroding.

In an increasingly appearance-focused culture, expectations of attractiveness intensify, but the significance of reconstructive surgery transforms, too. Beauty is contextually bound and the longing for cosmetic surgery is, in large part, motivated by cultural imperatives. As a sociologist would say, cosmetic surgery is socially constructed. What is less obvious, perhaps, is that the same is true of reconstructive surgery. Culturally bound appearance norms also structure reconstructive surgery. What bodies are deemed "in need" is shaped by the very same beauty cultures that inspire "looking your best"—or, in other words, optimization.

The appearance spectrum is narrowing as norms are intensifying. It is not simply that meeting the conventional standards of beauty is increasingly possible; it is that interventions feel increasingly necessary. Being attractive is not simply achievable; rather, it is often expected. This raises a critical question: What are the consequences of this cultural shift for those faces located at the devalued end of the appearance spectrum? Might the very emphasis on attractiveness that resulted in both my own childhood anxiety and the rampant expansion of beauty culture also produce a context in which more and more bodies can be labeled "disfigured" and thus stigmatized? The good life may be contingent on having a beautiful face. But living itself may be compromised by a face that looms too close to the devalued end of the appearance spectrum. This book demonstrates that conditions not historically understood as antithetical to life—ugliness, for example—are now treated in such bleak terms. As a result, aesthetic intervention becomes akin to lifesaving work.

1

About Face

The face is nothing but an instrument panel registering all
the body mechanisms: digestion, sight, hearing, respiration,
thought.
—Milan Kundera, *The Unbearable Lightness of Being* (1984)

In 1994 writer Lucy Grealy published *Autobiography of a Face*, a memoir tracing her life as a self-identified facially disfigured person.[1] The
book chronicles Grealy's experiences with facial difference resulting
from Ewing's sarcoma, a cancer of the bone and soft tissue. The cancer
metastasized in her right jaw, and the illness and subsequent surgeries resulted in a highly asymmetrical face. Grealy's book was a national
bestseller, earning distinctions as a *New York Times* Notable Book and
one of *USA Today*'s Best Books of the Year. Reviews praised the book
not only as an exceptional work of nonfiction, but also as a deeply
insightful account revealing what is it is like to be "disfigured." Given
the acclaim the book received, let's consider what it is about Grealy's
text that so captured critics and readers. What does *Autobiography of
a Face* suggest about the author's experience of facial variance and her
persistent attempts to "fix" the face? And more broadly, what does the
response to Grealy's story tell us about the vital significance Western
societies attribute to appearance in the twenty-first century?

Autobiography of a Face explores one young woman's bodily and
psychic suffering, but more specifically, it chronicles her attempts to

cope with facial disfigurement. At nine years old, Lucy Grealy was diagnosed. Following that moment, she tells us that her life was irrevocably changed. As a child, she began a series of treatments both to cure the cancer and to repair her appearance. *Autobiography of a Face* offers startling insight into the desire (and in moments, the compulsion) to "fix" the face. Like many others with faces defined as disfigured or nonnormative, Grealy's life story could be told through her medical records. Countless surgeries changed her face and ultimately her future. Most dramatically, the surgical construction of "pedestals," a procedure Grealy describes below, temporarily restored her lost facial structure:

> In the first operation, two parallel incisions would be made in my stomach. The strip of skin between these incisions would be lifted up and rolled into a sort of tube with both ends still attached to my stomach, resembling a kind of handle: this was the pedestal. The two incisions would be sewn together down its side, like a seam. Six weeks later, one end of the handle would be cut from my stomach and attached to my wrist, so that my hand would be sewn to my stomach for six weeks. Then the end of the tube that was still attached to my stomach would be severed and sewn to my face, so that now my hand would be attached to my face. Six weeks after that, my hand would be cut loose and the pedestal, or flap, as they called it, would be nestled completely into the gap created by my missing jaw. This would be only the first pedestal: the whole process would take several, plus additional operations to carve everything into a recognizable shape, over a period of about ten years altogether.[2]

Ultimately, though, each surgery failed to offer Grealy the permanent fix, the unremarkable or "normal" facial appearance for which she desperately longed. While her pursuit of bodily transformation relied on the same concerted attention and constant cultivation directed toward many kinds of aesthetic interventions, the significance of facial disfigurement imbued Grealy's bodily repair with particular weight.

Interspersed with descriptions of her interactions with the medical profession, we see Grealy as a child, an adolescent, and later as a twenty-something writer. Throughout the memoir, she searches for some sense of normalcy either through interventions that could repair her face or in relationships that could lend her some sense of self-worth. As a child, she worked in a horse barn. Of the experience, she writes,

> The horses remained my one real source of relief. When I was in their presence, nothing else mattered. Animals were both the lives I took care of and the lives who took care of me. Horses neither disapproved nor approved of what I looked like. All that counted was how I treated them, how my actions weighted themselves in the world.[3]

In her twenties, Grealy attended graduate school at the University of Iowa Writer's Workshop. There and in the writers' colonies that followed, she eagerly sought men for casual sex but with the hope they would love her in spite of her supposed ugliness. In adulthood, she was forced to look in the mirror after the doctors with their promised technological miracles had given up and the possible boyfriends intrigued by her tenacity and way with words had moved onto the next girl, one not so "different." The details of Grealy's story, and of her experience, are deeply shaped by cultural norms of appearance and gender. The face matters for everyone, but aesthetics carry a particular significance for women. Each of Grealy's stories centers on her constant quest for normalcy, her desire for male validation and love, and the fragile social status of women with facial difference.

Autobiography of a Face suggests that one's life is predicated on one's face and its relationship to one's sense of self. The "tragedy" of Grealy's face and the tragedy of her life become one and the same. She writes,

> There was only one fact of me, my face, my ugliness. This singularity of meaning—*I was my face*, I was ugliness—though sometimes unbearable, also offered a possible point of escape. It became the launching pad from which to lift off, the one immediately recognizable place to point to when asked what was wrong with my life [emphasis added].[4]

Despite an optimistic few final pages, it seems clear that Grealy's deep desire to be normal and valued will never be satisfied as long as her facial difference remains.

Autobiography of a Face humanizes Grealy, and in the process works to "normalize" facial disfigurement. As a memoir, the book offers an intimate depiction of Grealy's experiences. She speaks for herself, and her voice rises in stark contrast to the standard approach of talking *about* (others') facial differences. Be it the carnival barker who points to the sideshow performer with facial variance (the "bearded lady" or "elephant man") or the reconstructive surgeon who describes the techniques used on a face ("grafts replace scar tissue"), disfigurement is *talked about* in ways that position people with faces defined as disfigured as objects. By contrast, Grealy describes what it feels like to look different and how that experience inspires obsession with normalizing interventions. Midway through her memoir and after yet another disappointing surgery, Grealy makes the startling and bleak admission, "For the first time I wished I were dead."[5] Ultimately, she suggests that disfigurement is far worse than those with "normal" faces could ever imagine.

Perhaps the most gripping detail of Grealy's story is one that could not be chronicled in her memoir: Lucy Grealy is dead. The details of her death, most widely publicized in her close friend and renowned novelist Ann Patchett's 2004 book *Truth and Beauty: A Friendship*, are vague. Grealy was an admitted heroin user. Shortly before her death, she was committed to a psychiatric facility for clinical depression and suicidal ideation. On December 18, 2002, her body was found in a bathtub in a friend's New York studio apartment. Underlying every account of Grealy's death is the story of her face.[6] The drugs and depression may have facilitated her demise, but the story of Lucy Grealy's life and death is always and forever about facial disfigurement. In all of these accounts, including her own, it was her face that killed her.

But why is this explanation a believable and perhaps even appealing (to some) account of her death? The narrative that positions Grealy's disfigured face as the cause of her death rests on assumptions about what disfigurement means, the significance of the face in everyday life, and the supposed limits of living with facial difference. If facial disfigurement is unequivocally tragic (as it is depicted in so many accounts) and if our faces are who we are to the world, then life as a facially disfigured person is seemingly not viable. Reviews of *Autobiography of a Face* both reflect this assumption and reveal what critics found especially compelling about the book.[7]

In the *New York Times*, A. G. Mojtabai describes *Autobiography* as an "unblinking stare at an excruciatingly painful subject." A *Mademoiselle* review refers to the "horror" of Grealy's disfigurement, while a *Mirabella* review references her "unbearable fate." Reviews also suggest that Grealy's disfigurement provided her with significant, expert insights about beauty and attractiveness. A *Seventeen* magazine review notes, "Grealy beat cancer, but this almost seemed inconsequential compared to the horrors of coping in a world that measures a woman's worth by her looks." And a *Ploughshares* review concludes, "she makes a lyrical statement about the complex relationship between beauty and self-worth in our society."

Autobiography of a Face tells one remarkable story about the significance of disfigurement and one woman's deep desire to repair her face, but Grealy's story is not the only one. I tell a sociological story about the relationship between faces defined as disfigured and the surgical "repair" of these faces. As Grealy's life and the responses to her memoir demonstrate, facial disfigurement is socially and culturally significant. A physiological state and morphological condition, facial disfigurement is also a social status in the sense that it informs one's position in society. The power of a bodily state to determine a person's status is not unique to facial difference. Status is thoroughly informed by the body, and hierarchies of race, gender, age, size, physical mobility, and attractiveness are all attributes of bodily status. Particular categories or social locations carry more social value; others carry less. In effect, humans are varyingly and unequally defined and valued in accordance with our bodies.

The specter of disfigurement, however, saturates our collective imagination. It appears not only in *Autobiography of a Face* but throughout popular culture as a haunting reminder about the fragility of human bodies. Consider the ways facial variance is used as a plot device to signal a character's vulnerability in Hollywood films like *Mask* (1985) and *The Man Without a Face* (1993), or the young adult novel *Wonder* (2012). In these stories, disfigurement looms as particularly startling and an especially awful experience rather than as a variation of human life.[8] The significance of the face physiologically—as a mechanism for communication and as a means of eating, breathing, smelling, hearing, and seeing—accounts in part for the ways facial variance is routinely thought of as a particularly compromising disability. But it is a central argument of this book that in appearance-obsessed cultures, facial difference is treated as a threat compromising notions of self and identity and profoundly affecting social relations.

Consider the controversial British reality show *Beauty and the Beast: The Ugly Face of Prejudice* (2011), which pairs a self-identified "beauty addict" and a person with facial difference to live together for one week. Throughout each episode, participants suggest that life is essentially determined by appearance—albeit in very different ways, depending on whether one is considered ugly or beautiful. Ultimately, *Beauty and the Beast*, not unlike other television shows that take up the issue of appearance (and isn't all television and cinema, really, about appearance?), suggests that "disfigurements" undermine our social identity precisely because appearance matters so much and because faces are typically, especially in the West, uncovered and always visible.[9] This cultural matrix of body, self, and other provides the backdrop for this book, in which I take up what the face means and, more specifically, the responses facial variation ignites.

The Human Face as Sociological Object

It may seem curious to premise a sociological account on a particular body part, and yet this is exactly where I begin.[10] In doing so, I suggest that there is a need both to theorize "the body" as an experience and a social construct *and* to analytically take up the material body and specific body parts.[11] Consider, for example, that aesthetic interventions are disproportionately aimed at features like breasts and noses and very rarely at elbows and bellybuttons. Understanding why this is so demands not only a social account of medical technologies but also a cultural history of breasts, noses, elbows, and bellybuttons. The specter of disfigurement coupled with the importance accrued to physiological functions of the face imparts a particular social, political, and moral significance to the technical work of repairing faces. Here, I consider the singular significance of the face and explore how, within institutional sites of aesthetic surgery, facial disfigurement does not simply confer low status on a person but rather is routinely positioned as deadly. Ultimately, this book offers an ethnographic account of the meanings attributed to facial repair and the practices of facial intervention while also exploring the consequences for individuals and society of shifting meanings of aesthetic surgery.

The face, uniquely, is the locus of many organic functions and social processes. Physiologically, "face" describes the conglomeration of body parts including the mouth, lips, nose, eyes, ears, cheeks, forehead, eyebrows, philtrum (the tissue that joins the nose and upper lip), and the skin that covers these features. The face facilitates vital functions, most obviously eating and breathing, but it also mediates each of our "five senses" or methods of perception (taste, smell, vision, hearing, and touch). Thus, the face is a critical *functional* organ. Yet it is simultaneously a means of communication, a marker of identity and personhood, a signifier of social status, and a form of capital. It is no surprise then that bioethicist John A. Robertson would conclude: "Faces are the external manifestation of our persons (our souls?). They provide information about age, gender, ethnicity, and emotional states, and help to form the image that others have of us. Indeed, our face often provides the image that we have of ourselves."[12] The face, then, is akin to other body parts that enable critical organic functions, but it is unique, too, given its centrality in facilitating social life. As an object, it is thus ripe for sociological investigation of its material and cultural properties.

As a sociologist deeply concerned with issues of social inequality, for me the face is particularly salient for understanding difference and devaluation.[13] While it is certainly true that looks can be deceiving—many of the inferences we make based on another's face may not be accurate—every face-to-face human interaction is premised on the "social fact" that our faces tell us something about each other. The face ostensibly betrays our age, our race and ethnicity, our gender, and our social class. What the face tells others about who we are determines our status in social relations and systems of power. Its lines, colors, features, and adornment are all evidence upon which people are labeled, differentiated, and potentially stigmatized or celebrated.

Put another way, the face is a powerful biosocial resource, directly affecting what Max Weber deemed "life chances" or the opportunities one has to improve one's social standing.[14] Facial appearance, then, is akin to race, class, gender, citizenship status, and sexual identity, and as such, the face might be construed as a form of physical capital, a resource that can be exchanged for other kinds of capital, specifically social status.[15] Thus, facial appearance is a currency. Material results ensue from one's face, be they racial privileges or modeling contracts. Similarly, one's face can grant one access to a social circle, based on perceived ethnicity or class, for example. Yet facial appearance works both ways. While attractiveness can translate into high status, so too can facial difference undermine one's value.[16] Specifically, stigma can compromise a person's ability to trade on physical capital. In a real sense, then, we can talk of "uglyism" or "facism" as a pattern of bias that systematically disadvantages those whose appearance is at odds with dominant conventions of attractiveness.[17]

Our faces not only serve to rank us within the social order, but also work as mechanisms for communication and core facets of our identities. In the 2003 book *Unmasking the Face*, psychologists Paul Ekman and Wallace V. Friesen identify seven primary facial expressions: anger, disgust, fear, happiness, interest, sadness, and surprise. They argue that these are universal expressions, displayed by and recognizable to humans in every culture. Whether or not these facial features are biologically derived, as Ekman and Friesen suggest, this research points to the pervasive ways in which the face is an instrument of communication that can even transcend language barriers. Given the very fact that our faces are typically more visually accessible compared to most other parts of our bodies, our faces are the primary points of reference for those we encounter. Unless they are veiled or otherwise covered, faces are the basis upon which we are recognized, and thus the face is bound up with our social identities. We "put a name to a face." Viewed in this way, the face is both body part and critical social symbol, capable of mediating human subjectivity and public personhood.

Given the centrality of the face in social life, it follows that appearance, and specifically facial difference, are phenomena worthy of sociological inquiry.[18] In order to understand the transforming significance of appearance, among other concerns, this book examines interventions aimed at repairing facial disfigurement. But what *is* facial disfigurement? Disfigurement has no static intelligibility, no objective point of reference, no stable shared meaning. It is not a health status or condition clearly defined by, for example, the World Health Organization. Diagnostic criteria for "disfigurement" do not live in any medical text. Nor is there a shared collective understanding of what kinds of appearances might be deemed disfigured and what might simply be called unusual. Like "normal," which shifts historically and culturally, "disfigured" is also rife with multiple meanings. Yet despite the term's ambiguity and elasticity, it has a very definite, deeply felt social reality.

What kind of facial appearance counts as disfigured is subject to interpretation. Ultimately, experts know it when they see it, but what they see (or focus on) depends on the tools at their disposal and their institutional, cultural contexts.[19] As a diagnostic category, "disfigurement" materializes through the medical gaze.[20] "Facilitated by medical technologies that frame and focus the physician's optical possession of the patient, the medical gaze abstracts the suffering person from her sociological context and reframes her as a 'case' or a 'condition,'" according to cultural theorists Hsuan Hsu and Martha Lincoln.[21] In the biomedical sciences—for example in a maxillofacial clinic, a facility focused on treating the face, head, and neck—disfigurement is understood in physiological terms and approached as a target of medical intervention. The cause of facial difference is of primary importance in calculating how to proceed.[22] Congenital variance includes cleft lip and palate, conditions that result when the lips or roof of the mouth do not fuse in utero. In the United States alone, approximately 2,651 babies are born with cleft lip and 4,437 babies are born with cleft palate each year.[23] Probably due to ranging environmental exposures, rates vary by nation, but worldwide the World Health Organization estimates that cleft lip and palate occur in one in every 600 births.[24] Such differences are often surgically treated at birth, especially in industrial nations. In these clinical sites, facial reconstruction is also used to normalize appearance in cases of other congenital conditions, such as hemifacial microsomia (in which facial features are small compared with what is considered normal) or even Down syndrome.[25] By contrast, repairing facial difference resulting from illness (e.g., cancer) or trauma (e.g., burn injury) may be medically more complex. These forms of "disfigurement" are more likely to require multiple surgeries and highly specialized techniques. In medical contexts focusing on innovation of aesthetic surgery, such disfigurements are primarily conceptualized as bodily conditions to "fix."

Within mental health fields like psychology, the emotional experience of facial difference is routinely investigated. The picture of disfigurement painted in psychological research is stark—both self-image and social encounters are profoundly and negatively impacted.[26] Children with craniofacial anomalies are more likely to be ignored by their parents.[27] Facially variant children are less likely to be held, played with, and looked at by their mothers.[28] Worse yet, research indicates that children with facial difference experience more abuse than children with "normal" faces.[29] Disfigurement structures adulthood, too. For example, people with facial difference are significantly less likely to be hired even when compared to those with other physical disabilities.[30] Given the profound prejudice directed toward those seen as disfigured, it is perhaps surprising that research demonstrates that severity of disfigurement does not predict the degree of psychological adjustment.[31] According to social psychologists Nicola Rumsey and Diana Harcourt, "the extent to which a visible difference results in social disability involves a complex interplay of social and individual factors."[32] High levels of self-esteem, an optimistic outlook, a strong social support network, and meaningful social interaction all mediate the isolating effects of facial difference. This research suggests that extrapolating how someone with facial difference experiences everyday life based on the type or severity of disfigurement is erroneous. Rather, a range of intervening factors shape subjective experience, such that two people with precisely the same facial anomaly may experience everyday life quite differently. Ultimately though, psychological approaches capture individual experience with the goal of innovating methods for resolving the personal distress associated with disfigurement.

Yet facial disfigurement has been rarely explored through a sociological lens, and as such it is not altogether clear what social significance characterizes appearance disabilities, specifically facial differences, and how these meanings influence the work of experts who directly intervene. The central exception lies in the work of Frances Cooke Macgregor, a social scientist and photographer who worked as a graduate student under Margaret Mead. Soon after World War II, Macgregor met Dr. John Marquis Converse, a surgeon who worked on the faces of injured soldiers. Using Converse's patients, Macgregor began a sociological study of facial disfigurement, which resulted in publication of *Facial Deformities and Plastic Surgery: A Psychosocial Study* (1953) and *Transformation and Identity: The Face and Plastic Surgery* (1974).

Macgregor's work is remarkable in that she offered a sociological perspective on that which was often understood exclusively as a physiological or psychological problem to be fixed.[33] Her later text begins: "Facial disfigurement is one of man's [sic] gravest handicaps."[34] Throughout her work, Macgregor suggests that the face is so central to human life that having an atypical face is *a social problem and not simply a personal trouble*. Even Macgregor's *New York Times* obituary points to the extraordinary sociological significance of facial difference:

> As for those whose faces happen to deviate from the norm, there was and is, a special irony with which they must contend. Their problems have their roots in the inextricable relationship of the face to the person and its role in human relations. Moreover, it is a situation made even worse in a society whose frenetic efforts to look young and beautiful makes looking different a social stigma—a stigma that has the potential for social and psychological death.[35]

While facial difference is an overlooked stigma within sociology, Macgregor's work hints at how powerfully it affects those who experience it and how the social milieu intensifies the weight of appearance. Whether disfigurement is approached as a biomedical condition, as a psychological trauma, or as a social problem, facial difference is treated largely as something to be fixed, healed, and solved. By contrast, this book shifts the critical focus from the face itself to the complexities and social meanings of facial intervention, or "repair."

Facial Work and Sites of Repair

In 1955, symbolic interactionist Erving Goffman introduced the term "face-work" to describe a technique of interaction through which individuals gain recognition as social beings. Whereas breakdowns in interaction undermine the integrity of the social self, facial disfigurement is routinely positioned as a perilous social status. Aesthetic surgery might then be understood as a material practice of face-work or what I call "facial work," also aimed at facilitating social life. In relation to aesthetic surgery, the rationale to intervene, the designation of acceptable risks, and even what benefits are accrued to a patient are informed by the meanings attributed to facial difference, specifically a "disfigurement imaginary" or a shared way of thinking about facial variance and intervention itself. The disfigurement imaginary, discussed more fully in chapter 2, rests on multiple assumptions about the experience of disfigurement and the benefits of medical intervention, yet the ideological assumptions embedded within this way of thinking and the material interests driving intervention are largely masked within spaces in which facial work unfolds.

I use the term "facial work," quite deliberately borrowing from Goffman, to collectively refer to surgery aimed at repairing the face. Facial work is a complex and contradictory process wherein the face is technically repaired *and* what disfigurement means is negotiated. Facial work is not simply an interaction between a medical provider and a patient, but a social practice through which meanings about bodies emerge. The functional imperative in reconstructive surgery is most obviously repairing the human face, but facial work both relies upon and actively constructs meanings about the significance of the human face, the costs of disfigurement, and the redemptive claims and effects of science and medicine. This analysis lays bare the ways in which facial work relies on *ideological* links among aesthetics, disability, and medicine. In her book *Future Face*, Sandra Kemp writes, "Facial surgeons have historically been associated with the restoration of physical appearance as opposed to surgery that saves lives."[36] Here, I demonstrate the reverse. Facial work *is* portrayed as lifesaving work in the sites in which it is accomplished, rather than an intervention simply focused on improving appearance.

Each of the four cases analyzed in this book—the reality television show *Extreme Makeover*, facial feminization surgery, medical not-for-profit Operation Smile, and face transplantation—are engaged in the general project of surgical facial work. And although the faces that appear in each look quite different from one another, as we will see, all of the faces subject to interventions described here are perceived through the disfigurement imaginary. Thus throughout, I do not employ an a priori definition of disfigurement that emphasizes, for example, the loss of facial function or a radical departure of facial appearance from some mythic norm. The "disfigurement" examined here is less about what a particular face looks like—although it is that—and more about the responses the specter of disfigurement calls forth. While all four examples rely on surgery as the primary means for remaking faces labeled disfigured, the technical sophistication of procedures used in each site differs, as do the risks and consequences.

My analysis begins with *Extreme Makeover*, a superficial moment from popular culture, and culminates with face transplantation, an innovative and controversial reconstructive technique. Over the course of the book, the potential reach of each aesthetic intervention expands, as the patient population potentially subject to each technique grows larger. So too, stigma intensifies in each successive chapter. Importantly though, each example demonstrates the social significance of disfigurement and the shifting meanings of "vital" and "nonvital" in relation to appearance. By analyzing interventions alternately characterized as ridiculous and groundbreaking, cosmetic and reconstructive alongside one another, we can see how distinct forms of aesthetic intervention on the human face increasingly have something in common.

Unlike cosmetic surgery—an intervention regarded as elective because it aims to improve the quality of life—facial work carries a vital significance. If elective cosmetic surgery is a reaction to beauty culture, facial work is an effect of the disfigurement imaginary. If cosmetic interventions are consumed with the hopes of making the body more beautiful, facial work is tacitly treated as a lifesaving—as opposed to life-enhancing—technique, warding off a particular form of death. Facial work, though distinct from cosmetic surgery, is implicated in the exponential growth of medical products and procedures dedicated to optimization, one significant outcome of the biomedicalization of American medicine.[37] The emergent fixation on optimization depends upon intensifying individualization and an ever-growing emphasis on embodiment as a critical site of self-transformation.[38] The resulting biomedicalization of identity has established a slippery vocabulary, wherein enhancement is increasingly framed as a "need." In these sites of facial work, stigma has been biomedicalized such that the language of aesthetic intervention transcends "elective" and "need." As each case analyzed here demonstrates, medical practitioners routinely equate atypical faces with social death. This way of seeing difference is only possible because of broader transformations with regards to biomedicine and identity. Stigma takes on life-and-death significance, and thus becomes subject to biomedical expertise in entirely new ways. Put another way, biomedicalization makes it possible to refigure facial work as lifesaving work.

What constitutes death, material or social, is not as clear-cut as it might seem. Instead, death is a status designated when various criteria are satisfied. Multiple notions of death inform medical practice. In many clinical contexts, brain death is declared when a patient first demonstrates unresponsiveness—no physical response to pain and no cranial nerve reflexes, indicated by several measures, including fixed pupils and a lack of spontaneous respiration.[39] To be sure, the diagnosis of brain death informs how a patient is treated. For example, in the intensive care unit, the diagnosis of brain death often leads to the end of life support measures.[40]

But as I describe in greater detail in chapter 2, brain death is just one form of death that shapes clinical practice. Within sites of facial work, assumptions about disfigurement undergird medical practices. Specifically, facial difference is routinely treated as a socially deadly condition, and this way of understanding atypical appearance inspires both individual patient participation and collective support of the enterprise. Unlike the diagnosis of brain death, which is guided by established institutionalized protocols, facial difference is diagnosed as socially deadly through routine, largely informal accomplishments. Based on my research, I identified three criteria that trigger the implicit diagnosis of social death in response to facial difference:

1. Indispensable facets of human living including but not limited to economic, emotional, social, bodily, and intimate life are severely impacted.
2. The facility of essential social interaction is threatened.
3. Bodily features conceptualized as *universal* human traits are significantly impaired or absent.

In the four cases analyzed here, facial difference is attributed with these consequences, and as a result disfigurement becomes positioned as a (potential) cause of social death. Like brain death, social death carries practical consequences both in terms of medical intervention and in relation to social status more broadly.

Chapter 3 takes up ABC's *Extreme Makeover*, the definitive plastic surgery makeover show. In each of the 55 episodes, "real-life" people moved to Hollywood to undergo extensive aesthetic surgery to dramatically transform their appearance. The narrative structure of the show demonstrates how various actors understand a range of human experiences as contingent on appearance and approach facial work as a global solution to a range of problems, physical and otherwise. *Extreme Makeover* vividly demonstrates how the first criterion of social death—essential dimensions of life have ceased—is continually invoked when diagnosing and treating facial difference.

Chapter 4 explores another set of procedures aimed at "fixing" the face. In the 1980s and 1990s, reconstructive and cosmetic surgeons developed a set of procedures collectively identified as facial feminization surgery (FFS). The procedures are marketed to trans women for the purposes of affecting a "feminine"-appearing face. FFS is positioned as a vital intervention; the "disfiguring" effects of gender nonconformity are described as deeply threatening to social interaction. Given the indispensability of sociality to human life, potential FFS patients are especially vulnerable to the second criterion of social death. While faces subject to extreme makeovers and facial feminization are not immediately intelligible as "disfigured," participant/patients are routinely referred to as such. Taken together, these two cases demonstrate that what counts as disfigurement and repair is contextually bound. More importantly though, each illustrates how the disfigurement imaginary can be employed to reposition bodies using conventions of disability. Interventions traditionally understood as elective thus are reframed as necessary.

Chapter 5 considers the international charitable organization Operation Smile, which conducts medical missions to impoverished countries throughout the globe. In these countries the organization completes routine reconstructive surgery to repair facial anomalies, like cleft lip and palate. Prior to surgery, children occupy a deeply tenuous status due to both endemic global poverty and congenital facial difference. Through surgery, patients acquire the capacity to smile—an effect that is emphasized through the organization's name and promotional materials. Given that smiling is described as an essential and, in fact, universal facial expression, the facial work accomplished by Operation Smile is continually positioned as a vital accomplishment for children who are particularly susceptible to the third criterion of social death.

Chapter 6 examines an emerging biomedical technology developed to treat what is often referred to as "severe" facial disfigurement. Face transplantation is an experimental procedure in which a donor face is surgically removed and replanted on a recipient's skull. The procedure remains highly contested, with doctors vying to complete a transplant, bioethicists predicting devastating consequences, and a public simultaneously dazzled and horrified by the technology. Given that the side effects (including death) are framed as acceptable risks for treating facial difference, the debates about face transplantation explicitly convey the transformation of aesthetic interventions from life-enhancing into lifesaving work.

The first three sites of facial work analyzed in this book highlight how the disfigurement imaginary inspires "ways of seeing" that position patients as already socially dead or with social death imminent.[41] Notions of vitality routinely inform talk about facial surgery, and the practice of framing aesthetic variation as a deadly condition goes largely unchallenged by surgeons or patients. The final empirical site, face transplantation, opens up the question of the relationship between social death and clinical death. Just as the diagnosis of brain death has tangible outcomes, most notably the removal of life-sustaining technologies and the pronouncement of legal death, positioning living humans as socially dead has life-and-death consequences, too. Facial work demonstrates how the concept of social death shapes medical practice. More importantly, facial work demonstrates how conditions not traditionally understood as deadly can be reconceptualized as such with real consequences not only for those diagnosed as disfigured, but for every human navigating embodied life in an increasingly aestheticized twenty-first century.

Based on the four sites analyzed here, I raise sociological and ethical questions about the meanings of aesthetic intervention and the significance of facial differences. The specter of disfigurement, specifically the idea that human lives are not possible without a "normal" visage, lends itself to an imperative to repair. Repair is not *a* mode of coping; rather it is conceived of as the inevitable response. Of course, positing intervention as necessary is not unique to reconstructive surgery. Contemporary medicine is built upon its status as indispensible to modern living. Vaccines and antibiotics, dental fillings and Pap smears, are all deemed requisite methods for coping with embodiment in the twenty-first century. But in the case of facial repair, stories, images, and metaphors are invoked to characterize aesthetic surgery as not simply necessary, but rather as *vital*. Aesthetic intervention becomes more than the material practices of altering facial tissue and skull morphology. When the face is positioned as essential to human social life, aesthetic surgery is tacitly framed as lifesaving.

But what does it mean to characterize a particular intervention in such spectacularly vital terms? What are the consequences of this distinction? As medical anthropologist Emily Martin so beautifully demonstrates, conceptualizing women's bodies as machines or the immune system as flexible has shaped the very ways laypeople and professionals understand and interact with human bodies. Likewise, positioning facial difference as deadly and aesthetic intervention as lifesaving work marks the emergence of a new and profound metaphor.[42] To wit: In a new century characterized by widespread aestheticization and biomedicalization, what are the consequences of conflating facial appearance with "life itself"?

2

Facial Work

Aesthetic Surgery as Lifesaving Work

We can speak of all manner of living things as having faces.
—Daniel Black, "What is a Face?" (2001)

Metaphors that invoke the face abound. We take things "at face value."
Sometimes we "face the facts." We make an "about face." We "fly in the
face" of tradition. Ultimately, the word "face" is remarkable in its capacity
to communicate a wide range of meanings. This is not unlike the variation
and nuance that exists amongst human faces. We see faces everywhere—
on billboards, in the supermarket line, via social media like Facebook,
across the dinner table. In fact, faces may be the single most commonly
beheld entity in our daily lives, and yet no two are precisely identical.

It is curious, then, that the discipline charged with "studying society"
has virtually ignored something that so saturates and shapes social life.
The most significant theoretical exploration of the face in sociology is
contained in the work of Erving Goffman.[1] Goffman's "On Face-Work:
An Analysis of Ritual Elements in Social Interaction" first appeared in
1955 in *Psychiatry: Journal for the Study of Interpersonal Processes*, marking Goffman's initial efforts to understand mundane, and yet essential,
facets of social interaction. Its 1967 reprint in *Interaction Ritual* ushered
in a new, and what would become a core, focus of sociological analysis,
namely the study of face-to-face interaction.

Goffman defines the concept "face" as "an image of self delineated in terms of approved social attributes."[2] Put more simply, our face is our projected self or the self-image we deploy in interaction with other human beings.[3] Face is not inherent to an individual. Rather, as Goffman notes, face is "on loan to him [sic] from society."[4] Others respond to and, in the process, affirm our face, but the threat of losing face demands ongoing attempts to save face. For Goffman, "face-work" describes the "actions taken by a person to make whatever he is doing consistent with face."[5] Throughout social interaction, we routinely engage in face-work, and this tacit cooperation preserves our self-image and the face of others. Face-work may be an essential condition of human life, but it is anything but mindless behavior. Maintaining face relies on processes of avoidance (circumventing potential threats to interaction), defensive measures (guiding interaction away from particular topics and activities), protective maneuvers (employing discretion and deception), and corrective processes (fixing threats to one's face). Face-work involves calculation and social cunning. It is not consciously manipulative work necessarily, but it is deeply strategic.[6]

Without face-work, social interaction falls apart.[7]

Essentially, social interaction involves processes of meaning making, through which human sociality is forged.[8] The significance of social interaction cannot be overstated. Consider that the establishment of human culture relies on the emergence of shared meanings, which only emerge via interaction among humans. Traditionally, symbolic interactionism has focused on the traffic of words, gestures, and symbols, but the material human body is a highly significant though underexplored element of this process. Goffman employs "face" as a metaphorical concept, suggesting "the person's face clearly is something that is not lodged in or on his body, but rather something that is diffusely located in the flow of events in the encounter."[9] Yet face-work is a deeply embodied process enacted through facial expression and articulation too. Social interaction relies on the human face. Faces function as mechanisms for communication. Verbal language is delivered though the mouth; eyes, brows, and cheeks facilitate nonverbal communication. In addition, faces distinguish one person from another. Recognition is made possible largely by the human face, which we think of like a fingerprint— each might resemble another, but no two are *exactly* the same. It is the human face that is the locus of self-image and public identification, and as such the face is not merely a conceptual process but rather a material feature of interaction.

Aesthetic surgery is, in essence, a material, biomedical form of face-work. And yet more is going on here, both materially and symbolically. I innovate the term "facial work" to denote surgery that is both technically on the face and as such bound up with the various functions and meanings that the human face carries. While we tend to collapse corporality by referencing "the body," body parts matter differently, and unpacking intervention with regards to anatomy yields unique sociological insight. Instead of analyzing aesthetic intervention, writ large, we might consider the sociohistorical significance of different body parts in order to understand why some body parts command attention and management in ways that other parts do not. By reframing our analyses around "facial work" or "genital work" or "fat work," for example, we can consider distinct yet analogous interventions side by side. How might our understandings of body politics, biomedicalization, and embodiment evolve if we consider the ideological formations and technical histories that guide interventions on the same body part? What happens when we consider transgendering "bottom surgery," clitorectomies used to normalize infant genitals, and penile enlargement techniques employed by cisgender men alongside one another (rather than as disparate, unrelated inverventions) in order to query the significance of "genital work" and human genitals?[10] What do we learn about the sociopolitical significance of body size if we question the social construction of the "obesity crisis" and look at gastric banding for significant weight loss and liposculpting used to contour the thin body as analogous forms of "fat work" rather than as procedures for discrete populations?

In the cases of "facial work" examined here, human faces are work objects, particular for the actors who mark, measure, photograph, cut, rearrange, and stitch them.[11] And although both face-work and facial work are intrinsically social processes through which the social self is established, negotiated, and maintained, the medical interventions described in this book are simultaneously symbolic and technical practices in which the human face is materially reworked. Thus, aesthetic facial work is distinct from Goffman's face-work, but the concepts are theoretical kin in three distinct ways too. Both the interactional dynamic (face-work) and the material, symbolic practice (facial work) rely upon technical collaboration, ritualistic practice, and restorative procedures.

First, face-work/facial work is a collaborative process that involves multiple social actors who together are invested in the maintenance of face. Goffman suggests that social actors engage in face-work to create and maintain their respective faces. This is ongoing work and a necessary condition of interaction, without which a shared reality breaks down. Thus, everyone embedded in an interaction is invested in one another's face. Social interaction is obviously a collective undertaking, but the surgical repair of the human face is a cooperative endeavor, too. Social actors (human and nonhuman) including surgeons, patients, popular films and network television, technologically generated images, bioethicists, plastic polymers, news media, flight patterns traversing the globe, antirejection medication, and cultural narratives about the face come together to infuse facial work with the particular meanings and significance that it carries. Thus, both literal and interactive facial work is accomplished in collaboration. Neither the surgeon with her technical skill nor the patient with his desire for a different appearance accomplishes facial work in isolation. Face-work and facial work only become what they are in the give and take among social actors.

Second, face-work/facial work is an interaction ritual.[12] Goffman conceptualizes the self as a sacred entity forged through social encounters that require ritualistic respect. The process of social interaction not only maintains social order, but also fortifies the collective consciousness.[13] Facial work aimed toward repairing the human face is also a ritual of sorts. For symbolic interactionists, ritual refers to processes that solidify the social order. Repairing facial difference has direct effects on those who experience surgery, but because atypical faces often elicit social anxiety, aesthetic surgery has indirect effects on others. The intervention is two-pronged, then. Facial work not only normalizes facial variance but also facilitates social ease and, ultimately, social solidarity in structures and contexts that are deeply ableist. Moreover, because the face is imagined as so essential to making us who we are and to facilitating everyday life, the repair of the human face is routinely described as miraculous, a designation that invokes sacred overtones.

Third, face-work/facial work involves strategies to recover potential threats to social interaction and generate a shared reality. In everyday life, avoidance practices stabilize social order. Corrective processes or attempts to "save face" are practices of repair wherein a social interaction is fixed. Similarly, aesthetic surgery recovers threats that destabilize social interaction and undermine shared notions of reality. Specifically, facial work produces human bodies that correspond to shared notions about what faces should look like and how they should function. In the very process of identifying who is a potential candidate for facial surgery, notions about what constitutes a "normal" human face and which conglomerations of flesh, skin, and bone are not sufficient are established. Facial work, then, aims to recover a "disfigured" face or to transform facial difference into an appearance that is unremarkable or perceived as normal.

The Disfigurement Imaginary

Within our (Western, US-based) cultural imagination, not all bodily differences are one and the same. Sociologically, it is crucial to ask how ways of thinking and seeing shape our responses or interventions. Which bodies are in need of surgical repair, and what differences are deemed so threatening that significant risks are considered reasonable? To understand the relative responses to a range of disabilities, it is useful to consider the notion of stigma, another Goffmanian invention. Stigma is explored most often in the sociology of deviance and disability studies, the latter an interdisciplinary field that interrogates how social context determines what disability means and generates the devaluation of bodily differences.[14] A stigma is not simply a discrediting or undesirable attribute, but one with significant consequences in everyday life. Goffman writes, "We believe *the person with a stigma is not quite human* [emphasis added]. On this assumption we exercise varieties of discrimination, through which we effectively, if often unthinkingly, reduce his [sic] life chances."[15] There is no question that appearance shapes how individuals are treated, but here Goffman suggests something even more profound—that certain stigmas call one's very status as human into question.

Given the impending threat of discrimination, the stigmatized constantly anticipate and react to what so-called normals think about stigma, employing self-isolation, avoidance, depression, hostility, and defensiveness to navigate social interaction.[16] To a large degree, stigma is disproportionately managed by the stigmatized themselves, despite the fact that "normals" are deeply implicated in the process of stigmatizing particular attributes. Given that stigma emerges in collaboration, it is important to understand how "normals" respond to ever-present stigma. How do so-called normals cope with "abominations of the body" or visible markers of difference like facial variance? If social *reality* is the result of social interaction, what realities do "normals" make possible for those with facial difference? Ultimately, reconstructive surgery is an enterprise largely accomplished by "normals," and facial work, specifically, is a practice that reveals the role unstigmatized parties play in managing stigma.

For Goffman, face-work describes those efforts aimed toward recovering a potential threat to one's face or public image. Stigma, specifically bodily difference, is one kind of threat. This book explores reconstructive surgery as facial work. In characterizing medical intervention in this way, we can understand surgery as more than the erasure of congenital variance or the grafting of unburned skin, for example. Rather, surgical facial work is *a technique of social interaction and a material practice deployed to cope with bodily stigma.* A threat to face, the material and the figurative, is neutralized, and the fragile social interaction is reordered. Viewed in this way, aesthetic surgery is not simply an intervention with corporeal effects but a technique with distinctly social aims that is guided by cultural notions about appearance.

Medical intervention is always shaped by and deployed in response to cultural narratives about sickness, disability, and chronic illness. In the case of aesthetic surgery, what facial difference means, specifically how threatening it seems to one's social status, deeply shapes how facial work is talked about and how intervention actually proceeds. Facial work reflects the biomedicalization of difference.[17] Constructions of disability, specifically aesthetic difference, are embedded in facial work. As the following four chapters demonstrate, "biomedicalization carries *within itself* the ideological, social, and cultural infrastructures that support and maintain" a specific form of ableism—the disfigurement imaginary.[18]

Sociologist Chrys Ingraham, drawing on Louis Althusser, employs the concept of "imaginary" as a way of thinking about reality that masks political, economic, and social interests.[19] In order to understand the specific stigma that surrounds facial difference, I describe ways of thinking and talking about facial difference as a "disfigurement imaginary." Framing the responses bodily differences often elicit in terms of an "imaginary" challenges that idea that stigmatizing reactions are natural or instinctual and, instead, highlights how our ways of thinking about disability are deeply shaped by ideological interests.

Faces are treated as objects of intervention based on the meanings attributed to them. First and foremost, the disfigurement imaginary presumes the tragedy of facial differences. The experience of facial difference is positioned *as inherently horrific*, thus reducing a range of human experiences to one of suffering. Second, the disfigurement imaginary naturalizes a "fix-it" response. Aesthetic surgery is understood as an indispensible method of coping; thus disfigurement is positioned as an emergency necessitating intervention. Third, just as the disfigurement imaginary provides a lens through which to think about facial difference, it is also implicitly a way of thinking about medical intervention. In other words, the disfigurement imaginary understands facial difference *in relation* to aesthetic surgery such that intervention is imbued with particular meanings. If a bodily variation is thought of as a deeply threatening crisis, then the work of "fixing" that difference carries extraordinary significance. As I demonstrate over the next four chapters, when facial difference is viewed through the disfigurement imaginary, aesthetic surgery that ironically yields an unremarkable or "normal" face is described as lifesaving work.

Aesthetic Surgery as Facial Work

If the disfigurement imaginary shapes how people see facial difference, how do we think about the effects of surgery on the face? Put another way, how do the practical techniques of surgery—cutting the face with scalpels, suturing those incisions, and bandaging the face—change a human life? Throughout this book, I demonstrate that facial work is approached as a three-pronged intervention: as a mode of repair, a technique of normalization, and perhaps unexpectedly, a lifesaving intervention. There are several reasons to complicate how we think about medical interventions. To think about a surgery, for example, as simply a medical technology misses the emotional and social significance treatment holds for patients. Additionally, because intervention carries risk, treatments of all sorts are always enmeshed in a set of social meanings and ideological interests that operate in weighing the benefits of intervention alongside the costs. If we want to understand the emergence of, and to anticipate the future of, medical intervention, we must complicate how we see medical treatment.

At the most basic level, aesthetic intervention is aimed at repairing or "fixing" facial difference. When viewed as repair, facial work is akin to many basic medical interventions, like the use of an antibiotic for the treatment of a sinus infection or rotator cuff surgery to mend a shoulder injury. Yet unlike some forms of medical treatment, facial work is not simply framed as repair, but as a form of normalization. Facial difference is refashioned to approximate a new, aesthetically "normal" face. Obviously, facial work is geared to facilitate facial functioning, but it is also oriented to craft an aesthetic that more closely approximates cultural standards of appearance. Unlike repair, normalizing techniques often take on coercive dimensions for patient populations. In this way, aesthetic intervention is ideologically charged. In a social context which thoroughly stigmatizes bodily differences broadly and appearance disabilities specifically, pursuing normal is often experienced as requisite for navigating life.

It is not altogether surprising that aesthetic surgery is approached as repair and normalizing work, but what is striking are the life-and-death stakes that come to be associated with facial work. How we characterize medical treatments as vital *or* nonvital, lifesaving *or* life-enhancing changes over time. In contrast to innovations like the artificial heart, the iron lung, and immune isolation chambers that were explicitly oriented toward extending or saving life, aesthetic intervention has been traditionally understood in terms of (merely) improving quality of life. Yet in the case of facial difference, distinctions between elective or necessary, vital or nonvital are eroding, thus creating space in which to situate facial work as a kind of lifesaving intervention. This emergent meaning of aesthetic intervention is both connected to and generative of the shifting "vital politics" of the twenty-first century and a new "politics of life itself."[20]

Facial Work as Repair

Humans are a kind of "repairing animal."[21] Not only do we invest resources in repairing our stuff—cars, houses, laptops—we repair ourselves through doctors, therapists, and spiritual guides. The work of repair is simultaneously the work of rehabilitation, restoration, and redemption. But what and how we repair, along with the urgency with which we do repair work, reveals something about our cultural values. What do we believe needs to be repaired, as opposed to disregarded, and what reasons do we employ to justify the work? What values are implicit in justifications for why a face needs repair? What lessons about economics, citizenship, family, love, sex, community, and humanity are embedded in arguments to repair the face? Identifying what logics inform facial work—the repair of the human face—reveals what the face, and by implication disfigurement, means.

In Elizabeth Spelman's 2002 *Repair: The Impulse to Restore in a Fragile World*, she distinguishes between two forms of repair work. *Bricolage* innovatively pieces together both material and nonmaterial remnants to repair an object. The car is rebuilt with salvaged parts and mechanical know-how. Junkyard finds and the work of multiple mechanics restore it to working order, although its brokenness may remain perceptible. In contrast, *invisible mending* aims to fix an object so that it appears to never have been broken. For example, art restoration and tailoring attempt to mend art works or garments in such a way as to conceal decay and damage. Facial work involves both bricolage and invisible mending. It aims to erase disfigurement and in the process make a face unremarkable, but the technological limits of surgery along with the complexity of the facial structure mean that facial work more often resembles a kind of bricolage, in which techniques are cobbled together to make for the best possible outcome. In most cases, people defined as disfigured undergo numerous surgeries. The hope is that a more desirable form will emerge, though the reality is that a good enough appearance may allow for improved living. In this way, the realities of erasing facial difference often fall short of the fantasy of facial work, as in Lucy Grealy's memoir.

Repairing humans is often accomplished under the guise of returning people to basic working order. Bodily interventions couched in terms of repair are distinct from body projects framed as self-improvement. In the latter case, intervention is accomplished in the service of enhancement. Botox injections diminish the appearance of fine lines and, according to some, consequently improve one's appearance. Most understand this as an elective intervention. By contrast, repair work is more like maintenance rather than optimization. Consider most routine dental work. Rather than making the body new and improved, regular cleanings sustain the working order of our mouths.

In the context of aesthetic surgery, images of disrepair abound, most often represented through the "before" image. Before images are almost always juxtaposed with "after" images, displaying the transformation possible through facial work. Before pictures depict the face in its original "disfigured" state, and these images exist in a state of suspended disrepair inciting fascination, pity, and fear—a deeply problematic kind of human ruin porn.[22] After pictures mobilize support and investment in facial work because the image works as evidence that a possible resolution exists.[23] According to Spelman, repair is so compelling because it is a process that reestablishes our sense of order:

> To repair is to acknowledge and respond to the fracturability of the world in which we live in a very particular way—not by simply throwing our hands up in despair at the damage, or otherwise accepting without question that there is no possibility of or point in trying to put the pieces back together, but by employing skills of mind, hand, and heart to recapture an earlier moment in the history of an object or a relationship in order to allow it to keep existing.[24]

One goal of facial work is to restore appearance and facial function. The basic reconstructive techniques that repair a cleft palate, for example, rehabilitate congenital difference and allow for improved ingestion and, subsequently, better health. In addition, our image of human bodies includes a mouth that does not have a gapped palate, and eating food (without it entering the nasal cavity and exiting the nostrils) is implicitly understood as a basic human function. Thus, facial work also restores our ideas about how the world works and what it means to be human.

Facial Work as Normalization

Bodily difference is almost never construed simply as a variation of human possibility. In the case of bodily characteristics like hair and eye color in which variability is widely accepted, there are still ideals. Blonde hair may not be universally celebrated over brown, but gray hair is routinely concealed, revealing its relative devaluation. Bodily difference almost always elicits great anxiety and immense mobilization of resources aimed at refiguring and resituating it.[25] Over and over again, the variant body is subject to normalizing techniques that aim to establish, in feminist philosopher Julia Kristeva's words, a "clean and proper body."[26] Difference is normalized again and again, sometimes violently. From genital surgery for infants born with disorders of sex development to cosmetic surgery that erases "ethnic" facial characteristics defined as undesirable, medicine routinely works as an agent of social control, a biotechnological handmaiden to social norms.[27]

The word "normal" emerged around 1840, and within 15 years its modern usage was commonplace.[28] New modes of production and governance demanded innovative ways to classify, manage, and control increasing numbers of citizens. Modern statistics, aided specifically by sociologist and mathematician Adolphe Quetelet's normal curve, established a new point of comparison for human variation.[29] Human characteristics were measured and plotted, and in turn a notion of average, and thereby normal, materialized.[30] Embodying the ideal, as encouraged by traditional Christian doctrine, remained compelling, but excellence began to lose conceptual stability as the primary standard of reference. Instead, "the normal body," a fictive collection of averages, inspired an altogether new way of thinking.

In *The Normal and the Pathological*, Georges Canguilhem queries how notions of normalcy operate throughout medicine and science.[31] Although normal is a numeric category and thus seems to be a straightforward distinction, Canguilhem suggests that within medicine, normalcy takes shape alongside perceptions of pathology. A body that falls outside of the numeric norm is not treated as different, but rather as defective. Medicine technically intervenes and diagnostically situates human bodies using normalcy as a point of comparison. Basic clinical encounters make use of visualization technologies like x-rays and MRIs in order to discover bodily difference, but in the process, those bodies deemed abnormal are stigmatized. Medical diagnosis and treatment work as "microsystems of social regulation," in which bodies are made to more closely embody typical features.[32]

While facial work certainly facilitates repair, it is also a technique of inscribing or cultivating bodily norms. In many cases, aesthetic surgery cannot comprehensively craft a face that is perceived as normal. Often, disfigurement remains perceptible. Scars remain after a cleft is repaired. Skin grafts do not always preserve facial features like eyebrows. Reconstructive techniques can restrict movement, eliminating nuanced facial expression. Yet it is precisely because the human face is defined as a normative facet of human experience that people remain compelled to seek out intervention.[33] Despite what can be modest outcomes, facial work is made to seem compulsory. According to bioethicist Arthur Frank, in relation to techniques of normalization, "the possibility of fixing renders inescapable the question of whether or not to fix."[34] In other words, interventions that promise some semblance of normalcy ignite a "fix-it" reaction.

Optimizing body projects are largely inspired by individual "choice" and facilitated through capitalist modes of consumption.[35] By contrast, normalizing interventions largely operate outside of this logic. Techniques of normalization—from face transplantation to tissue grafting like Lucy Grealy experienced—are deployed toward making patients more "normal" and more recognizably human. Viewed in this way, facial work is not simply a biomedical product for consumers to purchase, but an obligatory intervention. As Frank notes in reference to surgery on intersex infants, people are "acceptable *only if* their anomaly is fixed."[36] The difference between elective body projects and techniques of normalization is that life is not made better—but rather in the logic of normalization, life is made *possible*.

Interestingly, normalization techniques like limb-lengthening and genital surgery for individuals whose height and sex fall outside of the normal range are increasingly critically interrogated, but facial work or aesthetic surgery remains taken for granted. Frank writes of the Hastings Center project "Surgically Shaping Children," which examined the ethics of interventions aimed at anomalously sexed, facially variant, and short stature children:

This critique of surgical normalization is difficult to apply to the cranio-facial surgeries that our project group saw. Our seeing again took place through the conventional medical rhetoric of before-and-after slides, and these slides like the word *deformity*, depend on normative visual convention, and those conventions need to be contested. Yet it would challenge most observers to see these pictures and not feel the appropriateness of this language of deformity. Faced with such faces, it is difficult not to affirm the value of surgery as at least an improvement in what are readily (perhaps too readily) perceived as life impairing conditions. . . . *The public visibility of the face and the symbolic importance that links faces to character*—exemplified by the aphorism attributed to Lincoln that after a certain age a person is responsible for his or her own face—*make facial deformity a problem of a different magnitude, and that difference commands our respect* [emphasis added].[37]

Frank rejects the term "deformity" and suggests that ways of looking and diagnosing, and corresponding ways of intervening, must be critically assessed. At the same time, Frank reveals that even in the context of a bioethics working group interrogating the ethics of normalization at the renowned Hastings Center, facial work retains a kind of inevitable status. Aesthetic surgery is essentialized as a form of repair, even as other medical interventions are situated in a context of social imperatives and critically assessed.

There is, then, something about facial "disfigurement" that makes normalization so taken for granted. Disability studies scholar Rosemarie Garland-Thomson writes,

Appearance tends to be the most socially excluding aspect of disability [emphasis added]. Bodies whose looks or comportment depart from social expectation—ones categorized as visually abnormal—are targets for profound discrimination. Bodily forms deemed to be ugly, deformed, fat, grotesque, ambiguous, disproportionate, or marked by scarring or so-called birthmarks constitute what can be called appearance impairments that qualify as severe social disabilities. Perhaps the most virulent form of body disciplining in the modern world is the surgical normalization of bodies that deviate from configurations dictated by the dominant order.[38]

While those subject to facial work might express a desire to appear more "normal," these interventions also function in the service of societal norms. For example, those with facial variance often experience employment discrimination. Thus, disfigurement and subsequent ableism potentially compromise economic security. Then, aesthetic surgery simultaneously normalizes appearance and counters economic reliance on social support systems. Facial work yields bodies that more closely resemble aesthetic norms and, in the process, crafts citizens capable of greater economic productivity.

Facial Work as Lifesaving

Extraordinary medical technologies like deep brain stimulation—an intervention that channels electrical currents through the brain, eliminating both the tremors related to Parkinson's and the euphoric mania and debilitating depression associated with bipolar disorder—are routinely described as "life-changing."[39] More mundane interventions, such as the hormones used to transition gender and to manage the hot flashes associated with menopause, could also be described as life-changing. The fundamental practice of medicine is focused on making our bodies "better," on facilitating transformation from one state—most often sick or bothersome—to another state—most often well or manageable. While many medical interventions produce life-altering effects, very few get characterized as "lifesaving." It is radically different to claim that something saved, as opposed to changed, your life. When we describe an intervention as life-changing, we are pointing to the ways life was made different. When we describe an intervention as lifesaving, we are suggesting that the very act of living was made possible.

In early 2012, criticism erupted after several online news outlets released graphic video footage of an injured boy who had been caught in the crossfire of Syria's civil war. The images are shocking because the boy appears to be conscious. His eyes are blinking as he frantically looks around a hospital, yet his jaw is completely missing, leaving a bloody gaping wound in place of the lower half of his face. Due to the nature of his injury, he cannot audibly express either pain or fear.[40] Media critics questioned the ethics of releasing the tape via social media. On a February 20, 2012 episode of National Public Radio's *On the Media*, journalist Andy Carvin, senior strategist for NPR, defended his decision to disseminate the video via Twitter as an effort to raise awareness about the human costs of ongoing revolutions unfolding in Middle Eastern nations. Carvin also hoped that the video might help in mobilizing resources to help the boy. In order to warn Twitter followers about nature of the video, instead of flagging the video as graphic (the industry standard), Carvin went one step further by describing the content as an "abomination." Carvin explains, "I shared the video because I thought it would snap people out of their complacency . . . There was something about this image, something about the numbness. His soul was already beginning to disappear at that point."[41] Andy Carvin's reflection is telling. While the boy is clearly alive in the video, the nature of his injury elicits a description that conjures metaphors of dying and positions the unnamed Syrian boy as in need of "saving."

Given the relationship of appearance to a range of outcomes, facial surgery repairs and normalizes in a way that fundamentally alters a life. A postsurgical face that appears, relatively speaking, more normal might facilitate intimacy with a spouse or economic security made possible through steady employment. Yet characterizing an intervention as lifesaving suggests that it accomplishes something beyond transformation. Life is not simply different and, presumably, better; rather, lifesaving efforts circumvent death and make continued life possible whatever the quality of that life. The meanings attributed to facial difference shape the significance of aesthetic intervention.

To be sure, in rare instances facial injuries or differences, including in the case of the aforementioned Syrian boy, result in death if untreated. But most people subject to aesthetic surgery are not at risk of dying, at least as we traditionally understand death. Yet as I demonstrate throughout the next four chapters, the disfigurement imaginary not only reduces the experience of facial difference to one of suffering but also routinely implies that the life that endures is hardly life at all. It is in this context that facial work is routinely characterized as a vital intervention. Disabilities are repaired. Defects are normalized. And appearance, it seems, increasingly is seen as a matter of life and death.

Surgeons, families, philanthropists, bioethicists, patients, and even journalists and media pundits invoke death both explicitly and subtly through death imagery. But this is a different kind of death than the one we most commonly think about that is largely dominated by biological measures and rubrics. If we encountered what we suspected was a dead body, our immediate impulse would probably be to assess the person's pulse. In doing so, we would be gauging a physiological process as an indicator about a person's status as living or dead. Most commonly, death is understood as the cessation of breathing and of heartbeat. In the context of medical institutions, brain activity constitutes another dimension of life and thereby death. While other vital processes may persist, brain death signifies that a body has no hard drive, no mechanism for communicating between bodily systems, and as a result no method for orchestrating vital life processes. Consciousness is yet another dimension of human living, and neocortex death or brain stem death signifies the cessation of mindfulness. In short, given that there are multiple dimensions of somatic life, there are multiple points of reference for designating a person as dead.[42]

Social death, by contrast, describes the cessation of social viability. The status of social death might be described as the point at which a person loses the ability to fill given social roles.[43] Social death is not a synonym for social ostracization or even dehumanization, though to be sure these are dimensions of the experience of social death. Rather, as sociologist David Sudnow describes in his study of dying patients, social death is the "point at which a patient is treated essentially as a corpse, though perhaps still 'clinically' and 'biologically' alive."[44] In this way, social death describes a profoundly dismal and subjugated status that is deeply intertwined with one's status as biologically living. Interestingly, research on medical care indicates that patients are implicitly conferred the status of social death in many treatment scenarios. Moreover, this designation facilitates and may even expedite clinical death given that treatment of disease or resuscitation efforts, for example, often stop once a patient is understood as socially dead.[45]

But how do we know social death when we see it? In the case of brain death, criteria designate what conditions must be satisfied in order to legally and ethically pronounce brain death. For example, in clinical contexts like the intensive care unit at many hospitals, cerebral and brain stem unresponsiveness serve as a basis for diagnosing death.[46] A lack of reflexes and a flat electroencephalogram serve as indicators that a body is "brain dead." As the definitive report of the Ad

Hoc Committee of the Harvard Medical School outlines, when these criteria are met, "Death is to be declared and then the respirator turned off."[47] Per this protocol, the declaration of clinical death and legal death depends on the technologized diagnosis of brain death. Each is its own kind of death, separate and distinct, and yet highly contingent on one another.

Despite the availability of medical technologies that facilitate vital life processes, particular conditions that suggest limited cognitive function over the course of a lifetime are often determined to be deadly. For example, lifesaving measures are not necessarily extended to brain dead infants based on the premise that they would be unable to create and sustain human relationships.[48] Lifesaving measures are dispensed and withheld in the confines of the intensive care unit based on the same logic. The likelihood of regaining the ability to socially interact is a criterion upon which doctors' decisions are made.[49] In the context of hospice care, patients come to the understanding that they have "lived too long," and families see loved ones as "as good as dead."[50] Hospice patients are subsequently positioned as socially dead; hospice programs also reject the use of lifesaving interventions. Ultimately, subjective understandings of death infuse clinical contexts impacting patient care. In short, dead patients do not need saving. As Stefan Timmermans writes, "Social death might thus become a self-fulfilling prophecy of biological death."[51] Perception of viability impacts clinical decision-making processes that culminate in death of the organism. Put another way, social death not only precedes but may also facilitate clinical death.

Most research concerned with social death explores how the status precedes biological death. For example, aging researchers Helen Sweeting and Mary Gilhooly detail how people who undergo hospitalization for a potentially deadly condition experience a period of limbo in which both the body and their social status are tenuous. Loved ones respond with anticipatory grief that results in a patient's social death. Biological death follows and is responded to with rituals of mourning, the goal of which is to concretize that a human is now dead. In their model, fragile bodily conditions compromise one's social viability, which culminates in the cessation of vital life processes.[52] Essentially, this book explores the reverse. I demonstrate how constructing bodies as socially dead makes it possible to construct interventions as lifesaving. In the case of disfigurement, the attribution of social death generates possibilities for intervention rather than the withdrawal of treatment or lifesaving measures.

Though there may be conflict between and among laypersons and medical experts about what particular statuses like brain death mean, as the highly publicized Terri Schiavo case demonstrates, criteria for clinical death or brain death operate in the spaces in which these forms of death are declared.[53] Curiously, what constitutes social death remains unformulated even as social death continually shapes clinical practice. Social death is made even more difficult to pin down given that it operates as a way of classifying human experiences of illness and disability, and yet not all forms of bodily suffering are reduced to social death. While a range of bodily functions (or the lack thereof) might serve as a basis for designating social death, not all kinds of impairments are conceptualized as deadly. For example, lack of mobility or capacity for spoken communication does not typically suggest that one is dead, biologically or socially. By contrast, within the sites of aesthetic surgery analyzed here, facial difference is continually described as deadly, both explicitly and implicitly. How is it that facial disfigurement but not mobility impairments, for example, carry vital significance? In short, what makes appearance impairments, specifically those of the face, different from other kinds of disabilities?

As science has elaborated techniques for warding off death and prolonging life, life and death are increasingly nebulous categories. The invention of "brain death" means that a person with heart and lung activity might be legally dead. Ultimately, death then is a status based on the cessation of processes deemed vital. By contrast, life is a status to denote flourishing or at the very least vital activity; metabolism, reproduction, growth, and adaptation are all indices of organic living. The distinction of living or dead is negotiable based on the interpretation of activity. Put simply, the same human bodies are subject to being constructed as living *or* as dead depending on what is at stake. Facial work is guided by a set of assumptions—namely, the disfigurement imaginary—which presumes that life with facial difference is not worth living. Ultimately, the disfigurement imaginary equates facial difference with social death, although this is certainly not the only way to understand "disfigurement." Equating facial difference with social death lays the groundwork for positioning aesthetic surgery as lifesaving. But what are the criteria used to declare social death, and in what contexts? How is appearance routinely positioned as a vital dimension of human living? The following chapters disentangle the criteria implicitly used to pronounce social death in order to understand the significance of appearance and aesthetic interventions.

The Politics of Noninterventionism, the Promise of Social Change

As I researched and wrote this book, I was asked one question over and over again: Are you for or against these interventions? Implicit in this question are two assumptions—first that facial work is either good or bad, and second that anyone investigating the topic could uncover the definitive answer. It is important to note that the voices captured in interviews and fieldnotes and represented in these pages are squarely in favor of facial work. In the early years of this project, I was unsettled to discover that my analysis reflected a bias that I came to understand as a product of my training as a sociologist of medicine and bodies and as feminist scholar with a definite disability politic.[54] There was edginess in my writing, and what I had to say seemed, as time passed, more scathing than I ever intended. I sounded like I was against it.

I was not the first sociologist of medicine to find myself at odds with the subjects of my research. Given the longstanding history of using the tools at our disposal—close observation and analysis driven by critical praxis—the field has not come off as a friend to the practice of medicine, not that it functions as a foe exactly either. Rather, combativeness is a byproduct of disentangling the consequences of medicine within societies that situate medical expertise as paramount. As many sociologists and cultural critics have found, it is hard to think about medicine without finding yourself taking on medicine. My biting analysis was only one product of this tension. My work reflected a related disciplinary bias too. If I was against (albeit unintentionally) medicine, I had to be for something. As a sociologist, the something that I seemed to be for was, not surprisingly, social change. The trouble is that as of this writing I do not find myself unequivocally "against" facial work nor simply "for" social change.

There is a common refrain in response to normalizing interventions: Reject intervention. Contest medical expertise. Focus, instead, on resolving the stigma or challenging bodily norms. As a sociologist, I want to query this call for nonintervention that has come to dominate some bioethics assessments and social critiques of science and medicine. Like facial work, noninterventionism can function as a quick fix, and this uninterrogated logic has particular consequences on real people's lives. Instead of defending facial work as unequivocally good *or* promoting social change over facial work, I suggest from the outset that we can carve out spaces to critique practices of biomedicine while empathetically supporting interventions that impact daily living *now*.

Medicine is an applied practice. Bioethics is a normative discipline.[55] The overarching question for bioethicists is: Under what conditions could or should an intervention be used? By contrast, sociology of health and medicine exposes the social embeddedness of an intervention and thus the problematics of normative judgments, and as such tends to be nonnormative.[56] For many medical sociologists, the central question is: At what costs to individuals and to society do medical practices proceed? In both bioethics and sociology, dissatisfaction with medical practice regularly results in conclusions that endorse social change over intervention. It is not surprising, then, that critics of medicine and medical practitioners often find themselves at an impasse; each has opposing commitments.[57] But what kinds of medical intervention would emerge from a generous collaboration? Likewise, is there a politics of intervention that values the tangible coping that biomedicine offers *and* challenges the assumptions that position intervention as necessary in the first place?

Over the last two decades as scholars, activists, and patients have increasingly talked back to medicine, one significant point has been made over and over again with regards to normalizing interventions—hegemonic social institutions and discursive structures inspire intervention. Nothing is intrinsically "wrong" with bodies, the argument goes, and medicine should not be in the business of normalization under the guise of repair. Sometimes explicitly (but often implicitly), those talking back argue that social change is preferable to surgery, prescription medication, or medical monitoring.[58] Some critics have argued that the cultural desire for attractiveness is so compelling that facial work is saturated with socially derived expectations.[59] From this perspective, the desire for facial work cannot be disentangled from the stigmatization of disfigurement. This framing operates as a basis for arguing that facial work is intrinsically unethical.

Rather than surgery, the solution proffered is complete social overhaul. It is not the face that needs fixing, but rather it is "the society" that deems the face abject that needs fixing. Such "solutions" are not uncommon, but the path for accomplishing this sort of solution is not altogether clear. This logic is problematic on additional grounds, too. Because medicine inevitably operates within society and is relentlessly social, no intervention proceeds outside of social norms. If intervention is critiqued on these grounds, then the entire practice of medicine is suspect. Rejecting intervention in favor of widespread social change reads as euphoric and reflects tinges of technophobia, a reluctance to see any progressive or transformative potential in biomedicine. These responses are essentially tautological too. Because appearance norms are culturally determined, facial work is imbued with the normalizing impulse, and medicine should not be the handmaiden to societal interests, but medicine is embedded in the operations of society.

Ultimately, the impetus to *not* intervene demands as much critical attention as the impulse to intervene. When we are critical both of biomedicine and critiques of biomedicine, our questions look somewhat different. Upon what grounds is intervention promoted *and* resisted? Who gets to say that a desired intervention should *and* should not be made available? For whom are long and difficult solutions—namely the overhaul of social norms—reasonable and ethical alternatives to medical interventions? These are questions not posed often enough, but they are the questions to be asked of self-reflexive, feminist, critical accounts of medicine to expose even the assumptions that undergird "critical" accounts.

While the disfigurement imaginary is deployed to push for intervention, its effects tinge noninterventionism too. Those who support facial work employ the disfigurement imaginary to position those with facial difference as socially dead and, thus, in need of intervention. In the case of critics who oppose facial work and favor noninterventionism, the emphasis is on changing society. In effect, critics of facial work dismiss the powerful effects intervention could have in the present moment.

In this way, being opposed to facial work disregards the experiences of individuals who are facially atypical and deeply desire facial work. Both positions reflect the disfigurement imaginary's stigmatizing and dehumanizing underpinnings.

What those who take a noninterventionist approach seem to disregard is that there are consequences of promoting the transformation of aesthetic norms, a solution that grapples with what ails us all, over and above facial work. And yet even as I recognize the limits of social change as a pragmatic response, I do not want to dismiss the spirit of these critiques out of hand. Perhaps more than anything else, this book reveals the ways in which living with facial difference is untenable not because of something intrinsic to the face, but rather something endemic to society.

When I consider my own answers to the for or against facial work question over the last several years, I see myself trying to stake a position that works outside of these two camps. Feminist philosopher Margrit Shildrick suggests a framework for moving forward:

> Critique is not destructive per se. Its purpose is to expose the shortcoming, the unreflective assumptions, the hidden contradictions and elisions of hitherto unchallenged structures; *to bring them into question but not to make them unusable* [emphasis added] . . . The point is that things could always be otherwise, and that the answers we give ourselves—often the basis for far-reaching actions—must never be allowed to settle, to take on the timeless mantle of absolute truth or moral right or universality.[60]

Instead of providing a framework to evaluate facial work, this book attempts to bring to light the "unreflective assumptions" upon which intervention proceeds. The point is not to make these methods of facial work unusable, as Schilbrick suggests, but rather to ask how things could be otherwise, and for whom.

If noninterventionism is an untenable and perhaps even unethical response, intervention cannot be wholly embraced as innately valuable and unambiguously compulsory. It is certainly the case that medical treatment might be conceptualized as the less worse option. Unlike spaces in which facial work is unequivocally celebrated like the facial feminization surgeon's office or the Operation Smile brochure, real-life decision making is often premised on choosing what is less worse when there appears to be no "good" option available. Undoubtedly, there are physiological and social reasons that inspire people to pursue intervention, but I wonder if facial work can unfold outside of the disfigurement imaginary. Is there another lens with which to approach aesthetic surgery? Facial work could proceed outside of a totalizing narrative that reduces difference to suffering. We could approach intervention as one method of coping rather than as a requisite response to bodily difference. In essence, facial work could be promoted and consumed as a promising, rather than an indispensable, method of coping. Facial work need not be understood as a lifesaving intervention, and those with facial difference need not be positioned as socially dead.

As the following four chapters demonstrate, the disfigurement imaginary shapes the way we respond to facial difference and the meanings we attach to aesthetic surgery. To position facial work as lifesaving imagines disability as acutely threatening and medicine as innately miraculous. The craniofacial techniques used by Operation Smile to fuse a cleft palate are most certainly a form of repair. Facial feminization is a normalizing intervention that often facilitates being taken for granted as a woman. Facial work operates, undoubtedly, as a technique of repair and normalization, always already bound up with notions of functioning and social norms. Must aesthetic intervention also carry vital significance?

3

Making Faces

Life Makeovers through Facial Work

Face, of course, is a metaphor. But it is a very powerful
metaphor.
—Thomas Holtgraves, "The Linguistic Realization of Face
Management" (1992)

In 2002, ABC introduced *Extreme Makeover*, an innovative and controversial reality television show that chronicled makeovers facilitated
through cosmetic surgery.[1] In each of the fifty-five episodes that aired
over the course of three seasons and in subsequent syndication on the
Style Network, real-life people (most often women) moved to Hollywood to begin surgical, exercise, dietary, and other cosmetic regimes.
Under the supervision of the Extreme Team (comprised of cosmetic
surgeons, dermatologists, cosmetic dentists, eye surgeons, hair restoration specialists, physical trainers, stylists, make-up artists, and hair stylists), participants' appearances were radically altered—in many cases
making them unrecognizable to family, friends, and themselves.[2]
    While the format of episodes changed slightly over each of *Extreme
Makeover's* three seasons, the basic structure of the show remained
consistent, indeed formulaic. In fact, while the participants vary, each
episode is startlingly similar.[3] As cultural critic Brenda Weber puts it,
the "strict formula" of *Extreme Makeover* allows a viewer to anticipate
what is coming in each successive episode, establishing a solid narrative about "disfigurement" and aesthetic intervention.[4] The show opens

by introducing "tonight's candidates." Cameras capture the landscape of their hometowns to give viewers a sense of their lives, but the majority of the introduction in each episode focuses on crafting a story about why the candidates need an extreme makeover.

Each episode devotes considerable time to establishing that the candidate experiences significant problems due to his or her appearance. Family, friends, coworkers, and the candidate collectively describe why a makeover is necessary. This opening set-up is quickly followed by an on-camera surprise—the candidate has been selected to go to Hollywood. The show shifts location to Los Angeles, where participants meet with members of the Extreme Team. Each episode chronicles these consultations during which candidates identify which bodily features they most desperately want to change. In response, the Extreme Team outlines what kinds of aesthetic interventions can "fix" problem areas. Within days, participants are admitted for surgery. Each episode features a brief glimpse into the surgical suite with fleeting images of the blood and gore that are an unavoidable part of going under the knife. Equally limited attention is paid to participants' postsurgical physical pain and homesickness.

Significantly, more time is spent displaying candidates healing from surgery as they meet with personal trainers, aestheticians, make-up artists, and fashion stylists. Each makeover culminates in a "big reveal" where family and friends see their made-over loved one for the first time in months. Without exception, family and friends are amazed and elated to see the postmakeover results. No doubt the process is quick and dramatic, but perhaps the most startling component of each episode entails the final few minutes, in which "before" and "after" pictures fill the viewer's television screen. The announcer enumerates the staggering number of procedures required to produce the postmakeover aesthetic. Extreme makeovers are focused on redoing a participants' entire look, but interestingly, surgical intervention generally fixates on participants' faces.

In October 2006, ABC broadcasted the first episode of the fourth season of *Extreme Makeover*, but no additional episodes aired during the fall season due to low ratings. In June 2007, the network announced that *Extreme Makeover* was officially canceled and that three prerecorded episodes would air in summer 2007 to fill a summer time line-up.[5] While *Extreme Makeover* aired on a major network for only three seasons, it irrevocably changed American discourse about aesthetic intervention—and, by extension, Americans' relationships to these procedures.[6] Specifically, *Extreme Makeover* animated public debates about cosmetic surgery, reality television, and America's enduring pursuit of personal transformation. Reviews of *Extreme Makeover* revealed both an infatuation with and contempt for self-improvement measures that are far beyond what is generally attainable.[7]

The outcomes of the makeovers were considered astounding, but most critics agreed that the show made excessive use of cosmetic interventions. In a scathing review, *New York Times* television critic Caryn James wrote,

> As a reality show it's a flop, with bad casting and the tackiness of a cheap syndicated series . . . As a cultural barometer, though, *Extreme Makeover* is fascinating. It displays both the voyeuristic excess of reality shows and the cultural ideal of creating a purely artificial personality (everyone goes to Hollywood) . . . We all fantasize about changing something, but these Frankenstein dreams seem spooky . . . television is shifting our idea of what cosmetic revisions seem normal.[8]

When ABC added the show to its regular line-up, even the Academy of Cosmetic Surgery condemned the show, releasing a statement objecting to the glamorization of radical cosmetic intervention parading as entertainment.[9] Critiques centered on the fact that while participants wanted to improve their appearance, they did not "need" surgery. The disgust with *Extreme Makeover* relied on a shared sensibility that cosmetic interventions for "normal" faces should be kept to a minimum, the assumption being that only in the case of "real" disfigurement would it be appropriate to try to effect such radical, transformative results.[10]

While most of the show's participants are not exceptionally good-looking (based on Western notions about what constitutes attractiveness), neither are they extraordinarily unattractive. In short, the faces that appear on *Extreme Makeover* would likely go unnoticed in public spaces. But not incidentally, the show's narration and the candidates' self-description routinely reflect the disfigurement imaginary. Participants on *Extreme Makeover*, prior to intervention, are described using words often reserved for the faces of those who have experienced facial trauma and congenital difference: "Freak. Deformed. Defective. Damaged. Monster. Witch. Cursed. Nightmare. Abnormal. Disfigured."[11] In explicitly framing the faces subject to makeovers in this way, *Extreme Makeover*, a site of popular discourse and imagery, implicitly positions itself as a mode of facial work, a necessary and legitimate response to disfigurement, and simultaneously operates as a spectacle of cosmetic intervention.

This book is not an analysis of cosmetic culture or an inquiry into the ever-expanding markets facilitating attractiveness, but beauty culture—its tools and effects—is implicated in the story of facial work. Historically and technically, reconstructive surgery and cosmetic surgery are kin to one another. Specifically, contemporary technologies of cosmetic enhancement arise out of techniques developed in the service of reconstructive surgery.[12] While *Extreme Makeover* and facial feminization surgery (which is described in chapter 4) are often described as forms of cosmetic surgery, this analysis reveals the ways in which both can operate as facial work. Potential patients are viewed through the disfigurement imaginary, and the intervention is described as requisite, which stands in sharp contrast to cosmetic surgery patients who are often positioned as consumers. In this way, both extreme makeovers and facial feminization are interesting cases to understand how disfigurement functions within modern aesthetic surgery.

The very fact that both extreme makeovers and facial feminization operate in a sort of in-between cosmetic and reconstructive space provokes questions about the "real" differences between reconstructive and cosmetic interventions. While the methods of cosmetic and reconstructive surgery are similar, the driving impetus of each differs. Those subject to reconstructive surgery are routinely characterized as in *dire* need of intervention. By contrast, cosmetic surgery is often distinguished as elective surgery, under the assumption that patients-as-consumers do not need surgery but rather want it. Most sociological and feminist accounts of cosmetic surgery take for granted the purpose of reconstructive surgery.[13] In this way, the disfigurement imaginary shapes even critical accounts of aesthetic surgery. These analyses rely on assumptions about what kinds of faces and bodies need intervention, and this "need" is assumed to be self-evident.

Yet doctors and patients alike may understand elective procedures as "needed," and of course those with facial difference often "elect" to undergo reconstructive surgery. Indeed, the line between what constitutes reconstruction and what counts as cosmetic is not altogether clear. This messiness is telling: When is intervention restoration? When is it optimization? When is it both? What are the stakes of claiming that something is reparative or enhancing? How is the project of healing related to the project of optimization? And how do both the disfigurement imaginary and consumption in a for-profit health care system factor into the decisions?

In this gray area, then, a face deemed merely unattractive may be redefined as disfigured, and thus in need of intervention. So while cosmetic and reconstructive surgery are technically similar, examining reconstructive interventions alongside sites positioned as cosmetic allows us to unpack the ways in which these distinctions are deployed, and with profound consequences. Characterizing faces as disfigured refigures them in relation to need, and thus animates the imperative to repair. In this way, the disfigurement imaginary can be deployed to transform cosmetic intervention into a practice that carries the significance of reconstructive surgery. On *Extreme Makeover*, the disfigurement imaginary functions in precisely this way, as candidates are diagnosed as socially dead by the fact that vital dimensions of human life are compromised. Importantly, these shifting meanings of surgery and faces are disseminated via popular culture, specifically makeover television, making this evolving narrative about disfigurement widely accessible.

Makeover Culture

A makeover is a quintessentially American venture, with its emphasis on self-improvement and diligence. From Ben Franklin's *Poor Richard's Almanac* to John F. Kennedy's calls for volunteerism, Americans have been encouraged to embody, often quite literally, innovation and industriousness.[14] As television scholar Robert Thompson writes, "If you had to describe the American mythos in one single word, 'reinvention' really would not be a bad choice. One could argue that from the time of the Pilgrims' arriving at Plymouth Rock, a lot of at least the European settlement story of America has been about reinvention, leaving the Old World for the New. It's American culture as the annihilation of history, of the past. . . . In a very real sort of way, the history of the United States is one big fat makeover show."[15] Perhaps not surprisingly, makeover culture focused on personal development and aesthetic transformation appears to be on the rise. According to numbers released by the American Society for Aesthetic Plastic Surgery, cosmetic surgery rates began rising during the same period in which sales of self-help books increased.[16] But why are Americans increasingly obsessed with transformation?

Sociologist Micki McGee suggests that makeover culture is directly related to the new insecurity of American life.[17] Lifelong careers are the exception rather than the rule. Work life is now characterized by stagnant wages along with erratic employment opportunities, and social welfare programs that promised a safety net in hard times have been severely cut. Family life is more unpredictable than in previous periods. With divorce as a very real and quite common option (at least for people allowed to legally marry), marriage no longer lasts until death.[18] Flexibility around socially acceptable family configurations, including cohabitation and queer partnering, means that the forms intimacy takes over the course of a lifetime increasingly vary, too. While flexibility makes it possible for us to pursue what feels resonant, insecurity and unpredictability also require coping. Ultimately, makeovers are a method for making one's self appealing and securing desired outcomes—a job we want, a partner we like, and psychological stability—in an ever-changing world.

Feminist critic Deborah Caslav Corvino suggests, "Individuals, seemingly ineffective in changing society, make a decision to change themselves. In makeover and plastic surgery narratives, choice typically involves discarding the past, be it an old sofa or, as in the case of cosmetic procedures, an 'old' face. This shedding of personal history expresses the self through the body."[19] Often, aesthetic makeovers are about ridding ourselves of what we do *not* want—acne, cellulite, wrinkles, jowls, markers of ethnicity, and other "defects"—in the service of achieving something else entirely. For example, erasing the signs of aging might be accomplished by eradicating fine lines and age spots, but this is often done in the service of retaining a competitive edge in the labor market or attracting a mate in the dating pool. In short, aesthetic makeovers are not simply processes of transformation but efforts at eradicating stigmatizing features. The stories presented on *Extreme Makeover* hinge on this dimension of makeover culture, and this feature is also what makes the reality television show similar to other sites of facial work, albeit a unique site of intervention given that the process of diagnosis, the treatment protocol, and the surgical experience are chronicled on film and subsequently broadcast to millions of television viewers.

In the last ten years, reality television has saturated the television line-up. When shows like *The Real World* and *Survivor* first aired, critics remarked that within a few seasons Americans would be sick of watching themselves on TV.[20] They were wrong. As of the Spring 2013 television season, The CW's *America's Next Top Model* is in its nineteenth season, CBS's *Survivor* is in its twenty-sixth season, and MTV's *The Real World* was in its twenty-seventh season. In 2003 and 2004, the Primetime Emmy Awards, arguably a reliable barometer of television culture and industry, responded to the surge of reality programming with two new awards for the genre: Outstanding Reality Program and Outstanding Reality-Competition Program.[21]

Reality television is a medium that blurs the very terms used to distinguish genre. Reality television is simultaneously fact, fiction, education, and entertainment.[22] While it relies on the continual negotiation of the very qualities used to distinguish one genre from another, reality television has come to employ two identifiable and predictable plot devices—chronicle and competition—in order to construct an intelligible narrative. First, reality television chronicles the life of the cast as it unfolds in environments engineered by television producers. For example, shows like *The Real World* and *Big Brother* capture participants' lives over the course of a predetermined period of time as they live in a made-for-television set. The thrill comes in watching cast members respond to factors that are introduced throughout the time they occupy "The Real World" or "Big Brother House."

Reality television participants not only live their lives on camera, they also compete for prizes. On *The Apprentice*, contestants compete for a job in Donald Trump's empire. Some shows rely more heavily on documenting events than on competition and vice versa, but almost all reality shows employ both strategies to capture television audiences. For example, ex-Victoria's Secret supermodel Tyra Banks's massive television hit, *America's Next Top Model*, captures mostly gangly, sometimes catty, often anxious teenage hopefuls as they pose their way through a variety of highly crafted photo shoots that mimic those experienced by "real" models. The girls also participate in bizarre challenges that purportedly work to pedagogically cultivate America's next top model.[23] As a formula, chronicling "reality" and capturing "competition" have made for successful television.

In the world of reality television, makeover television is an emerging subgenre in and of itself. Not only *Extreme Makeover* but also television shows like MTV's *I Want a Famous Face*, TLC's *What Not to Wear*, Fox's *The Swan*, Bravo's *Queer Eye for the Straight Guy*, Style's *Style Her Famous*, and E!'s *Dr. 90210* have created a pop culture landscape exclusively devoted to cultivating new appearances through aesthetic interventions. Reality television has established a reputation for enacting the unthinkable and the crass (think: Fox's *Who Wants to Marry a Millionaire* and its denigrated spin-off *Who Wants to Marry a Midget*), and makeover television pushes the boundaries, too. *Extreme Makeover* stands apart from most other makeover shows. As opposed to shows that rely primarily on nonsurgical interventions, *Extreme Makeover* routinely employs numerous surgical interventions with the explicit aim of making participants unrecognizable to themselves, friends and family, and presumably the television audience.[24]

Extreme Makeover was not the first television show to broadcast cosmetic surgery. Documentary style television shows of the 1990s introduced Americans to the aesthetic possibilities afforded by ever-emerging surgical techniques, but rather than focusing on individual patients, these shows relied on an Enlightenment-tinged trope that emphasized the promises of scientific medicine. By contrast, makeover shows like *Extreme Makeover* deploy medical technologies within a narrative centered on individual biographies suffused with themes of personal transformation and self-improvement. In both cases, television featuring cosmetic surgery makes intervention increasingly accessible culturally, even if it remains materially inaccessible. Viewers become acquainted not only with the "facts"—the procedures, providers, bodily risks, and financial costs—but also with particular meanings of aesthetic surgery.[25]

Makeover television advances a particular understanding of aesthetic surgery—that is, framing who needs such interventions and what surgical techniques can make possible. And the meanings produced by makeover television infiltrate the culture; thirteen million viewers tuned in to the December 11, 2002 premier of *Extreme Makeover*.[26]

Cultural critic Melissa Crawley argues that via plastic surgery television, people witness the "medicalization of real people's everyday lives."[27] But it is not simply that people consume medicalization as a form of entertainment; rather, the biomedicalization of the audience's everyday life is also intensified.[28] While medicalization represents the extension of medical expertise more broadly into people's lives, biomedicalization is constituted through a range of interconnected processes. In economic terms, biomedicalization represents the ever-growing relationships between medicine and other for-profit ventures, most often informatics, managed care, and technology industries. Here, corporatized entertainment joins forces with biomedicine, and this merger generates another shift indicative of biomedicalization. Specifically, human bodies are transformed, yielding new identities or, in the language of *Extreme Makeover*, "lives." This represents a departure from the traditional medical work of "healing" (although the very notion of healing is transformed in this site too such that optimization is refigured as healing). This site then opens up questions not only about facial work but about the "consequences of patients becoming consumers and biomedicine staging itself through the language and sales strategies of other consumer products."[29]

Extreme Makeover is acutely conscious of its audience. Experts who guide the makeovers of participants routinely address the audience directly. For example, episodes feature segments in which Sam Saboura, *Extreme Makeover* host and Hollywood stylist, suggests ways in which the audience might incorporate the advice provided to *Extreme Makeover* candidates. These recommendations most often focus on fashion, make-up, skin care, and fitness rather than surgery, but the segments reveal ways in which the show approaches the audience as potential makeover subjects. By inviting viewers to intervene in their own appearance using the techniques modeled on *Extreme Makeover*, the show incorporates pedagogical moves into its approach to entertainment. Viewers are not only voyeurs peering into the surgical suite;

rather, television viewers are tempted to consider subjecting themselves to aesthetic surgery. *Extreme Makeover* trains the audience about how to view, assess, categorize, and manipulate appearance—their own and, perhaps as importantly, others'. These elements of content and style, specifically the broadcasting of diagnostic processes, illustrate another shift in increasingly biomedicalized societies. Medical information and expert knowledge are increasingly accessible, transforming the role of patients who are charged with being increasingly engaged in what we might understand as biotechnologies of the self.[30]

Throughout each episode, *Extreme Makeover* instructs the audience on how to look at and attribute meanings to others' appearances. In an episode featuring DeShante, a middle-aged black woman born with cleft palate that was repaired in childhood, the announcer explains that although we may think DeShante is unremarkable, she is, in fact, *not*: "From a distance seemingly normal, but closer you see it—the deformity that has cursed her life—cleft palate." Despite appearing "seemingly normal" to the untrained eye of the television audience, the announcer urges us to reconsider what we initially see, and to redefine DeShante's unremarkable face as a face marred by a "deformity." *Extreme Makeover* plays the role of aesthetic arbitrator deciding who needs intervention. It does not matter that DeShante seems normal at a glance. *Extreme Makeover* urges the audience to see DeShante's face as one in need of a fix. Ultimately, the show incites viewers to see many of the faces that appear through the disfigurement imaginary.

Early attempts to define reality TV emphasized "real life" and the participation of "real people" to demonstrate that the genre captured "reality." Critics have denigrated reality television as a genre that purports to chronicle reality, but instead fashions an inauthentic or pseudo reality characterized by a producerly aesthetic. The question of whether reality television is real or not is beside the point; it matters only that the program makes the "discursive, visual and technological claim to be 'the real.'"[31] While *Extreme Makeover* is mediated (and thereby "fake"), in the sense that it relies on a cadre of experts to enact the transformation, the fact is that it purports to intervene in candidates' "real" lives. In this way, *Extreme Makeover* shapes viewers sense of what is real, both what surgery makes possible and what kinds of real-life appearances are in need of repair.

Makeovers as Repair

Not everyone is a candidate for *Extreme Makeover*. To participate, applicants must convincingly persuade producers that they need aesthetic intervention. But how does one make a case for an extreme makeover? The application process reveals that the language of beauty culture that surrounds elective surgery is forfeited in favor of a vocabulary of need. In this way, the intervention that takes place on the show is talked about in ways akin to reconstructive surgery. As described earlier, the language of disfigurement is used to describe candidates when they are introduced to the audience, but the disfigurement imaginary actually undergirds the application process too.

The *Extreme Makeover* application, available online via the ABC television network website during the years in which the show was in production, is an artifact of the show. Given that the show is most obviously about making over participants' visual appearance, it would follow that the primary selection criterion would be applicants' looks. But appearance did not speak for itself in the process. Candidates were not selected simply based on a photograph or even an application video. Without a doubt, appearance was a basis for selection, but as we will see, what an applicant looked like was not the only or even the most significant feature of a candidate's application. Throughout, the application subtly suggested the ways producers understood the significance of appearance and the vulnerability expected from those who were ultimately chosen to participate.

As part of the application process, hopefuls submitted both a written application and an audition tape. Many reality television shows require applicants to make a video that gives producers a way to gauge an applicant's television appeal. In contrast to other kinds of auditions in which attractiveness and magnetism are crucial for making the cut, application directions suggest that *Extreme Makeover* producers were actually seeking the opposite:

The videotape must meet the following restrictions:
  1. Tell us who you are and why you deserve the Extreme Makeover. Explain how your looks have affected your life and how they continue to affect you.

2. We are looking for fun and outgoing people who want a makeover. Please be creative, exciting, and personable when making your tape. We are looking for people who America will love and root for.

3. Make sure you shoot a 30-second close up of your face and profile with NO MAKE-UP . . . We need to be able to see what problems you have.

4. DO NOT tape yourself in front of a blank white wall or window. Make sure there is color or a solid background behind you. Also, make sure there is good lighting so we can see your face and problem areas.[32]

In most audition tapes, make-up and lighting are used to complement appearance. By contrast, *Extreme Makeover* producers required applicants to wear no makeup and to use lighting to highlight "problem areas." At the same time, these directions encouraged applicants to be "personable," someone the audience would want to root for. Given that candidates were coached to highlight their most unattractive features, the *Extreme Makeover* application process reveals how producers anticipated mobilizing the audience's pity. Positioning participants in this way dislodges *Extreme Makeover* from the rhetoric of glamour and beauty culture. Instead, the application process hints at ways the disfigurement imaginary frames the extreme makeover process.

In the written application, too, applicants were asked to identify what features of their looks they found chronically bothersome.

27. If you are selected to receive the Extreme Makeover, list everything you would like to have altered.

28. What areas or parts of your body are you most unhappy with? Have you always felt that way? If not, what event changed your image of yourself?[33]

In asking hopefuls to describe what parts of their face and body they most disliked rather than selecting participants simply based on a photograph, the application process suggests that it was not just appearance but rather the story candidates could tell about the experience of being "unattractive" that was important for being selected to appear on the show. Applicants were asked to catalog facets of their appearance they most disliked, but the application probed further:

29. In what ways has your physical appearance affected your life?

This question presumes that appearance operates as a compounding factor in other spheres of life. Thus, the very process to appear on the show prompted candidates to understand status, trauma, and failure as a marker of what they already looked like.

The application process was not a disinterested one, but rather reflected producers' sensibilities about what stories they wanted to tell. Not only was appearance given a particular kind of significance, but questions included in the application also positioned the makeover as a globally transformative process, as demonstrated here:

30. If you were to receive the Extreme Makeover, in what ways would your life be altered?

In asking applicants to imagine what life would be like post-makeover, the question suggests that makeover interventions contain the potential to comprehensively change a participant's life. The process of posing and responding to these questions allowed candidates and producers to establish a definition of the situation that stigmatizes pre-makeover appearance, attributes life circumstances to what one looks like, and fortifies the aura of the makeover itself.

A substantial portion of the application asked potential candidates to share information about their lives that was unrelated to appearance in any obvious way, but the information revealed played a crucial role helping producers construct the story that unfolded over the course of each episode:

31. Tell us about your relationship with your parents.
32. Tell us about your relationship with your siblings.
33. Tell us about your relationship with your mate/significant other.
34. Tells us about your relationship with your friends.
35. Do you belong to any affiliations or organization (charitable or community or otherwise)?
37. Have you ever been treated for any serious physical or mental illnesses within the last five (5) years? (Circle One) Yes No

39. Have you ever been treated for depression? In your opinion, what trig-
gered your depression?

42. Have you ever been diagnosed with alcoholism or any other drug-related
addiction?

43. Do you have any sexually transmitted diseases? If so, please describe:

44. When was the last time you hit, punched, kicked, or threw something in
anger?   Provide details.

46. Besides altering your appearance, what is your biggest dream?

In asking these questions, producers elicited information about the
emotional well-being, sexual histories, family systems, social embeddedness, and general aspirations of applicants. Over the course of each
episode, these details, which were ostensibly unrelated to a candidate's
appearance, assumed great importance. Ultimately, the narrative structure of each episode centers on explaining *why* a particular recipient,
whatever their looks, requires an extreme makeover—and quite often,
one's aesthetic is not the central thread in explaining why someone is
a candidate. In makeover culture generally and especially on *Extreme
Makeover*, problems that are extraneous to one's appearance are precisely the point. This "cataloguing of inadequacies," both of the aesthetic
and lived variety, positions the makeover as a solution to a multitude of
personal troubles.[34]

In asking applicants to continually connect what they look like to
the quality of their everyday lives, the application processes elicited a
working narrative about the relationship between appearance and life
writ large, and the sheer range of topics covered by the *Extreme Makeover* application attests to the gamut of stories that producers anticipated telling about appearance. While *Extreme Makeover* chronicles the
transformation of participants' appearance, every episode was simultaneously organized around at least one other narrative of transformation. Stories about candidates' emotional, social, economic, intimate,
and bodily lives comprise the backdrop against which the physical
makeover occurs, suggesting that it is not simply a person's aesthetic
that is changed, but rather something more global. Especially when
intervention takes place on an aesthetic that has been characterized as
"disfiguring," the function of facial work, specifically, is repair not only
of the face but of life itself.

To illustrate the ways appearance comes to operate as the explanatory factor for a range of everyday life experiences and subsequently how aesthetic surgery becomes a global solution, I turn to stories straight from the small screen.

Emotional Repair

A January 2004 episode features Art, a fifty-five-year-old seemingly average American guy—medium build, brown hair, male pattern baldness. In short, he looks like millions of other middle-aged white men. Within minutes of meeting him, the announcer reveals that Art's wife died five years ago and his grief has grown into chronic depression. According to the *Extreme Makeover* announcer, in that time Art has been "asleep in every sense of the word . . . Art needs to chart a change of course." Art's path to recovery begins with an extreme makeover. In Hollywood, Art meets with a cadre of surgeons, dentists, optometrists, and stylists that help craft a new aesthetic. At the end of the episode, Art concludes, "I'd lost the winning edge, and now it's back." Art looks different postmakeover, but the success of the makeover lies in its ability to restore Art's verve for life and to give him the push to remake his life as a single person. In this episode, aesthetic intervention is aimed at repairing emotional heartbreak.

In a New Years Day 2005 episode, Amy cries as she describes her life and the way she feels about herself. The announcer suggests, "Beneath the pock marks on this woman's face—deeper scars." She is intensely insecure. "Pretty is not what Amy sees when she looks in the mirror." She points to gaps in her teeth, her nose, and her complexion. She tells us that as a child she was made fun of. She used to scrape her face with steel wool to make her acne go away. Her acne scars remind her of the humiliation she endured. The announcer tells us that there are very few pictures of Amy growing up. "When I was a teenager my mother never told me I was pretty . . . I hated how I looked," Amy says. Understandably, she never accepts a compliment: "It's always there. It's always in the back of your mind." In describing the frantic scrubbing of her face and the hurt experienced as a result of her relationship with her mother, Amy emerges as a woman deeply enmeshed in emotional pain. After a series of procedures including a nose job, brow lift, and laser resurfacing, Amy declares, "For the first time in my life I feel like I have a beautiful smile . . . It really is a dream come true." Her makeover has done more than change the look of her face. The announcer concludes, "Amy's *life* has turned around."

Social Repair

A February 2004 episode features Regina, a recently divorced, middle-aged mother of two. Like many women in her circumstances, she has little time for self-care or socializing. She wears her hair tied back. Her wire-rimmed glasses are not particularly stylish. If she wears any make-up, it is not visible. Although she does not seem to invest much in her appearance, she wants a makeover. Regina explains that before her children were born, she prayed that her kids would not look like her. She tells her children, "I don't want you guys to go through the hurt that I went through. People constantly talking about you all of the time." In short, it is social exclusion that has led her to so desperately want a makeover. After a regime of cosmetic surgery, Regina remarks, "I am the swan on the lake. I'm going to strut my stuff." Instead of being the outsider, Regina anticipates a postmakeover life as the center of the party.

Later in the series on a February 2005 episode, the audience meets Ray Krone, a man who has experienced profound social exclusion. After spending ten years on death row for a murder conviction, DNA evidence exonerated him. Dubbed the "snaggletooth killer," Ray was convicted of murdering a bartender based on a bite mark found on the dead woman's body. His crooked, mangled teeth resembled the bite mark. The announcer asks, "Was his only crime bad looks?" Ray concludes, "My crooked, irregular teeth and my haggard looks, I think that led to the outcome of me being sentenced to death." Now Krone works as an inspirational speaker encouraging others to look beyond appearance. As images of the Hollywood makeover fill the television screen the announcer declares, "the extreme team decriminalizes Ray's outlaw looks." In addition to dental implants and a custom toupee, Ray receives a brow lift, upper and lower eyelift, liposuction, nose job, and laser resurfacing. "Our whole goal is to give you a more innocent look," plastic surgeon Dr. Griffin tells Ray. The makeover works as a way of erasing the social stigma of Ray's "criminal" past, which presumably impeded his ability to navigate the free world. To conclude Ray's makeover, the announcer declares, "Prison took ten years from Ray. *Extreme Makeover* gives ten years back."

Economic Repair

In a December 2004 episode we meet Bill, who cites his inability to function in public as the primary reason why he needs aesthetic intervention. For Bill, an extreme makeover promises to fix problems he has had while working as a manager at Home Depot. "Bill's shyness has held him back at work," the announcer tells us. Bill elaborates, "I deal with a lot of people. It's hard when I have to directly face them . . . I feel like they're looking at my big lips. I feel like they're looking at my big forehead, and I feel a lot of insecurities because of it, so I had to step down as a manager." One of *Extreme Makeover*'s star surgeons Dr. Fisher agrees that Bill needs cosmetic intervention, but not because he is ugly. In a consult before his surgery, Bill explains to Dr. Fisher, "A lot of people tell me I look angry." Dr. Fisher replies, "You have really heavy bones that make you look very intense." To deal with Bill's "intense" bones, Dr. Fisher suggests a collection of cosmetic procedures including a nose job, liposuction on his chin, an eyelift, and a sculpted brow sanded down in surgery. In *Extreme Makeover* terms, new bones promise to make for new job opportunities.

An April 2003 episode begins by promising the audience a look at a dramatic new procedure. The announcer declares, "New weapons target the world's most rampant disease." What's the disease? Acne. Tammy's face is red and inflamed. She lives "her life in a darkened room" working as a telemarketer. She admits that although she wants to be a professional dancer, she works a job where no one can see her so that: "They [coworkers] don't have to see me or be judging me for my appearance . . . I can just let my inside out." After a series of facial procedures including a brow lift, nose job, upper eyelid lift, and dermatological treatments, Tammy exclaims, "When I look in the mirror it's definitely not the same person from eight weeks ago. I have more confidence. I don't have to hide anything." No more hiding means that Tammy is primed for the work she has always wanted to do.

Intimate Repair

Unlike many *Extreme Makeover* candidates, Aimee, featured in a January 2005 episode, is *not* looking for a partner. She is married to a man who tells producers in an interview preceding Aimee's extreme makeover that he loves her heart and soul, not her looks. Upon seeing Aimee, her surgeon Dr. Moellekan admits, "Aimee is the most difficult case of my entire professional career." Her mother, echoing Dr. Moellekan, seems to imply that even she thinks Aimee is ugly: "I know she's a beautiful person, but I'm her mother." Aimee suggests that her looks adversely influence her relationship with her husband. He tells the camera that she has trouble being completely naked, suggesting that their sexual relationship is troubled. "She's always saying that she doesn't like herself," he says. And yet after a three-month stay in Hollywood and some fifteen cosmetic procedures, Aimee declares, "I'm ready to . . . walk out with confidence," presumably into the bedroom with naked self-assuredness.

Pam is a respiratory therapist, a real girl-next-door type with sandy blonde hair and nondescript facial features whose story is told in an episode that originally aired in November 2003. She wants a makeover, largely to entice her boyfriend. Even though they have lived together for three years, he has not popped the question, and she wants to get married. Maybe a makeover will give him the incentive he needs? In Hollywood, she gets her ears pinned back, an upper and lower eyelid lift, a nose job, dental work, and Botox and collagen treatments, along with a slew of body work. Two weeks after surgery, she is still extremely swollen. While her recovery proceeds slowly, her makeover produces the very effect she longed for. At her big reveal, Pam's boyfriend, who is waiting to see her, drops to one knee and proposes. More than the makeover, Pam seems excited about the idea of her upcoming marriage. Problem solved.

Health Repair

As a November 2003 episode opens, we meet Sara, shirtless, sitting on her bed. She speaks into her home video camera, attempting to convince the producers why she needs a makeover. Her left arm covers her right breast. A large scar marks her chest where a breast used to be. Sara is a "victim of breast cancer." Sara has "aged ten years" during her treatment, and she has also developed a deep sense of fear. "When I found out I had cancer, I was devastated because you think you're going to die," she explains. Sara receives a number of interventions including a facelift, laser skin treatments, and breast implants. The climactic scene of her stay in Hollywood is bra shopping, as if she is whole again: a sharp contrast to the vulnerable woman marked with mastectomy scars.

"By all appearances Rachel Myer from Colorado is a normal, lovely young woman . . . but appearances like beauty itself can be deceiving," the announcer explains in the opening for a January 2004 episode. Rachel looks "normal," but Rachel needs a makeover because she has alopecia, an autoimmune disease that results in hair loss. We are told that "Rachel is headed to Beverly Hills to be beautiful, *to be normal.*" In Hollywood, Rachel meets with the extreme team and undergoes a variety of procedures including a brow lift, facial fat injections, tattooed eyebrows, and laser skin treatments. What Rachel most desires is a wig that would allow her to go swimming and to "not worry if there was a wind storm." But a custom wig accomplishes more than diminishing Rachel's anxiety. According to the narration, "We're [the extreme team] going to give back what nature stole." At her reveal, Rachel concludes, "I feel like a person with a real head of hair." The implication is that the makeover has conquered the ravages of Rachel's disease and in the process repaired Rachel's life.

Social Death in Makeover Culture

As the episodes described above demonstrate, the intervention that takes place on *Extreme Makeover* is not offered to participants simply as a life-enhancing intervention, but rather as a method of repair.[35] Reality is the problem, and television (or rather, televised medicine) offers the solution. But how is it that the facial work that transpires on *Extreme Makeover* functions as a multifaceted and far-reaching mode of repair? For example, how does a new face make for more satisfying intimacy or a nose job help a spouse grieve the loss of his wife? How does laser resurfacing absolve the humiliation of childhood torment or facial surgery resolve the experience of breast cancer? How does an eye lift facilitate a more resonant career? How does aesthetic intervention operate as a technique of social, intimate, economic, emotional, and health repair? The answer lies in the ways participants are situated within the disfigurement imaginary such that their life circumstances are interpreted within a framework of social death. Without intervention, we're told, these people are as good as dead. The narrative is made possible by the norms of the reality television genre.

Reality television has been hailed as a profoundly democratic medium—for the people, by the people, and about the people.[36] As cultural critic Mark Andrejevic explains, participants do the work of being watched, and reality television relies on "a form of production wherein consumers are invited to sell access to their personal lives in a way not dissimilar to that in which they sell their labor power."[37] The medium is seemingly democratic in the sense anyone can do this kind of performative labor, and shows do not typically exclude participants based on educational attainment or experience. In this medium, though, participation is only possible in exchange for exposure and vulnerability. The radio and television program *Queen For a Day* (1945) popularized this narrative. Throughout its twenty-five year run, the show featured interviews between the host and female contestants, which culminated in questions about financial and emotional hardships. The winning contestant was chosen by the Applause Meter, which measured the studio audience's response to each woman's story. Routinely, the woman describing the harshest circumstances and expressing the most palpable suffering (think sobbing) ignited the loudest applause and thereby won. On the television version, the winner was draped with a red velvet cape, escorted to a gold gilded throne, bedecked with a rhinestone crown, and presented with a bouquet of roses. She was then presented with prizes—a washing machine or similar appliances, a trip away for her and her husband, or stylish fashions—all provided by the show's corporate sponsors. Runners-up left with consolation prizes, a form of remuneration nonetheless.[38] While television blogger Mark Evanier has described this format as "utterly degrading to the human spirit," compensation for vulnerability persists especially on makeover television and uniquely so on *Extreme Makeover*.[39]

When television makeovers function as a reward on shows from *The Ellen DeGeneres Show* to NBC's *Today Show*, aesthetic intervention is used as a prize for a participant's life of meaningful work—exceptional mothering, community organizing, extraordinary volunteering.[40] Makeover candidates are "normal" folks who, like everyone else presumably, could look better through the efforts of experts. The makeover is a fun and compelling enterprise wherein daily obligations are put on hold and access to services is provided yielding a new and improved look, even as participants are often required to appear on television bare faced and in everyday frumpy attire. But on *Extreme Makeover*, surgery does not function as a reward. Rather like on *Queen for a Day*, participation requires a tragic story. As the application for participation suggests, one trades vulnerability for access to interventions. Specifically, participants—their appearance and the stories of their lives—become mired in the disfigurement imaginary. As a result, extreme makeovers are not indulgences, as makeovers are on other television programs, but rather extreme makeovers operate as repair. Life, the show suggests, hangs in the balance.

Documentary television that features behind the scenes images of surgery has been described as "trauma TV."[41] Like other plastic surgery shows, *Extreme Makeover* documents the bodily wounding that is part and parcel to any surgical procedure. Describing surgery television as trauma TV also points to the effect graphic depictions have on an audience. In fact, the entire experience, not simply the surgery, could be understood as traumatic. Here, "trauma" refers to bodily or psychic injury often inflicted from an external source that compromises well-being. The plotline of the show could be described as "traumatic" too. Participants often struggle alone with the effects of profound isolation and the pain of cosmetic interventions. The narrative constructed on *Extreme Makeover* capitalizes on life events regularly characterized as "traumatic" (death of a spouse, a miscarriage of justice, profound social isolation, memories of school yard bullying), and the show requires participants to continually offer detailed and sensational accounts of painful experiences. In this way, the show not only relies on stories of trauma, but arguably it produces a trauma all of its own by exposing participants to emotionally vexing and physically invasive procedures. In this way, the show uses "trauma" strategically. Critical trauma studies scholar Maurice Stevens writes,

When we imagine we are "seeing" trauma or the signs of its passage, we know immediately that something spectacular and catastrophic has transpired and we fear, also with a sense of immediacy, that normal systems for understanding the event and any of its survivors will be overwhelmed and rendered incapable of adequately capturing its immensity or the subtlety of its sublime pervasiveness.[42]

In other words, trauma makes us pay attention and anticipate what is coming next. Even improvement is gauged by invoking participants' trauma, as when the *Extreme Makeover* announcer declares, "A lifetime of heartache mended and healed."[43]

"Trauma" and its diagnostic kin posttraumatic stress disorder (PTSD) saturate our lexicon in unprecedented ways, but critical trauma theorists analyze what counts as trauma, who successfully makes claims to trauma, and what the symbolic and material consequences of labeling an experience "traumatic" are. The processes of invoking trauma on the show (and even of describing *Extreme Makeover* as "trauma TV") function strategically. Of the ways trauma is deployed, sociologist Monica Casper writes,

Trauma reveals, unsettles, and/or reaffirms social classification systems. Thus, "trauma" has as much to say about history, social relations, politics, and cultural meanings as it does about discrete events or experiences (Simmons and Casper 2012). Moreover, in theorizing disruptions, breaks, shocks, and ruptures, "trauma" marks a deviation from situations that are perceived as normal or mundane. The naming of something—an experience, a memory, an encounter, an interaction—as trauma denotes a before and after, a changed subjectivity, a revised embodiment.[44]

Extreme Makeover may be a critically panned, over the top, "cheesy" reality television show, but by embedding its narrative in notions of trauma, the abnormal status of participants is reified and the intervention escapes associations with other, arguably more frivolous, makeover shows. The invocation of trauma bolsters the disfigurement imaginary, which helps the interventions come off as "real" facial work. In effect, trauma strategically functions to overcome the show's farcical elements.

Undoubtedly, *Extreme Makeover* engages in the work of "eradicate[ing] embodied anxieties."[45] To be fair, cosmetic surgery has always framed its work on appearance as an intervention in the service of psychological wellness. In fact, cosmetic surgery only emerged as a respectable medical specialty when cosmetic interventions were situated within prevailing discourses about medicine's therapeutic or healing function. Stakeholders, specifically surgeons, initially put forward the idea that changing a patient's outer appearance profoundly impacted a patient's well-being. Gradually, professional associations acquiesced.[46] Viewed in this way, cosmetic surgery operates on logic similar to psychiatry. Instead of prescription medications, cosmetic surgeons utilize scalpels. Instead of conversation about a patient's emotional state, cosmetic surgeons talk with patients about what needs changing while viewing "before" pictures (as if these pictures speak for themselves). Both enterprises use medical techniques to intervene in extraneous features of a patient's life. Yet psychopharmaceuticals aimed at brain chemistry or talk therapy focused on patients' perceptions are decidedly targeted at the source of a problem. By contrast, *Extreme Makeover* uses aesthetic surgery as a means for repairing psychological well-being alongside financial, social, intimate, emotional, and bodily facets of life.

While the program technically transforms the faces of makeover candidates, it simultaneously proliferates collective understandings about what aesthetic intervention can (and should) accomplish. The intense narrative work invested in explaining *why* candidates need surgery centers on facets of the candidates' lives that are not working. Being unattractive is *not* a sufficient reason for receiving an extreme makeover. Rather, recipients' facial appearance is made over in the service of transforming—or more specifically, repairing—their lives. It is because extreme makeovers are projects of repair that they are prefaced by a story of defeat or destruction. *Extreme Makeover* stories outline the financial, emotional, intimate, and health problems experienced by candidates. In any sociological framing, these would be seen as social problems. Yet the makeover works as a superficial repair mechanism: aesthetic solutions for life's impasses.

Extreme Makeover ends a makeover declaring, "Mission Accomplished!" as if radical transformation happens instantaneously via aesthetic intervention. Whether this happens or not is unclear, but undoubtedly this is what both experts and makeover participants claim at the end of an episode. As these shows continually frame psychologi-cal well-being and bodily health along with work, family, and intimate life as fundamentally dependent on one's appearance, these shows help to propagate "endless insufficiency."[47] *Extreme Makeover* predicates all other projects of self-improvement on a desirable aesthetic. If every facet of our lives depends on our appearance, it is *the* most important facet of ourselves, and one worth investing incredible resources into repairing. All else will fall into place postmakeover, or so it is claimed.

Self-improvement narratives, generally, rely on notions of inad-equacy and sometimes deficiency. Financial guides assume that the reader does not know enough about economics. Dating books assume that the reader does not grasp how successful social interactions should proceed. What makes *Extreme Makeover* unique is that it approaches the participants as aesthetically inadequate, but rather than positing that appearance interventions will make the participant more attractive, the show goes much further. In fact, the show suggests that an entire life is made over as an effect of the alteration of appearance. Part and parcel to being viewed within the disfigurement imaginary is that candidates' very existences are depicted as fragile. *Extreme Makeover* suggests that participants' preexisting faces perilously impact indispensable facets of human living. In this way, they are socially dead. In reaction to stories of compromised lives, appearance is stigmatized, and a "fix-it" reaction emerges. Aesthetic intervention is credited with staving off social death.

The degree to which aesthetic makeovers can work in the service of repair, writ large, is a question. While appearance undoubtedly shapes all areas of social life, can aesthetic intervention repair lives in the ways *Extreme Makeover* suggests that it can? And perhaps more importantly, what are the consequences of positioning facial appearance as socially deadly—as a threat to indispensable facets of human life—and facial work as a means for alleviating that with which we struggle? Most nota-bly, in conflating a changed appearance with a changed life, life itself is reduced to appearance. The aesthetic is triumphant as a register of living. While the real power of makeovers to transform and, in effect, to repair the subject's life are inadequate, in popular culture aesthetic transformation is continually purported as the solution for whatever ails. The potential consequences of this development cannot be over-stated. If aesthetic transformation takes on this kind of significance, it becomes an increasingly indispensible mode of navigating human life, even when the changes that are effected fall short of what is promised.

Focusing on aesthetics forgoes any kind of structural analysis that locates the causes of participants' problems in sociohistorical-cultural context. Subsequently, individualized intervention, in this case facial work, is favored over broader social change. This model for transformation is readily available for incorporation into the audience's lives, particularly because it is so compatible with contemporary American consumerist culture and the rise of the aesthetic register. Transformation happens through consumption.[48] Makeovers require purchasing clothes, beauty products, aesthetic services, and cosmetic surgery. Insofar as life transformation is forged through aesthetic intervention *and* popular culture, individual enhancement cannot help but solidify and exacerbate an aesthetic glamour culture that depends on and expands consumption. *Extreme Makeover* provides viewers with language to identify bodily flaws and information about expensive interventions, in effect broadening the ever-expanding market of appearance-related industries and reifying the very notion that aesthetic transformation is lifesaving work.

Extreme Results?

I have shown here how the disfigurement imaginary operates in the context of popular culture via a reality television series. Candidates are routinely described as not "normal," and yet *Extreme Makeover* does not dispense with the rhetoric of glamour-driven makeover television. Rather, the disfigurement imaginary unfolds alongside tropes that are typical of the genre. Extreme makeovers take place in Hollywood, America's center of fantasy production, and employ the services of many self-professed celebrity surgeons and style-makers. It is a biomedicalized Cinderella story, except that rather than becoming a princess, candidates are primed for becoming celebrities or, more precisely, looking like celebrities. In fact, *Extreme Makeover* explicitly positions itself as a proverbial fairy godmother: Through the magic of television (and the resources available to primetime network shows), producers turn "beasts" into beauties.

Cultural critics of *Extreme Makeover* take for granted that producing celebrity look-alikes is exactly what is accomplished.[49] For example,

Brenda Weber argues that "*Extreme Makeover* offers viewers the promise of the exceptional (coded as high-glamour beauty) built on an economy of sameness."[50] The sameness that Weber refers to is an aesthetic of celebrity culture. But if *Extreme Makeover* offers the promise of celebrity exceptionalism, as I agree that it does, viewers might be sorely disappointed. Promising celebrity look-alikes is not the same as actually producing a celebrity aesthetic, and it is critical to actually look at what makeovers do on real bodies in order to understand what physical effects are celebrated as vital interventions.

To be sure, *Extreme Makeover* rhetorically invokes the glamour of celebrity aesthetics. At the end of each makeover, the process is recapitulated in catchphrases that give viewers a framework through which to attribute meaning to the images of each candidate post makeover:

> "From the girl next door to the girl of her dreams."
> "From snaggletooth to a jaw-dropping dazzling beauty."
> "Bill looks like a movie star."
> "A nightmare transforms into a dream."

The narrative, as conveyed by the announcer, remains one of glamorous transformation. Understanding *Extreme Makeover* as a site of cosmetic intervention that culminates in the production of celebrity look-alikes relies on a fantasy of cosmetic surgery that ignores the ordinariness of postmakeover candidates' faces.

During the years the show was in production, the *Extreme Makeover* website featured "before" and "after" pictures of recipients. Undoubtedly, the after photographs are slick—faces are well lit and candidates are smartly posed. Candidates are also more stylized. Most go from wearing little or no make-up to a full face of professionally applied cosmetics. Most arrive at the *Extreme Makeover* mansion in jeans and sweatshirts and leave in designer suits and gowns. And surgery has erased (or at least diminished) facial characteristics conventionally defined as unattractive. A scar that remains after multiple surgeries to repair a cleft palate is lightened. The prominence of a brow is reduced. A nose is broken and set at a straight angle. Acne is lasered away.

While participants look *very* different at the end of the process compared to how they looked in the beginning, they do not look like celebrities who embody the ideals of beauty culture. Ultimately, the pageantry of the show obscures the fact that while many candidates look different at the end of the makeover, they are still relatively unremarkable vis-à-vis most celebrities (who themselves have likely had interventions). Episodes sometimes feature updates. We meet candidates postmakeover who have returned to their "real" lives. Not surprisingly, these candidates look significantly different than when they appeared at their big reveals and in their postmakeover glamour shots. High-maintenance hairdos have been traded for ponytails, for example. Despite all of the surgical intervention, without the Extreme Team candidates appear like everyday folks, the opposite of celebrities whose aesthetic is built around enduring exceptionalism.

Setting aside instances in which consumers use cosmetic procedures for the purposes of inscribing classical art works onto their bodies, as in the case of French performance artist Orlan, or embodying animals, as in the case of Seattle's CatMan Dennis Avner, there are few examples of cosmetic intervention going further than what occurs on *Extreme Makeover*. The level of intervention most candidates experience is extraordinary, and many would say excessive. In each episode following a candidate's big reveal, before and after images of the candidates wearing only their underwear are projected onto the television screen. The announcer narrates as the images are turned, revealing a side profile with a newly achieved ski slope nose or a strong jaw line enhanced by a chin implant. As the image shifts, the announcer offers a comprehensive list of the procedures undergone. Often candidates have experienced ten cosmetic procedures. Sometimes, they have undergone twenty. The techniques of intervention are undeniably extreme, but rather than extraordinary, the results are surprisingly mundane. Candidates are made over into a radically different version of themselves, but ultimately an unexceptional version. Rather than celebrities, candidates appear like different versions of everyman and everywoman.

Extreme Makeover as a cultural artifact is emblematic of not only makeover culture but also beauty culture. The show employs prototypical makeover tropes in promising exceptional results, and in doing so it speaks to our cultural obsession with attractiveness. At the same time though, interventions undertaken on *Extreme Makeover* are driven by the stigmatization of candidate's premakeover appearance. As I have shown, a discourse of stigma and disfigurement is frequently used to describe candidates. Yet while *Extreme Makeover* participants are constructed through image and narrative as disfigured, most participants look (in their before *and* after pictures) like unremarkable people. The before pictures resemble photographs of persons some might describe as dowdy, unkempt, or even ugly, and after pictures feature faces that more closely conform to dominant notions of attractiveness. But there is no self-evident facial difference that firmly situates the facial work accomplished on *Extreme Makeover* as reconstructive surgery; these candidates are not, for example, burn survivors. Nevertheless, the disfigurement imaginary situates candidates as having, preintervention, experienced profound suffering and compromised lives due to their appearance—just like people clinically defined as "grossly disfigured." In both cases, the face is understood and experienced as profoundly disabling.

But what is the difference between a face "marred" by crooked teeth, wrinkled skin, or a nose with a bulbous tip and a face that displays the signs of third-degree burns? In the world of *Extreme Makeover*, there is no difference. The bodies subjected to extreme makeovers are disfigured discursively in the hyperreality of twenty-first century reality television culture. This is a site engaged in the production of disfigurement—faces that in many contexts would be thought about as normal are redefined as disfigured—and arguably disfigured through intervention. Not coincidentally, the imperative to repair has emerged simultaneously with the tools to intervene. *Extreme Makeover* is devoted to repair, to facial work, but also to the creation of its very work objects.[51] In this way, *Extreme Makeover* unavoidably produces and expands notions of "disfigurement."

The very fact that results of extreme makeovers are unremarkable intensifies the repair impetus motivating extreme makeovers. Just as the enhancement effected by cosmetic interventions both encourages the pursuit of beauty culture and marks the consumer as someone invested in self-improvement, facial work that produces unremarkable results, which are then defined as vital, refigures recipients as especially fragile preintervention. As statuses, average, "normal," and unremarkable only garner attention and celebration when the one embodying them has been formerly characterized as subpar, anomalous, or ugly. Consider that to be called unremarkable is an insult if you imagine yourself to be more than mediocre. For some of us, to be average is, in itself, a kind of failure. But if one is already botched, becoming normal seems like something worth attaining. As the other cases described in this book will demonstrate, facial work yields unremarkable appearing results, and yet routinely much fanfare surrounds postintervention effects. The implication is that whatever face came before was so untenable that restoring and establishing an unremarkable appearance is an astonishing accomplishment. Ultimately, then, the disfigurement imaginary is fortified.

4

Not Just Another Pretty Face

The Social Value of Unremarkability

You don't know what it means to a woman not to be beautiful. For us beauty is everything. Living only to be loved,
and attractiveness being the sole condition for love, the existence of an ugly woman becomes the most terrible, the most
harrowing of all torments. I have hated myself very much, I
have deeply hated my unattractiveness, but never as much as
I have detested and still detest my heart.
—Iginio Ugo Tarchetti, *Fosca* (1869)

The pictures of Arlene Lafferty's face featured in a 2005 *San Diego
Union Tribune* story are startling. Not unlike most women over fifty,
her face exhibits signs of aging. Wrinkles and frown lines etch the
contours where her facial muscles move thousands of times each day,
and some loss of elasticity, what we commonly call "sagging skin," is
apparent too. But Lafferty's face is altogether different from the faces
of most women her age. Globular masses of congealed industrial grade
silicone contour her profile. The substance, commonly used as window
sealant, floor wax, and bathroom caulk, was injected into Lafferty's
face in order to make her appear "more feminine." According to Lafferty, the silicone, which is not contained in a protective container, as
is the case with silicone breast implants, worked initially. Her face was
rounder and softer—effects that helped to de-masculinize her appearance. But Lafferty's pictures are also a stark demonstration of the long-
term effects of subcutaneous silicone injections.[1] News stories about so-
called pumping parties are reaching mainstream news outlets in record
numbers.[2] In this media coverage, photographs feature faces and bodies
that bear witness to the limits of free-floating silicone as an aesthetic

enhancement method. Because the material has not been manufactured for cosmetic use and because "pumpers" are not trained or licensed, silicone may produce the desired effects at first, but eventually the plasma often amalgamates into surreal globules and migrates to other regions of the body.

In my early twenties, I was tangentially immersed in drag culture, filling the role of "dresser" for a friend who was a rising performer. Regularly, backstage conversation drifted to "pumping" and "pump girls," slang for women who participate in the underground silicone market. Some entertainers guesstimated how many "Dixie cups," a measure referencing the three-ounce disposable cups sometimes stocked in bathrooms for use with mouthwash, it took to produce a range of effects— from startlingly defined "cheek bones" to lips so plump they would put Angelina's Jolie's pouty mouth to shame. One commonly told story involved a performer who was allegedly a pump girl *and* a compulsive tanner. Supposedly, tanning beds raised the temperature of her silicone such that she had to hold her face in place to minimize "pump" migration caused by the heat.[3] While I could never be sure if the story was an urban legend or some amalgamation of fact and defamation, it served as a warning about the downsides of do-it-yourself aesthetic intervention.

The disadvantages of industrial silicone are not simply visual. Recent arrests for "murder by silicone" speak to the insidious consequences of using industrial silicone for aesthetic purposes.[4] Migrating silicone can result in a number of chronic autoimmune illnesses and fatal conditions, including pulmonary embolism caused by free-floating silicone entering the bloodstream and pooling in the lungs.[5] This begs the question: Why would individuals seek out body modification with highly toxic materials injected into their bodies by nonmedical personnel? Tracie Jada O'Brien of the Transgender Community Coalition of San Diego, in an interview for the *San Diego Union Tribune* article, suggests one answer: "It's about being able to get up in the morning and walk down the street without being ridiculed or physically abused."[6] Pumping, as it is practiced by trans women, is not simply about creating a beautiful visage; it is, first and foremost, about crafting a reliably female-appearing face. As O'Brien suggests, this is high-stakes aesthetic transformation. Silicone is one avenue for changing the gendered appearance of the face. Facial feminization surgery is another.

In the 1980s and 1990s, a Northern California plastic surgeon with extensive experience in reconstructive surgical techniques developed a collection of procedures identified as facial feminization surgery (FFS). These procedures are marketed to trans women for the purposes of changing facial appearance.[7] As of 2008, facial feminization surgery was promoted and practiced as "facial feminization surgery" by four surgeons in the United States.[8] While FFS consumers may desire a pretty face, what distinguishes facial feminization from cosmetic surgery more generally is that the work is expressly aimed at making the face more feminine, rather than simply more attractive—although some accounts of what constitutes beauty suggest that the most feminine faces are often perceived as the prettiest.[9] Facial feminization is accomplished through a variety of procedures including but not limited to a brow lift, a trachea shave, a jawline reduction, a chin reduction, and a face and neck lift. While surgeons are often reluctant to provide cost estimates except in private consultation, patients' websites report that FFS can cost between $20,000 and $60,000. Like other kinds of aesthetic intervention, FFS can cost less if one is willing to go outside of the United States for surgery. This practice, increasingly dubbed "medical tourism," remains a popular option for transgendering interventions. Many cosmetic surgeons offer facial interventions that have the effect of feminizing trans women's faces, but FFS is a distinct and cohesive set of surgical techniques explicitly marketed to refiguring a face perceived by potential patients and FFS surgeons as "too masculine."

Like other forms of reconstructive surgery, facial feminization requires intensive surgery lasting hours, sometimes as many as ten. Because procedures are aimed at radically altering multiple facial features, patient's faces (and skulls) undergo serious surgical manipulation. For example, jawline and chin reduction may require actually breaking or severing the bones of the face with a surgical drill. Facial bones are then resecured with screws, wires, and bone pastes. Brow shave or forehead recontouring involves removing a section of the skull, reshaping it with a device that resembles a dremel drill, and reattaching it to the skull.[10] To reduce the distance between the hairline and the eyebrows, a cut is made along the hairline, a section of skin is removed, and the scalp is pulled forward, bringing the hairline down lower on the forehead. As with all surgical interventions, swelling, bruising, and scarring are common. Some patients experience changes in the face's range of motion, reducing the facility with which one moves one's jaw, for example. Others report a loss in facial sensation, typically a sort of numbness that leaves a face unable to perceive human touch or a searing burn. Like all forms of surgery, infection and death loom as potential side effects. And of course, the results may not resemble what one had hoped for. Facial feminization is an invasive, expensive, dubiously successful intervention, and yet it remains a highly sought after technology of gendering the face.[11]

Passing from the Neck Up: Faces versus Genitals

In *Vested Interests: Cross Dressing and Cultural Anxiety*, Marjorie Garber's classic cultural analysis of transsexuality, she asks, "Does a transsexual change subjects? Or just bodies—or body parts?"[12] Garber uses trans identity to pose questions about the category crisis precipitated by living at odds with sex and gender binarism. To be sure, querying gender writ large by way of transgender identity is an objectifying and politically problematic practice. Yet other scholars have followed suit and overlooked complicated questions of lived experience and gender politics, instead focusing narrowly upon the implicit meanings of surgical transformation of the genitals through "bottom" surgery.

For example, Janice Raymond's scathing account of transgenderism, *The Transsexual Empire: The Making of the She-Male* (1979), positions sex reassignment surgery as *the* crucial act. Her argument, which is rampantly transphobic, is that genital surgery is fetishized by trans women during the process of transitioning.[13] In Sander L. Gilman's *Making the Body Beautiful* (2001), "transsexual surgery" is reduced to surgery aimed at the genitals (and breasts, in his discussion of trans women).[14] Similarly, social scientific research often queries the "success" of transitioning, focusing on genital surgery as the crux of change.[15]

In the aforementioned texts there are occasional references to the bodily effects of hormone usage and even nonsurgical gendered practices of embodiment like dress, but relatively little attention to other technologies of transgendering. And there *are* other technologies employed in the process of cultivating trans bodies, as the market for

underground silicone and the existence of facial feminization surgery suggest. Thus the scholarly preoccupation with genitals is curious for many reasons.[16] First, not all trans people choose to undergo
genital reassignment surgery as research often implies. Given the range
of transgender identities, bottom surgery may not be a desired form
of body modification. In fact, people choose to "do transgender" in a
range of ways, employing particular technologies and resisting others, if
not all medical intervention. Financial constraints may also mean that
one must prioritize medical interventions, and genital surgery may be
deemed less crucial or desired in comparison with other costly interventions. Second, positing genitals, a facet of the human body most
often hidden in everyday life, as the locus of transgender identity is
peculiar. Social identity is less determined by actual genitals and more
determined by what we assume is true or known about others' genitals. In the course of everyday life, most people do not typically have
firsthand knowledge about another's genitals.[17] We might think that we
know, but in most cases, we have very little evidence upon which to
base our assumptions.

Perhaps academic attention to the genitals simply mirrors the preoccupation with genital surgery reflected in the 2001 Harry Benjamin
International Gender Dysphoria Association (HBIGDA) Standards of
Care.[18] While the Standards were updated in 2011 and reflect a more
inclusive vision of trans health care, the 2001 Standards of Care have
deeply shaped both treatment protocols and public understandings of
trans identity.[19] The Standards, touted as clinical guidelines for helping
professionals who work with patients diagnosed with "gender identity
disorders," outline treatment paths.[20] Inherent in the Standards is the
assumption that patients will undergo a process of transitioning facilitated by medical technologies. The initial sections of the document
focus on diagnosis, followed by a discussion of therapeutic treatment
of patients. Subsequent sections discuss technologies of transitioning,
with an emphasis on "triadic therapy" involving counseling, hormone
treatment, and genital surgery. The Standards are structured as a universally applicable model of treatment that progresses from one step to
another. Psychological counseling precedes hormone treatment, which
precedes genital surgery. In this way, the Standards of Care position the
genital overhaul as *the* definitive step in the process, such that genital

surgery operates as a litmus test for determining if transition is complete. Overall, the preoccupation with another's most intimate body parts contributes to systematic othering of trans people. Put another way, this fascination with genitals appears to be transphobia masquerading as benign curiosity or "objective" research.

Feminization of the face appears briefly in the 2001 HBIGDA Standards for the first time in the document's history. A section entitled "Other Surgery for the Male-to-Female Patient" reads: "Other surgeries that may be performed to assist feminization include reduction thyroid chondroplasty, suction-assisted lipoplasty of the face, rhinoplasty, facial bone reduction, face-lift, and blepharoplasty."[21] This is the only mention of facial procedures in the document. Thus, the very standards intended to guide treatment aimed at transitioning largely ignore technologies aimed at the face. Interestingly, the 2011 revision does not explore facial feminization in any greater depth than the 2001 Standards of Care. While scholarly, professional, and popular interest in "transsexualism" has disproportionately focused on surgery of the genitals, facial work is a crucial part of transitioning for many, and in terms of navigating everyday social life, the appearance of the face is arguably more significant.

In a June 16, 2006 letter published on her widely accessed and cited website www.tsroadmap.com, transgender activist Andrea James encourages HBIGDA to reconsider its position on facial feminization surgery in future revisions of the Standards of Care.[22] James argues that facial feminization is "medically necessary for male-to-female transitioners." Based on her own experience, James argues that "vocal and facial cues are far more likely to be factors in how others respond to a trans woman and are in my opinion the key to being accepted more easily in one's target gender. These cues affect everything from one's personal and professional relationships to one's ability to move through the world safely."[23] According to James, the very fact that the face is so visually accessible makes its appearance more crucial for navigating everyday life unencumbered by threats to one's privacy or safety. Consequently, James encourages both medical practitioners and trans women to redirect their attention to "passing from the neck up." Her first-hand experience attests to how significant facial appearance is.

Feminization of the Disfigurement Imaginary

But how are interventions aimed at passing from the neck up a kind of facial work? How does facial feminization constitute a case through which we can understand normalization and repair of facial difference? The faces subject to facial feminization are not immediately intelligible as "disfigured" faces, yet within sites of facial feminization, the faces of trans women are positioned using the fix-it imperative. References to disfigurement appear frequently in subtle and obvious ways. Faces are described using the specter of defect and the language of repair rather than enhancement. Thus, the disfigurement imaginary is deployed in ways that are similar to the case of *Extreme Makeover*. This case also makes especially clear the ways in which compromised social interaction is yet another criteria used to position certain patients, in this case trans women, as socially dead.

The data upon which this chapter is based comes from my fieldnotes taken at conferences featuring seminars on facial feminization, namely Southern Comfort and the International Foundation for Gender Education (IFGE). These conferences featured seminars that addressed a wide range of topics including politics, spirituality, mental health, and activism, but a significant number of speakers addressed topics related to body modifications made possible by and forged through medical technologies. Seminars on hormone therapy and genital reassignment surgery appeared throughout conference schedules. In addition, each of the primary US-based facial feminization surgeons appeared at transgender conferences to discuss and market facial feminization.[24] Seminars provide opportunities for potential patients to meet and consult with surgeons, to learn more about facial feminization techniques, and to view the faces of other trans women who have undergone facial feminization. Thus, seminars are simultaneously information sessions and commercial advertisements. In addition, I analyzed the materials— pamphlets, medical journal articles, and promotional materials—distributed to attendees during these seminars.

Facial feminization seminars and surgeons' promotional materials reveal the ways in which the disfigurement imaginary infuses the marketing of FFS. Trans women's presurgically altered faces are discursively constituted as disfigured via brief, but revealing, references.

In one facial feminization seminar, a surgeon pointed to a photograph of a seemingly unremarkable face, noting, "You can see her forehead deformity."[25] Words like "deformity" suggest that a face is seen not simply as masculine but rather as disfigured. In a different seminar, another surgeon explained why somebody might choose facial feminization: "This is the same thing as if you were in a car wreck and you want to look like who you really are."[26] Here, trans women's faces are equated with an injury or a trauma and in need of repair. From this perspective facial feminization is hardly elective surgery, but is rather positioned as unequivocally necessary—not coincidentally, perhaps, by those who stand to benefit commercially. The ways disfigurement and the prefeminized face are referenced interchangeably trickle down, shaping trans women's perceptions of facial appearance too. Consider this excerpt from Lynn Conway's personal website, which describes her own FFS experience: "Many thanks to Douglas Ousterhout [FFS surgeon] for understanding and caring about the masculinization *facial disfigurement* [emphasis added] problems of transsexual women, for applying his creative and innovative capabilities to figure out how to solve those problems, and for applying his unmatched surgical skills to artistically feminize the faces of so many, many TS [transsexual] women."[27] Facial disfigurement is qualified here with the word "masculinization," similarly to how the words "congenital" and "severe" are regularly interjected to mark specific forms of facial disfigurement. Used in this way, masculinization, like congenital, also points to an etiology of trans women's "problems"—they were "born male." Put in a decidedly less transphobic way, trans women were assigned male at birth.

Perhaps even more revealing is a strategy used by Dr. Elliot Peterson, an established surgeon with a vibrant practice specifically focused on transgendering interventions.[28] The first time I attended a seminar presented by this surgeon, I watched as his personal assistant connected his laptop to a digital projector. As Peterson and his assistant readied themselves for their presentation, images flashed on a large screen set up in the front of the hotel meeting room. When I saw the photographs, I was sure that his assistant had opened the wrong PowerPoint file. What filled the screen were images of children with a range of cranio-facial anomalies. These particular images seemed startlingly out of place. I wondered: Why begin a lecture on facial feminization with the faces of facially variant children?

My fieldnotes from a second, different seminar presented by Peterson reveal why it made sense within the guiding framework of FFS to begin with such images:

> Dr. Peterson tells the audience that he spent 20 years running a center focused on the repair of cranio-facial anomalies. He's worked on hard cases, "horrible" facial anomalies. He flips through slides of people with a variety of congenital facial differences. One has a cleft palate. One has an unusual skull shape. It is not spherical. The surgeon refers to the photograph as an example of "clover leaf skull." One picture of a baby illustrates asymmetrical facial features. The eyes and the nose appear randomly placed as if in a Picasso painting. One has eyes that upon profile extend dramatically beyond a recessed eye cavity. You can see the shape of the entire eyeball, and they look as though they may fall out of the skull. Next to each is an "after" picture that shows the face post-surgery. Each face looks remarkably different, more "normal." Dr. Peterson remarks, "Those three patients show what I do to feminization patients."[29]

Certainly these images convey the kinds of cases treated by reconstructive surgeons and what surgical "success" looks like, but this introduction to FFS accomplishes much more than that. By beginning the presentation with images of children with craniofacial anomalies, the audience is immediately engaged with representations of disfigurement. While looking at these pictures, the audience is, not surprisingly, solemn. No one speaks, and that particular hush of silence that emerges in the face of something painful is palpable. The display of such photographs taps into an enduring (and ableist) cultural disposition to see images of children with disabilities with reverence, as "tragic" representations of human life gone terribly wrong.[30] By claiming that "those three patients show what I do to feminization patients," the faces of the trans women are positioned as somehow just like the faces of the children pictured. All are anomalous. All are in need of repair. Such a claim also suggests that facial feminization as more akin to reconstructive surgery than elective cosmetic intervention.

Other surgeons provide potential patients with a carefully crafted narrative about their careers that firmly locates their work as facial feminization surgeons within a trajectory of reconstructive surgery. A pamphlet distributed by an East Coast surgeon, Dr. Ivan Thomas, describes his educational history and professional affiliations:

> Advanced training was obtained with fellowship in Facial Plastic and Reconstructive Surgery, and Microsurgery through Harvard Medical School. He currently devotes his practice to facial plastic surgery and head and neck cancer reconstruction. The busiest component of his practice is Facial Feminization Surgery (FFS).

Another, Dr. Laurence Adams, emphasizes similar career ties in a handout distributed to potential patients entitled "Head of Plastic Surgery of Nation's Oldest & Busiest Military Hospital Relocated to Chicago." The feature describes the techniques innovated by Adams while serving as the chief of the Plastic Surgery Department at Naval Medical Center, Portsmouth, VA. Plastic surgery departments located at military hospitals often function to innovate reconstructive techniques that address disfigurement resulting from war injuries. Work as a plastic surgeon in the military locates one's professional history firmly within the domain of reconstructive—and often lifesaving—surgery.

I am not arguing here that it is unique for cosmetic surgeons to have training in reconstructive techniques; rather, I am interested in the ways in which surgeons use that training to communicate something about the work they do as facial feminization surgeons. By positioning facial feminization as a logical extension of training in reconstructive surgery, surgeons both produce and rely on associations between the work of repairing facial anomalies or injury and the work of feminizing trans women's faces. As a result, the articulation of professional history establishes surgeons' expertise while simultaneously feeding the stigmatization of trans women's appearances. Invoking and thereby fortifying the stigma associated with congenital aesthetic difference and facial trauma helps to mark trans women as "disfigured." This is the disfigurement imaginary at work, as fear and ableism are employed to expand notions of who is in need of aesthetic intervention.

It is not simply that facial feminization and reconstructive surgery are discussed as technically comparable and that trans women's faces are portrayed as similar to those with facial difference. Rather, facial feminization surgeons routinely invoke reconstructive surgery to lend particular meanings and moral authority to FFS. The effects of facial feminization are characterized as equivalent to the effects of more traditional kinds of reconstructive surgery. When asked by an audience member "Why do you do this?" Adams replies, "I came out of the Navy with a great set of tools . . . As a plastic surgeon, it is rare that I can make a difference. I have profoundly affected their [trans women patients'] life so that they can go in society and live their lives. We all know how cruel society can be."[31] This surgeon frames facial feminization as "profound," allowing people to "live their lives." This is quite a claim, and one that we will return to later in this chapter.

Similarly, Dr. Simon Nelson, a surgeon whose practice is divided between facial feminization and genital reassignment surgery, begins a presentation by explaining to the audience what makes a surgeon trained to "fix" facial "abnormalities" decide to start one of the country's preeminent centers for transgender related surgery: "What deformed people remember is what they looked like before."[32] He explains further that his patients are happy to be in the hospital and happy to see him, given that intervention will make life different and better. In explicitly linking trans women's experiences to the experience of "deformity," Nelson invokes the disfigurement imaginary in order both to clarify what FFS offers and to convey the personal significance and meaning his work has. In doing so, he echoes the sentiment expressed in other sites of facial work, that reconstructive surgery is both admirable and gratifying because of the extraordinary effects it has on patients.

Ultimately, the subtle inferences that liken FFS and reconstructive surgery aimed at facial difference coalesce to position the faces subject to each of these interventions as alike. This rhetorical work is indispensable in making FFS into a "lifesaving" intervention.

Sexing the Face, Diagnosing Disfigurement

Feminist accounts of cosmetic surgery have pointed to the ways in which cosmetic surgery consumption is gendered. Not only are women more prone than men to pursue aesthetic interventions, but what men and women hope to accomplish via intervention is largely determined by social conventions about men's and women's bodies.[33] As sociologists Diana Dull and Candace West argue,

> This [gender] is the mechanism that allows them to see the pursuit of elective cosmetic surgery as "normal" and "natural" for a woman, but not for a man. The accountability of persons to particular sex categories provides for their seeing women as "objectively" needing repair and men as "hardly ever" requiring it.[34]

Cosmetic surgery is an effect of gendered relations, and cosmetic surgery is a method for more closely approximating gendered cultural ideals. Women purchase faces (and breasts, for example) that might be described as beautiful or, perhaps, sexy. Men consume interventions that result in a good-looking, though certainly still masculine, face.[35] Yet not all women who seek cosmetic surgery change their bodies in precisely the same ways. For example, a woman may choose any number of surgically constructed noses—the ski slope, the upturned, or the perfectly angular. The desired outcome is gendered in that whichever nose one chooses will presumably yield what is understood as a more conventionally attractive face for a woman. But in this sense, the techniques of cosmetic surgery are gendered in a very generic sort of way.

Facial feminization is different. It, too, is a method of surgically inscribing gender onto the body, and in this way, it is a method, albeit an extreme one, for doing gender in the classic sociological sense. But facial feminization takes up gender as its very object of intervention and invention. Facial feminization is about surgically constructing gender itself. Cosmetic surgery is a method of doing gender through which women achieve prettier faces; FFS is a surgical method for producing a face that is itself perceived as female. To this end, facial feminization relies on and reproduces essentialized notions about what distinguishes a male face from a female face.

In a 2007 issue of *Clinical Plastic Surgery*, in an article entitled "Transgender Feminization of the Facial Skeleton," the idea of facial feminization was explored in a general plastic surgery journal.[36] The article begins by defining "transsexualism" and describing multiple modalities employed in the treatment of "gender identity disorder," specifically genital reassignment surgery and hormone therapy. Yet the authors, a group of Dutch surgeons, contend that these are crucial though insufficient means of addressing gender identity disorder: "For passing in public as a member of the opposite gender, facial features are of utmost importance for the transsexual individual."[37] The surgeons propose the following:

> There is a need for more objective standardization of the differences in the facial features of the two sexes, to facilitate surgical treatment planning and more objectively assess the outcome of the facial surgery on psychosocial functioning and appearance, not only from the perspective of those treating, but also from the patient's own point of view.[38]

> By calling for "objective standardization," Becking et al. argue that rigorous scientific research aimed at *discovering* facial sex differences would help in elaborating a basis for surgical practice and a standard by which to judge success. Although there has been a limited amount of the kind of research they propose, the practice of FFS already relies upon circulating, albeit informal, "theories" of sex differences in facial appearance.[39]

In a pamphlet distributed by FFS surgeon Douglas K. Ousterhout entitled "Feminization of the Transsexual" and targeted to prospective consumers, techniques of facial feminization are described in detail. However, the pamphlet is not simply a list of surgical procedures often accomplished in the process of feminization.[40] The pamphlet also offers a theory of facial sex difference and a subsequent account of why facial feminization works. In the introductory section, the pamphlet reads:

> There are basic differences between a male and a female skull, differences long appreciated by anthropologists studying skulls but also by artists as well. Females have a more pointed chin, tapered mandible, and less nasal prominence than males. These areas must be modified from those more massive areas on the male . . . You must change the underlying structures to affect a real change. Changing the shape of the skull will markedly assist in changing one from distinctly male to female . . . REMEMBER: TO APPROXIMATELY FEMINIZE THE FACE, THE SKULL

MUST BE APPROPRIATELY REDUCED TO FEMININE SIZE AND PROPORTIONS.[41]

Here, Ousterhout asserts that anthropological evidence suggests that on average, the skulls of men and women differ in both shape and size. In this way, his pamphlet taps into a well-established history of employing scientific research in the service of identifying sex differences through cranial measurements, hormones, and skeleton size and shape.[42] This strategy lends a seemingly objective and "scientific" explanation that accounts for why facial work is important to transitioning from male to female. Ousterhout's theory of facial sex difference also posits that changing the skull through surgery will alter the appearance of the face, specifically the gendered effects of the facial structure. Ousterhout's account of facial feminization works to position facial work as a crucially important intervention for trans women, while simultaneously advancing essential, naturalized accounts of sex/gender differences.

The pamphlet continues by expounding upon the differences between male facial features and female facial features, including the brow, forehead, hairline, chin, mandible (jaw), cheeks, lips, neck, and nose. In reference to each facial feature, the differences between male and female features are identified, and then surgical techniques are described and prescribed, which purportedly erase facial sex differences. In regards to the forehead, the pamphlet emphasizes the "prominence" of male bone structure: "As the male forehead is so different than the female forehead this may be one of the most important areas to modify. Males have brow bossing with a flat area between the right and left areas of bossing while females have a completely convex skull in all planes and markedly less prominence." To deal with the masculine forehead, skull contouring is used to reduce the bossing or bone ridge that appears across the forehead.

The distance between the hairline and the browline also becomes salient: "In physical anthropology studies, it has been shown that men have a longer distance from the brows to the hairline than do women. . . . A long forehead is generally acceptable for the male but not for the female." The pamphlet suggests that this distance be shortened by way of scalp advancement and in some cases a brow lift. The chin also works as a sign of sex: "The chin varies markedly between the male and the female. The male chin is generally wide and vertically high while the female chin tends to be more pointed, narrow, and vertically shorter . . . Thus the chin is an extremely important area in gender recognition." To address this "important" feature, Ousterhout suggests a sliding genioplasty, which involves the cutting and removing of sections of bone to reduce the "squareness" associated with male chins.

The underlying theory of facial sex difference articulated in Ousterhout's pamphlet also structures the facial feminization seminars of the FFS surgeons I studied. Facial features are first dissected for sex differences. Then, surgical techniques, which purportedly can intervene in these differences, are described in detail. Given that facial feminization seminars are intended to *inspire* facial work, it is important to critically interrogate how surgeons position the intervention itself and trans women's faces, given that surgeons have direct incentives to increase demand for FFS.

The theory of facial sex difference is the most commonly used strategy to diagnose trans women's face as untenable, and its rhetorical weight is amplified by the disfigurement imaginary. My fieldnotes reflect the format of an FFS seminar and the way the theory of facial sex difference fundamentally structures the seminar:

> Then, the doctor suggests that "anthropological differences" matter, that "anthropologists can tell the difference between male and female" . . . On his PowerPoint presentation he clicks to a graphic of two different skulls and two different faces (one male and one female). He then begins to point out the differences between the two skulls, demonstrating how each feature of the face varies between men and women . . . "There are basic differences between the male and the female skull."[43]

FFS surgeons do not subscribe to a monolithic, standardized theory of facial sex difference, which speaks to its very nature as an emergent and contested basis of diagnosis. For example, each surgeon puts a varying degree of emphasis on the importance of soft tissue work relative to bone work. In his seminars, Dr. Laurence Adams stresses soft tissue work:

> The doctor posts two pictures side by side on the screen. A male skull and a female skull. He begins to point out male and female facial

characteristics. "When you look at your female counterparts, I'm not trying to be rude, but there are differences." Dr. Adams points a number of facial features—the temporal ridge, facial hollowing, the cheeks, the eyebrows—and points out the differences between the male skull and the female skull. "Soft tissue is the magic . . . Procedures on the upper face are the most feminizing . . . The forehead is the most critical thing."[44]

By contrast, Dr. Ivan Thomas highlights the significance of bone work:

The surgeon poses the following question to the audience: "What is it about the face that allows the distinguishing of gender?" He compares slides of men and women's skulls and argues, "The thing that's really making the difference—the bone. The skin is just the skin." Dr. Thomas goes through parts of the face one by one and describes what is needed to make the face appear more feminine.[45]

Regardless of whether a surgeon employs physical anthropology or his own experience regarding the relative effects of tissue versus bone on facial appearance, every surgeon deploys equivalent rhetorical strategies in his seminars in order to establish and to foster notions of facial sex difference. Herein is the dilemma of employing a theory of facial sex differences in this context. Each surgeon disagrees about where the crucial determinant of facial sex appearance lies. For one, bones matter most. For another, it is soft tissue. Another privileges some facial features over others. The fact is that while forensic anthropologists do use skull measurements to "sex" human remains, the physiological element that accounts for our overall gendered facial appearance remains subjectively determined.

Anomalous sex is an interesting point of reference here. Cultural ideas about gender fundamentally shape how individuals with disorders of sex development are medically treated. For much of recent history, surgical intervention, for example, proceeds with the guiding premise that bodies, specifically genitals, should either be able to penetrate another body or, more likely, be penetrable. Of course when a case of atypical genitals presents itself at birth, doctors do not always make these assumptions explicit in interactions with infants' parents. Medical providers may not even be cognizant of the gendered assumptions that drive genital surgery on infants. And yet even as culturally constructed notions of sexual intimacy and gendered bodily habitus saturate the clinical environment, reference to scientized ideas about sex and bodies shape the ways many doctors interact with parents instead.[46] As feminist sociologist Judith Lorder has intimated, biology is ideology.[47]

In the case of FFS, selective images are invoked as "proof" that the male face is demonstrably different from the female face. Rather than using images as *examples of* male and female faces, they are used as *evidence about* general patterns, which then inform surgical practice and patients' notions both about what is "wrong" with their presurgical face and what a new face might look like. Ultimately, facial feminization surgeons take a reductionistic approach. Single images of a male skull and a female skull are positioned to represent sex and gender *writ large* and as they are in "nature." In this way, surgeons rely on a theory of sexual dimorphism that presumes real, measurable difference between men and women and downplays variability in appearance among the categories of men and women. This strategy works to reify the differences between facial appearance in men and women, and thus to reproduce sex/gender differences.

"The female face" is dissected and disassembled into individual parts. FFS surgeons make reference to things like "a female nose," even though outside of the discursive landscape of FFS it is not at all clear what such a nose might actually look like. In the process, a surgical standard is constructed by way of fetishizing facets of femininity, in this case feminine facial features, and positioning these features as constitutive, as opposed to indicative, of femininity. "The female face" becomes an ideal against which a patient's real face is compared. Those features that do not evoke the female face are designated masculine. Masculinity becomes an empty signifier, a repository for all features not defined as female. This stands in sharp contrast to a long history wherein female bodies have been conceptualized simply as not male.[48] Within sites of FFS, however, masculinity is stigmatized and subsequently becomes an object of intervention and repair.

These surgeons do not simply position male and female faces as dissimilar from one another; the difference is conceived of as thoroughly problematic for trans women. Dr. Ivan Thomas, for example, articulates the degree of difference in this way: "It's not just bone work and pull some skin, you need a global change."[49] By "global," the surgeon implies that facial feminization is a surgical overhaul. This radical change is not simply elective, that is desired, but according to Thomas, for the trans woman it is "needed." Dr. Laurence Adams similarly suggests that the change needed is drastic: "In order to look female you must change your skeletal appearance. To do less is absolutely wrong. Less is not more."[50] To accomplish the objective of facial feminization, that is looking appropriately female, requires not only *some* surgical intervention, but rather, as the previous excerpt suggests, an extreme reworking of the skeleton. Potential FFS patients are met with treatment protocols that emphasize the immediate need for drastic intervention, resembling the diagnostic process *Extreme Makeover* participants experience.

In the course of stressing how invasive facial feminization needs to be, surgeons imply that the male face for trans women is, in short, a problem, as Dr. Elliot Peterson suggests in a seminar: "He turns to pictures of 'real' men and says that the pictures illustrate a 'female face on males.' Dr. Peterson says this is 'not a problem.' Then he shows a picture of a 'male face on a female' and says, 'but a male face on a female really is [a problem].'"[51] What makes traces of masculinity so unsustainable is not altogether clear in the surgeons' discourse, but the diagnosis is simple enough: If one is a woman trans or not, then one's face cannot appear masculine.

Facial feminization is, to be sure, a form of gendered body modification, but FFS has a markedly different significance than other gendered bodily practices. Sociologists Candace West and Don H. Zimmerman approach gender as a "routine, methodical, and recurring accomplishment."[52] Gender is an iterative process, enacted through dress and style, voice and gesture, along with roles and statuses. Like other aesthetic methods of feminization, facial feminization is a way of "doing gender." But unlike aesthetic methods of feminization like make-up, primarily employed to give the face a decidedly more socially valued appearance, FFS is positioned as a necessary intervention aimed at repair, not simply a means of "looking better." It is not just that gender gets constructed and enacted through facial feminization, but it is also the case that a bodily stigma becomes managed.

The stigma, in this case the masculine face, is a product of gender binarism. There are two, and only two, socially intelligible gender categories. As sociologist Mimi Schippers writes (drawing on Judith Butler),

> Gender is the socially constructed binary that defines "men" and "women" as two distinct classes of people. The discursive construction of gender assumes that there are certain bodies, behaviors, personality traits, and desires that neatly match up to one or the other category.[53]

Trans women, by the very nature of transitioning, already challenge the social prescription that one is born sexed and that one's gender follows from one's sex assignment at birth. In this way, trans women embody what Schippers deems "pariah femininities," traits that contaminate hegemonic gender relations. These characteristics function as master statuses and, if not contained, carry material consequences. Facial feminization and other techniques of transitioning are in one sense elective, but interventions like facial feminization are desired partially because within a culture of sexual dimorphism, gender difference generally, but pariah femininity specifically, must be eradicated. In discussing female erotic dancers' cosmetic surgery pursued to maximize their earning potential, sociologist Eve Shapiro writes,

> On an institutional level, the outcome of the biomedical construction of hyper-normative femininities by the women was an erasure of difference. By producing a very narrow set of femininities in line with hegemonic paradigms and gendered body scripts, the women naturalized a feminine body that was virtually unattainable without the use of body technologies, and in the process they erased the very real differences that had existed between each of their bodies.[54]

FFS is, then, both like and unlike cosmetic surgery pursued by cisgender women. For both, gender is a heavily enforced normative category, but facial feminization takes on additional significance as a technique of normalization.

The theory of facial sex difference relies upon the stringency of gender expectations, but it is also superimposed with the disfigurement imaginary to resolutely position trans women's faces as in need of intervention. For trans women, masculine facial appearance is a direct challenge to sexual dimorphism. Subsequently, the theory of facial sex difference positions the masculine face not simply as unattractive but rather as untenable. The narrative that treats the masculine face of a trans woman as disfigured maps gender and normalization onto one another. What a surgeon purports to do to facial feminization patients is to give them faces that make it possible to lead a "normal" life.

Social Death in a Gendered World

There is a story in my experiences conducting this fieldwork that stands out. It is a story that speaks to the trickiness of ethnography, the complications of positionality, and the deception that may be unintended but may always already be part of the work of the social scientist:

> I am sitting in the hotel lobby. I am working on my laptop, and I notice someone slightly behind me. She is standing too close. "You were in Dr. Adams's presentation this morning," she tells me. "You shouldn't spend the money, girl. You look okay. You don't need it." Later a friend, who identifies as a trans woman, will tell me that the same thing has happened to her at Southern Comfort. A stranger has commented that she doesn't need surgery, that she looks okay. I try to think of another context in which strangers can begin a conversation by telling you their personal opinion about what you look like. Generally, offering judgments about another's body is agreed to be an egregious invasion of privacy. Not here. In between opportunities to consult with surgeons who will tell you what exactly is wrong with your face, strangers will offer their two cents. "You shouldn't spend the money, girl. You look okay. You don't need it."[55]

This interaction reveals something significant about FFS, namely that looking "okay" means that someone does not "need" surgery. We all could pursue surgery to have fuller cheeks, tapered chins, and shorter foreheads in order to be "prettier." But in the context of facial feminization in which presurgically intervened faces are viewed through the disfigurement imaginary, the relevant questions are: What does "okay" look like? And *what*, exactly, is it that trans women supposedly *need*?

Surgeons commonly conclude seminars by demonstrating what facial feminization can achieve. Often this is done with the use of "before" and "after" pictures—just as in other sites of facial work. Undoubtedly, patients look different postsurgery. Yet many of the after pictures capture faces that are not exactly beautiful according to dominant cultural ideals. Nor are they ugly. They are simply unremarkable. Taken with the experience described above, it seems that looking "okay" *is* the palpable outcome of FFS. This is yet another way in which FFS is unlike cosmetic intervention and more akin to reconstructive surgery. As opposed to elective procedures, which are deemed successful based on their ability to enhance bodily appearance, facial work operates under the framework that faces are stigmatized to the degree that normal, as opposed to extraordinary, is a satisfactory postsurgical result. In fact, looking "okay" comes to take on a vital significance given how life prefacial work is understood.

In addition to after pictures, some surgeons share success stories to demonstrate what facial feminization can accomplish in the context of a life. In the last few minutes of one seminar, Adams talked fast, giving one example after another of how facial feminization can benefit patients:

> Dr. Adams begins telling stories. A trans woman post-facial feminization walks into a Chicago GLBT bar. A patron says, "Miss, did you know you were in a GLBT bar?" The trans woman replies, "No, but I think I'll stay." A trans woman lawyer gets on a train from New York to Philadelphia for this conference. She sits next to a fellow passenger. He asks the lawyer, "Where are you headed?" She replies that she is headed to Philadelphia. He tells the lawyer that he too is headed to Philadelphia to give a presentation at a transgender conference. The lawyer replies, "That's nice." The train arrives and the two depart the station. Over the course of the conference, the lawyer runs into the passenger from the train. Upon realizing that she is a trans woman, his face drops. He looks at her and tells her, "I didn't know." Dr. Adams tells us that he often gets in touch with patients when he travels. One met him on a family vacation in Disney World. He tells us, "It's amazing how many boys she had at the table with her." Another met him on the beach in Hawaii. It was "full of hot bikini bodies," and she walked the beach "turning heads." Another has "30 boyfriends" in Vegas. An audible gasp rises from the audience.[56]

These stories of success hinge on one effect of feminization—that "no one will know"—a phrase that several surgeons regularly use. These stories position anonymity as the promise of facial feminization. Dr. Adams's final story of the woman with 30 boyfriends suggests that facial feminization (and other interventions) can produce attractiveness, but it is the promise of passing that gives these stories an overarching rhetorical force.

Other surgeons use passing as the ultimate end of facial feminization surgery too. As Dr. Peterson blatantly says, "Our basic objective is for you to pass. You want to look, appear, and act female. Without doing anything else—putting on make-up, fixing your hair—I want you to be that female."[57] This surgeon suggests that after facial feminization, no other methods of aesthetic enhancement—make-up or hair—will be needed to be taken for granted as female. Again, the promise is not that one will be beautiful, but rather that one will look like "just another female." Dr. Thomas promises extraordinary effects: "We have the ability to get excellent results. There is nothing to suggest that these are trans women."[58] By "excellent," though, Thomas does not mean to suggest that patients will be beautiful. Instead, success is achieved by eradicating that which "suggests" masculinity. "Excellent results" is again code for "no one can tell." Passing is posited as the net benefit of facial feminization. In rare cases, beauty might be a side effect, but passing is the stated and, seemingly, the desired aim.

The idea that aesthetic intervention facilitates a kind of passing is not new. Cultural historian Sander Gilman situates contemporary cosmetic surgery as an extension of surgery employed by Jews in postwar Germany, arguing that aesthetic intervention inherently constitutes a form of passing. For example, face-lifts allow women to "pass" as younger.[59] Following Gilman, feminist scholar Kathy Davis, in a piece entitled "Surgical Passing: Or Why Michael Jackson's Nose Makes 'Us' Uneasy," frames cosmetic surgery on "ethnic" facial features as both a mode of assimilation and means of upward mobility, and she questions the politics of surgeries that enable "passing."[60] Additionally, cultural anthropologist Eugenia Kaw's work on surgery aimed at Asian facial features queries the tensions of passing.[61] For these scholars, passing refers to the taking on of another identity both as a means of distancing one's self from stigma (ones fortified through ageism and racism) and acquiring privilege accrued to another status.[62] In the case of cosmetic surgery aimed at racialized facial features, changing the face is a way of

approximating dominant (usually white) aesthetic standards. This surgery may or may not actually culminate in identification with or acceptance by the dominant racial group, but it typically transfigures stigmatized bodily characteristics into something more socially desirable.

What constitutes passing in the case of trans women is being taken for
granted as a "real" woman, in FFS surgeons' parlance. Passing in this way
is different from passing as another race. Whereas racial passing is almost
exclusively understood in terms of a racial minority assuming the identity
of or being read as the racially dominant group, in the case of trans women,
passing involves taking on a *devalued* status, that of female. Clearly, the
stakes of "passing" as thirty-five for the fifty-something cosmetic surgery
crowd and passing as *not* Jewish or white in postwar Germany or in "post-
racial" racist America are very different. To be sure, though, the stakes of
"passing" as female for trans women are highly consequential.

Given that there are real costs of challenging the gendered social
order, doing gender and doing it in normative ways is compulsory. As
West and Zimmerman note, "Doing gender is unavoidable . . . because
of the social consequences of sex-category membership: the allocation
of power and resources not only in the domestic, economic, and political domains but also in the broad arena of interpersonal relationships."[63]
Not only is access to resources contingent on doing gender in normative
ways, but as Judith Lorber suggests, there are profound consequences
for rejecting or living outside of normative gendered statuses: "Political
power, control of scarce resources, and, if necessary, violence uphold the
gendered social order in the face of resistance and rebellion."[64] Passing as
female requires that one is not being perceived as trans, and FFS is a tool
used to achieve this goal. As Eve Shapiro explains, gendered body interventions reflect both progressive and regressive tendencies:

> We are clearly living in a moment when gender paradigms, scripts, bod-
> ies, and identities are all being simultaneously refined and renegotiated.
> New technologies are being deployed to re-entrench hegemonic mascu-
> linities and femininities and erase race and gender differences in bodies.[65]

Thus, transgendering body modifications function simultaneously as
practices of identity formation, methods of self-determination, and
strategies for managing the social cost of difference.

As the publicized murders of Gwen Araujo and Sanesha Stewart demonstrate, the stakes of being "read" as trans as opposed to passing are, in some cases, those of life and death.[66] Other instances of violence, while not deadly, result in serious injury. According to the 2008 National Transgender Discrimination Survey, twenty-five percent of respondents reported bias-based violence. The rate for those transgender respondents who self-identified as gender nonconforming was even higher, suggesting that not passing is a critical risk factor in experiencing physical attack.[67]

FFS surgeons elide talk of actual violence and tend to characterize not passing as a form of social death, though this way of understanding the relationship between social status, body modification, and life chances is not without problems.[68] To be sure, consequences for not passing can include employment discrimination, interpersonal hostility, and street harassment, impacting people's ability to effectively and safely navigate everyday life. Ultimately social interaction—the essential humanizing process, as Goffman suggests—is compromised by not passing in a culture that requires adherence to gender binarism and rejects perceived violations of sex assignment at birth. According to this logic, one should fit into one—and only one—category, and it should align with the status one is assigned at birth. Even as gender transition increasingly becomes a part of public discourse, the presumption is that one will transition from one sex category to the "opposite" sex category, and that efforts will be made (via the use of biomedical technologies) to visually mask physical characteristics or embodied traits that do not align with the "new" status. The presumption that gender conformity is the central goal of transgender individuals, what community organizer Holly Boswell describes as the "tyranny of passing," exacerbates the social consequences of not passing. Boswell describes the benefits of passing and, by proxy, the costs of not passing:

> Society rewards us for filling its prescribed roles, for successfully assimilating. Those family members and friends who still associate with us can breathe a sigh of relief. Neither do we risk making others in public embarrassed or uncomfortable. We no longer have to keep explaining ourselves to the uninitiated, and seldom have to impose our gender issues on others. No longer an obvious target, our security and chances of survival are enhanced. We no longer arouse fears in others, and are not perceived as a

threat. We experience less hassles and stares. In fact, we are taken just as seriously as anyone else, and can be perceived as a credible, worthwhile and effective human being. We can get a job, be self-supporting, and even have a decent career. If we can pass, we can actually thrive. We are granted equal opportunity for growth and happiness.[69]

In a transphobic society, social status hinges on passing.[70]

Within sites of FFS, passing functions so persuasively as a surgical outcome because requisite social interaction is attributed to the intervention. Gaining and maintaining employment, accessing resources from state agencies, and interacting safely with neighbors are critical elements of social interaction that stand to be compromised by facial stigma. In the seminar described above, the story of the woman with 30 boyfriends is the only one in which FFS is described as augmenting. What is more common is that looking female, which is coded as not looking like a trans woman, is held out as the promise of FFS. Like other forms of facial work, FFS is squarely focused on reducing stigma: one not only fortified by transphobia but also though the disfigurement imaginary. It is also positioned as a solution to social death.

While compromised social interaction might be construed as disabling, facial atypicality is positioned as prohibitive to viability. The difference between something being disabling and something being socially deadly is that the stigma associated with bodily status gets magnified and transformed into something beyond stigma. As a result, life, in this case as a person whose face is defined as disfigured, is routinely imagined as not possible. This fortification process happens through routine accomplishment, but it is through these efforts that the nature of facial atypicality changes forms and the significance of facial work takes on vital weight. Consider the following (somewhat awkwardly worded) excerpt from a pamphlet entitled "Feminization of the Transsexual" distributed by the self-described founder of FFS, Dr. Douglas Ousterhaut:

Helping transsexual women to look like women, a healthy mind is a healthy soul. The first step to feeling like a human being, FFS is a very big part in that process. Looking feminine, appearing as a female, is of course extremely important to you. First impressions are often made based just on your face. That which is first seen in an initial contact is what frequently defines you. It establishes not only just who you are but frequently what you are as well.[71]

Here, "feeling like a human being" depends on one's face "appearing female." The weight of this rhetoric is made especially apparent when one considers the converse—when one's face does not appear "female," one does not feel like a human being. This is qualitatively different than sites of elective biomedical interventions that propose that enhancing procedures will make one feel more like one's self—if we experience cognitive dissonance when we see the signs of aging etched on our faces, for example, cosmetic intervention can aid us in more closely resembling the younger self-image that persists for many of us. By contrast, the surgical effects of FFS do not operate solely within a vocabulary of enhancement and instead are increasingly characterized using the language of viability. The promise of facial work is not only quality of life but rather life itself.

One byproduct of applying the disfigurement imaginary to trans women, of equating trans women's "masculine" faces with social death, is that a culture of transphobia is perpetuated. In the process of selling intervention, surgeons situate life as a visibly trans person as not comfortable, not feasible, or even dangerous. But do trans women really need reminding about the violence, employment discrimination, and microaggressions that are potentially at stake by not passing? Ultimately, the rhetoric of FFS offers an individualized solution to the problem of transphobia. If FFS remained embedded in the discourse of elective, cosmetic surgery, then the intervention would likely be framed as a method for embodying the self. Instead, as FFS is framed as vital, intervention becomes a defensive measure to ward against impending threat. The ways FFS is marketed not only fortify stigma, but rather reinforce a culture of fear as social death is continually amplified. The social causes of transphobia go largely unchallenged, as if no other world is possible. Financial investment and physical risk become a taken for granted method of survival.

As feminist sociologist Raewyn Connell argues, the preoccupation with passing ignores trans women's process, "stating their membership in the social group women and their 'problem' as gaining recognition of that membership. That is to say, we should read the significance of transsexual women's practice as centrally concerning social solidarity rather than individual identity, normativity, or passing."[72] Viewed from a critical queer lens, the problem trans women face is not "not passing"; the problem is a lack of recognition.

Unlike the cases of cleft repair and face transplantation described in the following chapters, FFS does not expedite any functionality. Women who undergo FFS will not have improved ingestion facility or communication ability. In fact, FFS may result in compromised facial function. What they may gain, however, is greater ease in social interaction. Ultimately, then, the case of FFS vividly demonstrates how faces that do not conform to aesthetic expectations but do not present any impairment can be refigured as deadly with the added effect of solidifying social injustice.

Celebrating Unremarkability, Fortifying Stigma

Surgery can never perfectly create "the female face" deciphered by theories of facial sex difference, both because the standard is an ideal and the results of surgery are never fully knowable or predictable prior to surgery. As Dr. Nelson notes, "You can only go so far. That's just the way the anatomy is."[73] At the same time that surgeons identify differences *between* male and female faces to diagnose trans women, they admit variability in facial appearance *among* "real" women—or as one surgeon put it, trans women's "biological counterparts." In this way, surgeons acknowledge that in reality, a range of faces may appear female. Comments by Dr. Adams reveal this concession: "Everyone else uses a cookie cutter approach but we all know there is a wide range of feminine."[74] According to his logic, if there are a wide range of female faces and if more than one kind of face "counts," then there is presumably decreased need for feminization. Similarly, Dr. Thomas concludes his seminar by admitting, "There are ranges. However, for someone who is transitioning you want to change everything you can with surgery to appear feminine."[75] Taken together, surgeons seem to undermine both the transformative potential of FFS and the very theory upon which FFS rests.

Even as surgeons rely upon theories of facial sex difference, they acknowledge that facial appearance widely varies for "biological" women. While they seemingly contradict their own assertions about facial sex difference, they emphasize that radical change *is* needed to sufficiently feminize the face. As Dr. Peterson explains, "I cannot explain completely and exactly why but in my experience the transsexual needs to eliminate every remnant of facial masculinity as possible in order to pass."[76] Other surgeons also suggest that the change needed is "global" or, in other words, *all-encompassing*, but if there is such a range in female facial appearance, as these surgeons intimate, the theory of facial sex difference is potentially undermined. Selling facial feminization, then, is a precarious enterprise, relying on a stringent theory of facial sex difference while conceding that a range of faces are read as female.

At first glance, such strategic claims-making seems contradictory. In the process of deciphering facial sex difference, male and female faces are conceptualized as radically divergent from one another but also as simultaneously coherent and homogenous within each category. In essence, the theory of facial sex difference is a discursive formation aimed at eradicating the perception that multiple kinds of faces are sufficiently "female." This contradiction begs the question: Why do surgeons rely on discourses seemingly in tension with one another?

Put simply, the theory of facial sex difference, in conjunction with the links surgeons draw to reconstructive surgery, animates the imperative to repair by locating trans women's faces as unacceptable, disfigured, and outside the norm. Elaborating the differences between male and female faces undergirds the need for surgery by continually deploying a notion of "the female face" that positions the faces of trans women as untenable. At the same time, recognizing the variability among female faces opens up the standards by which surgery might be deemed successful, and, importantly, acknowledging range actually intensifies the disfigurement imaginary through which trans women are viewed. Both in relation to the standard female face premised in theories of facial sex difference and in relation to the range of female faces that surgeons acknowledge exist in reality, trans women's faces are deemed deficient.

While "the female face" works as the point of reference for surgical intervention, there is no such thing as "the" female face, just like there is no definitive standard for "disfigurement." In both cases, we seem to know it when we see it. Here, the female face is a constructed conglomeration of histories, cultural stories, and measurements, which depend on averages (via references to skulls) in their making. It is not only an ideal but an ideal type, in the Weberian sense, an analytic comprised via reference to particular characteristics that do not correspond to any individual case. The logic that undergirds intervention positions a standard—"disfigurement," or in this case "the female face"—as the reference point around which surgeons organize practices of facial work and patients understand them. Ironically, because the female face is a conceptual ideal as opposed to an empirical point of reference, FFS can never *literally* produce the female face. Surgeons get around this limitation by positing passing as the ubiquitous goal of FFS. In this way, in addition to feminizing the face, facial feminization is directly aimed at expunging masculinity—the defect. Gender binarism requires both. The difference encapsulated by a masculine face is positioned as fundamentally threatening to passing, which surgeons suggest is critical for living a "normal" life. Through this web of stigma and intervention, FFS is promised as a method to ward off social death.

In all sites of facial work aimed at disfigurement, normalcy operates as the point of reference. In the case of FFS, the standard is a gendered norm, "the female face." Yet norms are tricky points of reference at least with regards to the aesthetic. At what point would one appear *definitely* normal? Like the female face, facial normality is a conceptual ideal that is surgically elusive. The female face and facial normalcy might well be hard to pin down, but passing is infinitely more pragmatic. Interventions can and do facilitate passing, because passing only requires being seen without being "clocked" or read as trans in specific social settings. Unlike normalcy, one can approximate how successfully one passes based on the ease of social interactions. In this way, passing is tangible in a way that ideals like normalcy and "the female face" never are. The case of facial feminization puts into sharp relief how aesthetic taken-for-grantedness is desired, sought after, and crafted via facial work. Sometimes it is not about embodying an ideal, but rather appearing unremarkable.

Facial feminization specifically, and facial work more broadly, takes unremarkability as its end point. There is something besides beauty to be attained via aesthetic intervention. The desire for unremarkability is the desire to go unnoticed, to blend in, to pass. The desire for beauty, on the contrary, is the desire to appear remarkable, even extraordinary. As a mode of normalization, facial work aims to recover a face defined as disfigured. In this line of work, there is little to suggest that beauty is even hoped for by potential patients or ever promised by facial workers. Perhaps something exists between or outside of beauty and ugliness? To desire unremarkability is, at the most basic level, the desire to live outside of the stigma of ugliness *and* the extraordinariness of beauty. If one cannot embody the ideal or approximate normalcy, one can at least hope to live outside of stigma. Unremarkability structures bodily interventions, both mundane and innovative, in this sociohistorical moment, and more than beauty, it drives facial work. This desire for unremarkability is an often unstated but critical impetus for aesthetic intervention. It is, in essence, the corporeal objective of facial work. For bodies perceived as disfigured, it is an aesthetic end aimed at circumventing social death.

In early 2011, the *New York Times* featured a story about the city's underground silicone market. The piece included an interview with Zaira Quispe, who desperately sought to appear more feminine. The irony is that the intervention, which promised a viable life, has deeply compromised Quispe's life. Silicone is slowly poisoning her body, which is in an unrelenting state of inflammation combatted through continuous steroids and antibiotics. Her heart is also under threat. A steady regimen of blood thinners wards off pulmonary embolism, which could be caused by migrating silicone. But the effects of silicone have also left Quispe socially isolated. As the *New York Times* reports, "'I'd rather be inside my place because everyone looks at me like I'm an alien,' she said, wincing and shifting uncomfortably on the chair. 'I'm a human being just like everyone else.'" Yet the demand for pumping persists, even as stories of pumping gone wrong proliferate.

Understanding why such an intervention remains desired in light of the very real consequences associated with subcutaneous silicone may seem baffling, until one considers how fears of social death drive the pursuit of risky interventions. However, listening more empathetically to the stories of trans women who pursue pumping reveals the hope that silicone will make life possible, even as it may expedite death. While the consequences of FFS are, by comparison, less threatening, the aim is essentially the same—to eradicate the stigma of a masculine face in order to more easily navigate social life as a woman. In this case, as in other sites of facial work, social death is swapped for threatening, even deadly, interventions. The social life made possible by aesthetic intervention, it seems, trumps the risk of bodily death.

5

Saving Face

Redeeming a Universal Face

In access to the face, there is certainly also an access to the
idea of God.
—Emmanuel Levinas, *Ethics and Infinity* (1985)

Each year, vaccination campaigns funnel over $1 billion dollars from
international aid organizations and private foundations to eradicate
polio in Nigeria, Pakistan, and Afghanistan.[1] Travel cautions circulate,
warning of impending global pandemics from Avian flu to the recently
identified "Middle East Respiratory Syndrome Coronavirus."[2] In a historical moment increasingly defined in "global" or transnational terms,
relationships between nations and populations are forged through
global health crises (and, relatedly, the specter of impending catastro-
phes). Cadres of international medical philanthropic organizations,
such as Doctors Without Borders, the ONE Campaign, and Mercy
Corps, have emerged to cure, fix, and treat bodies around the globe.
These organizations rely on the traffic of biomedical interventions from
the United States and other industrialized nations to places defined as
"in need."

Without a doubt, global health crises have incited panic because
of the threat of massive fatalities, especially in settings where there
are few resources to deal with outbreaks of infectious diseases. For
example, the World Health Organization (WHO) reports that AIDS/

HIV—certainly not a "new" phenomenon—is the *leading* cause of death among adults in Africa.[3] Warnings forecast the impending death of entire generations. But AIDS is not the only global health emergency. The specter of disfigurement motivates international efforts to repair the face, too. In fact, facial work, specifically repair of cleft lip and palate, has advanced as a vital intervention at the same time and in the same places that children die of HIV/AIDS, malaria, and malnourishment. Facial work might appear to be a trivial intervention when deaths due to disease and hunger persist and when international health experts have developed a "human suffering index" in order to rank places in intense need of global attention.[4] And yet, unlike the forms of "disfigurement" treated via extreme makeovers and facial feminization, the phenomena of untreated congenital facial difference in particular parts of the world is both produced and exacerbated by structural violence—the political and economic arrangements that expose populations to harm. Ultimately, the persistent unavailability of necessary resources—medical care, medicine, clean water, or food—in parts of the globe due to enduring disparities underlies these largely preventable emergencies.

Transnational facial work is conducted by several medical philanthropic organizations, but one in particular, Operation Smile, spearheaded the effort and has dominated the enterprise. The story of Operation Smile recounted on its website and in many media accounts about the organization begins in 1982 in the Philippines. During a trip with other medical volunteers, Dr. William P. Magee, a plastic surgeon, and his wife Kathleen Magee, a nurse and clinical social worker, encountered "hundreds" of children "ravaged by deformities." After encountering such overwhelming need, the Magees founded Operation Smile. Through what the organization terms "medical missions," free reconstructive surgery is provided to "indigent" children to repair facial anomalies.[5]

The most common facial anomaly treated is cleft lip and palate. Simply put, cleft lip describes an opening in the lip, while cleft palate refers to a gap in the roof and soft tissue of the mouth. Sometimes, cleft lip and cleft palate co-occur. While these congenital disabilities are fairly simple to repair using basic reconstructive techniques, cleft lip and palate have significant consequences if left untreated. For example, untreated clefts impede nursing and ingestion. Given the rates of malnutrition in the places Operation Smile operates, starvation is a real risk. Cleft lip, by contrast, undermines a child's ability to communicate, and this carries its own set of long-term consequences.

While the precise cause of cleft lip and palate are unknown, epidemiological research indicates that there are both genetic and environmental risk factors that trigger atypical craniofacial development.[6] Congenital differences may run in families, but cleft lip and palate are simultaneously effects of poverty, malnutrition, and compromised maternal health. For women with access to prenatal vitamins containing folic acid, rates of clefts are lower than for women without access.[7] Recent studies in Pakistan suggest there may be a correlation between consanguineous (between blood relations) marriage and the rate of cleft lip and palate.[8] Thus, the phenomenon of cleft is both more prevalent and more problematic in poor, geographically isolated regions of the world.

These particularly vulnerable places, sites of extreme structural violence, are precisely where Operation Smile intervenes.[9] Since 1982, the organization has conducted "missions" in 25 countries.[10] Over 100,000 children have received reconstructive surgery through the efforts of Operation Smile. According to the 2010 Annual Report, the operating budget expenses (i.e., programming, fundraising, administrative costs) hovered around $65 million. During the same time period, the organization accumulated $67 million in revenue, mostly through donations and grants. The value of donated medical services was around $33 million dollars. In 2010 alone, Operation Smile "changed the lives" of 16,113 children through medical intervention.[11]

In 2006, the organization expanded its operations to Iraq, and 245 Iraqi children received free reconstructive surgery. This specific mission is significant because it highlights the ways in which facial work can intervene in patterns of structural violence. In war-ravaged areas, conflict inhibits access to surgical care. While cleft intervention was commonplace before the 2003 Iraq war, new concerns about safety resulted in a sharp decline in the number of medical services dispensed in Iraq. The use of unconventional warfare both by US and Iraqi fighters impeded the work of medical humanitarian efforts too.[12] Thus, venturing into Iraq demonstrates how the organization, intentionally or not, responded not only to the problem of cleft but also to the ways that problem was exacerbated by ongoing US military presence.

In addition to providing surgery, Operation Smile offers physician training to local medical providers, dispenses referrals to US-based clinics, and provides support services, including speech therapy. US-based high school and college student groups sponsored by the organization build awareness about Operation Smile's efforts in local communities and on campuses. According to its website, over 600 student organizations exist. In line with the growth of philanthropic tourism, active college students are invited to volunteer on medical missions as Patient Imaging Technicians.[13] The organization also increases public awareness of cleft lip and palate through ads, which function to generate donations, in media outlets such as the *Financial Times* and *National Geographic*.[14]

As compared with medical tourism—travel from the "developed world" to less expensive destinations for elective or even long-term medical care—and bioprospecting—the extraction of native resources for commercial gain by health industries—Operation Smile represents a reverse biomedical flow.[15] Instead of exporting resources from a vulnerable locale, Operation Smile invests locally. Both medical tourism and bioprospecting are highly problematic. Services and resources that could be used to meet basic health care needs are diverted from the public to the private sector, from local populations to relatively privileged recipients.[16] And yet the reversal of these patterns is not without its own distinct complications.

Because this site of facial work is a charitable international organization, its work is unique from other sites of facial work. Operation Smile, like other sites analyzed in this book, engages in technical work aimed at normalizing facial difference. But to complete this work it relies on donations and volunteer labor, and thus is also intensely invested in mobilizing public support for its missions. Given the fact that Operation Smile requires collective investment, it is imperative to ask: How does Operation Smile portray its work in order to elicit volunteer participation and donor dollars? Specifically, how is facial work represented and how is the disfigurement imaginary employed as Operation Smile continually negotiates its public image in order to raise funds to do its work?

In this site, cleft lip and palate are positioned as socially deadly—as a fundamental threat to key facets of human life. (And indeed, the inability to eat may lead to biological death, just as the inability to communicate may lead to social death.) As we see on *Extreme Makeover* and in sites of facial feminization surgery, Operation Smile adopts the notion that facial difference is a threat to key dimensions of human life and to social interaction. But Operation Smile patients are positioned as socially dead in another, perhaps more significant way: Universal features of humanness are described as fundamentally compromised by facial atypicality.

Popularizing the Aesthetic as Vital

In the years I analyzed the work of Operation Smile its homepage transformed in subtle ways, but regardless of its specific format, it remained a dense website—marked by an abbreviated organization mission, links to news and events, requests for financial contributions, portals for potential volunteers, and video footage documenting participation of celebrity spokespersons or "Smile Ambassadors" in Operation Smile missions. But one truly unique (and captivating) feature of the Operation Smile website is "Smile Stories," which provide photographs and details of an individual patient's story.

At different points in time, these stories are the most prominent feature on Operation Smile's homepage.[17] "Before" pictures of six children—five-year-old Venezuelan boy Arnoldo, three-year-old Chinese girl Min Zhu Lei, thirteen-year-old Kenyan boy Brigid, five-month-old Nicaraguan boy Guillermo, and nine-year-old Vietnamese boy Thanh—circulated sequentially so that each visitor randomly encountered a child's face and story. Like other displays of "disfigurement," the images appeal to a kind of voyeurism. Children with cleft palate and lip are pictured, and because most web surfers likely view these images on a personal screen, staring is made possible and almost invited.[18] Underneath each before photograph, one of the following captions appears:

"Every night before I go to bed, I pray for a miracle. Will it ever come?"

"My village is afraid of me. My papa hides me away. My mama cries. Happiness?"

"Fear. Shame. Sadness. Will there ever be a day when I do not have these feelings?"
"They call me 'Sut' [which means split lip in Vietnamese]. Will there ever be a day they call me by my name?"
"They point. They stare. They call me names, when will it stop?"
"Will I ever feel like smiling with the sun shining brightly on my face?"

These captions are posed to the viewer as if spoken by the very child whose face is depicted in the accompanying picture. It is not clear whether these are the actual children's words, though at best they are a translation, since it is unlikely that each child speaks English. A moment later, the word "someday" flashes next to each photo. Then, an "after" picture appears. Stylistically, after images are not altogether unlike before pictures. Both are tightly framed headshots, but as opposed to the before pictures, which feature dejected (in some cases crying) children, all with cleft lips or palates, the after pictures capture smiling, beaming faces. Only traces of facial difference—a light scar or minute atypicality in an upper lip—are visible. Below each after picture, the following text appears: "With your donation, you can make someday today."

At a basic level, the slideshow plays on the trope of pity to encourage visitors to get involved, specifically to make a financial contribution.[19] With a donation of as little as $240, a child can receive reconstructive surgery.[20] The slideshow is a marketing tool that strategically positions image and text toward tactical ends—soliciting empathy, financial donations, and perhaps volunteer labor. But as happens in other sites of facial work, Operation Smile's branding conflates social death and disfigurement with vitality and aesthetic intervention. The slideshow, along with other features of the website, portray what technical work is accomplished with financial contributions, but equally as important, visitors to the website are offered a narrative—with closure—about disfigurement and aesthetic surgery.

Through promotional materials including the Operation Smile website, print and online advertisements, and infomercials that I discuss in greater depth later in this chapter, Operation Smile, perhaps more than any global health entity, disseminates information to the public about cleft lip and palate and the stark consequences of untreated facial disfigurement. But Operation Smile's work is covered extensively in news media, too. News coverage is data, in and of itself, about the ways in which the disfigurement imaginary and notions of aesthetic intervention as vital transcend sites of facial work and seep into the popular imagination.

At the most basic level, news coverage reifies one idea consistently—that children "suffer" from "defects," "deformities," and "abnormalities." Some accounts offer details about how children's lives—their physical and psychological health, their relationships with other children and with their families, their status as normal, and their futures—are affected by their faces. This kind of story resembles the plot of *Extreme Makeover*—that "disfigurement" precludes emotional, intimate, and economic dimensions of human life and thus amounts to a kind of social death. Suffering stories embody a "before" narrative, one that details the kind of social death children experience due to cleft lip and palate. It is critical to point out that this pattern of emphasizing what life is like before facial work is indispensible to constructing new meanings of aesthetic intervention. In other words, the "after" effect generated by Operation Smile only carries the meaning that it does in relation to what comes before.

Regularly, news accounts of Operation Smile emphasize the physiological effects of craniofacial anomalies. Images of children pictured in promotional materials display visual difference, but descriptions of children in news accounts emphasize physical impairment. Taken together, children are characterized as not only aesthetically variant but also functionally compromised. An *Africa News* article demonstrates this pattern: "Facial deformities are not only a physical defect but can be a huge handicap from an emotional level . . . 'These children can't speak clearly. They can't even eat properly because the food goes flying so they have very low self-esteem.'"[21] Another account echoes this emphasis on the "handicapping" effects of cleft: "Inability to feed well eventually leads to malnutrition and then ear and chest infections. Also, speech defects later occur as the child grows up and there are also other problems such as poor mental development, social maladjustment among others . . . These kids with cleft palate can get fluid into their middle ear which can result in hearing loss."[22] Even as appearance difference is acknowledged as hugely stigmatizing, news coverage works in conjunction with Operation Smile's efforts to convey that facial difference is a "huge," or perhaps real, disability. Describing the physical consequences of facial variance provides a sense of the "costs" of disfigurement and serves to amplify the mission of the organization.

Accounts make connections between the physical costs of disfigurement and the emotional or psychological consequences, portraying children as doubly disadvantaged. Operation Smile's recipients are depicted as both physically disabled, like the children featured in Jerry Lee Lewis telethons, and socially ostracized, like the children featured in the recent documentary *Bully* (2011). Of course, for telethon participants and bullied school children, the experience of a disability, be it cerebral palsy or Tourette syndrome, often occurs in tandem with the socially disabling consequences of stigma and peer rejection. In fact, social response is in itself disabling. Consider another news account that draws on an interview with an Operation Smile worker: "'These children are unable to have a normal life. They can't breathe, eat or speak properly, are often not admitted in schools, and are ridiculed. Our aim is to restore normal life to these children,' said Mr. Racel Wawn, development director, Operation Smile India."[23] Descriptions of the physiological effects of cleft lip and palate are regularly intertwined with references to the socially disabling dynamics that are a result of social stigma, rather than the disability itself. The ways in which basic bodily functions like eating and breathing are not disentangled from the social consequences of facial atypicality both reflect and propagate the disfigurement imaginary, which conflates difference and suffering.

In depicting the costs of cleft lip and palate, media accounts also stress that children untreated resolutely experience problems with social interaction, in ways that are similar to how facial feminization surgeons describe the costs of a "male" face for trans women. The *Irish Times* writes, "The condition can cause children to be shunned."[24] These facts could be depicted in an alternative way. News accounts could explain that the cultural stigma of facial difference results in social exclusion, for example. Instead, "the condition" is regularly attributed as the sole cause of a wide range of social interaction failures. Stories routinely emphasize the ways in which peers bully visually atypical children, but family relationships also become important in demonstrating what is at stake.[25] An *Africa News* article asserts, "Even some parents do not want to be associated with their [the children's] deformed faces."[26] Parent-child interaction is an emotionally charged human dynamic, thus parents' rejection suggests the severity of social isolation some experience, but this "cost" puts children's lives especially at risk. Because abject poverty characterizes the places Operation Smile works, nutritious food, basic medical care, and clean water are often difficult to access. Caregivers' investment in children's well-being is indispensible for attaining essential resources. Stories like these intimate that intervention to fix the "deformity" is a child's only hope if he or she is actually to survive. Here, the disfigurement imaginary is popularized, but vital notions of facial work are disseminated, too.

Most significantly, stories suggest that children with craniofacial anomalies have at best an uncertain future, and at worst are facing a fate worse than death. One article describes a child who "cannot blow out the [birthday] candles."[27] This reference points to the functional effects of cleft lip and palate but also plays on the uncertainty of the child's maturation. The very ritual that signifies passing from one year to the next is used to suggest that the child's body and relationship to time is fragile. Another article in the *Irish Times* suggests: "Without surgery, these children in the developing world don't stand a hope. They are never part of the school going population. Many are hidden at home, and in some countries, they will be placed in institutions."[28] In this account, the improbability of attending school, the certainty of social isolation, and the chances of institutionalization amount to "hopeless" futures or, in other words, social death. Other stories conjure similar images of impending despair, using language like "plight," "bleak," and "very lonely."[29]

Most who read these news accounts, who click on an Operation Smile ad on their Facebook sidebar, or who turn the channel to an Operation Smile infomercial will never volunteer for a mission. Many more will never meet someone with untreated cleft lip or palate, and yet all who encounter Operation Smile's promotional materials or news coverage about the organization take away some sense about the costs of disfigurement and the benefits of facial work. By unpacking the narratives embedded in these materials, I do not mean to suggest that these descriptions are not true or valid. Physical consequences of cleft palate are real, as are the insidious effects of social isolation spurred by extreme stigma. But at the same time that facts about cleft lip and palate are promulgated, ambient messages are dispensed, too. The disfigurement imaginary and its linkages to social death permeate these stories, and the ways they begin to shape widely held notions about facial difference are largely taken for granted. It's just a simple news story after all.

Creating Smiles, Saving Lives

The name Operation Smile is an interesting one. Most obviously, it refers to the literal surgeries or operations the organization conducts. The word "operation" also carries connotations of travel and adventure, in part because the name capitalizes on militaristic imagery. ("Join the military, see the world!") The word "operation" is sometimes used to describe military incursions, including Operation Desert Storm and Operation Iraqi Freedom. In these contexts, "operation" is a substitute for the term "war." Like military conflict, the work of the organization unfolds across geopolitical borders. But as opposed to propagating democracy, this is an operation ostensibly aimed at bestowing smiles. And smiles abound in this site: The name of the organization emphasizes smiling, the "after" photographs prominently feature smiling faces, and Operation Smile's most prominent slogans include "Changing Lives One Smile at a Time" and "Together, we create smiles, change lives, heal humanity." Undoubtedly the name is catchy, especially when compared with a more factually descriptive alternative, something like International Travel for Craniofacial Anomaly Repair. And of course, philanthropic organizations like Operation Smile that rely upon volunteer hours and donations must effectively mobilize imagery. But like "operation," "smile" has its own subtle dimensions.[30]

The techniques used to repair cleft lip and palate yield functional effects through fusing congenital fissures in the face, mouth, and nasal cavity. But in Operation Smile promotional materials and news coverage about the organization, the smile is referenced as the principle "after" effect. The smile operates as a sort of corporeal shorthand. As one account demonstrates, the result of intervention is described simply as a smile, without any real explanation about what that means: "But when they come here they know the stigma will go and they will go back home with a smile, said the nurse."[31] Of course, children presumably return home with a changed appearance and restored facial function, but the smile serves as the primary way of referencing the physical and existential change that has occurred.

The smile is characterized as a durable thing—something one can possess, rather than an action or a physiological expression that a face can make. One account describes the smile as "the best gift you can give a child."³² In this site, smiles are regularly characterized as "gifts" which are given to or bestowed onto recipients: "One campaign has literally brought smiles to faces of children."³³ In talking about smiles as things, the work of Operation Smile is positioned as an economic transaction, in which a valued durable good, a smile, is given to children in need. Of course, the meaning of a gift is not intrinsic to the gift, but rather determined by context. Flowers can function as a gift of love, a sign of sympathy, or gesture of apology. Thus, the smile as a gift carries an ambiguous meaning. Referencing the gift of a smile could simply be shorthand for restored facial function or a new appearance, and certainly facial work produces both of these effects. Yet the smile as a gift functions as a reference to a hopeful future, a possibility acquired *only* via aesthetic intervention.

The smile and the future are contingent upon one another in these accounts, as the following demonstrates: "The correction of deformities makes a world of difference for these children. It helps build self-confidence. It not just creates smiles, it also paves the way for a brighter future."³⁴ Another story quotes a volunteer for an Operation Smile Kenya mission, who describes how a relatively small amount of money can create a smile: "Most of these children are only Sh15,000 [$175 USD] from that precious smile that they will live with for the rest of their lives."³⁵ The smile carries a value because it embodies a kind of permanence. Once facial structure is restored in such a way as to facilitate smiling, presumably a child will *always* be able to smile.

Children's smiles are also referenced to describe what volunteers may accrue from their Operation Smile efforts: "The danger of challenging political and religious barriers is more than compensated by the smiles that eventually grace the faces of thousands of poor children every year—children who have been stopped from attending school, who have been locked away, ostracized by their communities and, often, by their own families . . . but it's the smiles that keep him [a volunteer] going back . . . the smiles are worth more than a million bucks."³⁶ What makes the smile such a gratifying outcome is that it operates as a framework for talking about something much larger; volunteers have given children the gift of hope, the gift of a brighter future, and, indeed, what greater gift can one give a child?

In the organization's name, its slogans and promotional materials, and news coverage about its work, the smile is made to speak for itself. The smile is a semaphore to describe the accomplishments of facial work. As the most commonly referenced "after" effect of facial work, a smile's meaning is deeply connected to how children's lives are understood before intervention. Hundreds of volunteers would not traverse the globe at personal risk nor would donors generate millions to produce a furrowed brow or a grimace. By contrast, the smile is a salient and desirable expression because it represents highly valued dimensions of human life. And yet, cultural critic Dellareese Higgs asks what is "behind the smile," and argues that white tourism imposes an identity on (nonwhite) "others" that requires the appearance of happiness to legitimate racialized power differentials.[37] Even as it is useful to think about how "smiles" function strategically, it is also worth asking how the smile echoes tropes about "happy natives" used historically to justify colonialist ventures.

In everyday life, smiles are associated with pleasure. When we're told to smile, as women regularly are, we are being asked to do the emotional work of appearing happy. Yet facial expression research indicates that what a smile means is contingent on context. As psychologist James A. Russell writes, "Whereas a smile in the context of just having received a gift might be interpreted as a sign of pleasure, a smile in the context of just having spilled soup might be interpreted as a sign of embarrassment, and a smile in the context of greeting an adversary might be interpreted as an act of politeness.[38] As opposed to this more nuanced social psychological account of what a smile means, in the context of medical philanthropic marketing, "giving the gift of a smile" is a way of bringing "joy to the world." Given that children with cleft lip and palate are routinely described as suffering, the (surgical) shift to happiness is momentous.

At the same time, happiness itself is an ineffable outcome. What precisely is happiness? And how do we know if someone is "really" happy? Answering these questions may be difficult if not impossible, but there seems to be a shared sense that everyone desires happiness and happiness is paramount for good living. Producing happiness, then, is no small thing. It is a highly valued outcome but one that is hard to pin down. By claiming to produce something that is so disagreeable to definition, the work of Operation Smile takes on an aura of wonder. Surely this facilitates financial contributions, but so too does it reposition the "disfigured" face as an object in need of miraculous intervention.

Another consequence of employing the smile as shorthand is to infuse facial work with vital significance. Psychologists who study facial expression and nonverbal communication agree that virtually everyone everywhere smiles.[39] Someone could encounter anyone from anywhere, and each would understand (at least in a general sense) what a smile suggests about the other. It may be cliché, but the idea is confirmed in the scholarly literature, making smiles one of the few human universals. This makes Operation Smile's deployment of the smile particularly striking. Because the smile is conceptualized as a *universal* expression, restoring a smile gives children access to an essentially human attribute. "Before" intervention, children are socially dead by proxy of lacking a universal feature of humanity. "After" intervention, children now possess this universally human trait. Like other forms of facial work, the intervention is imbued with lifesaving potential.

Certainly, the organization touts its work as life-changing, as implied in the slogan "Changing lives one smile at a time." Both news accounts and materials produced by the organization intimate that out of abject circumstances, life is made possible. This narrative works as an effective marketing tool and fundraising method. By focusing on what children are like "before" and then describing the "after" effects in vital terms, the facial work accomplished by Operation Smile is positioned as a shift from a life characterized by absolute dejection to hope, a transformation from socially dead to universally human. These are remarkable changes. By visually and rhetorically representing children before and after surgery, Operation Smile's work is positioned as a radical mode of social repair wherein children's faces are dramatically remade, and in the process new ways of being and experiencing the world are made possible. It is in this context of life-changing representation that the tangible work of Operation Smile can take on sacred tones.

Facial Work as a "Mission"

The word mission describes a range of practices and carries multiple connotations. The term itself has a deeply entrenched historical significance, describing global travel wherein "missionaries," representatives, or evangelists are sent from one place to another place, a "foreign" place as the Oxford English Dictionary explicates, to do good works, or god works. By characterizing its work as a "mission," Operation Smile positions its work in terms of goals and outcomes. But in another sense, "mission" portrays the enterprise as an intervention that unfolds between the "haves" and "have-nots" of the world. And even more, designating the work as a mission infuses facial repair with particular, often religious, subtexts and meanings. How might we begin to make sense of this?

Sociologist Robert L. Montgomery describes the sociological study of missions in this way:

> The sociology of missions may be defined as a comprehensive sociological study of the spread or diffusion of religions . . . What makes sociology of missions distinct from other sociological studies of religions or religious growth is its focus on the crossing of socio-cultural borders by religions. In short, the sociology of missions is simply the sociological study of religions and ideologies in their diffusing activities, not simply through migration, but primarily as they have spread across sociocultural boundaries by propagation or dissemination.[40]

In defining the sociology of missions, Montgomery provides a framework for knowing a mission when we see one. Ultimately, a mission is constituted by three elements. First, a mission is aimed at a goal, specifically the diffusion of religion, but also, as Montgomery notes, at the circulation of ideologies. Second, propagation, as opposed to passive diffusion, is the means for transmitting the mission's message. Finally, a mission takes place across sociocultural borders, including but not limited to geopolitical territories. Without ideological diffusion through propagation, moving across borders is simply travel. Without travel across borders (geopolitical, economic, racial or ethnic borders), a mission loses its zeal, and its work is more akin to mundane volunteerism.

These three elements are indispensible to making a mission the salvation venture it aims to be.

Interviews with Operation Smile staff and mission volunteers reveal a collective approach to facial work that maps precisely onto the elements of religious missions that Montgomery describes. While the surgical work of repairing cleft is altogether different from the colonial (and postcolonial) ventures of Christian denominations, the work is embedded in similar structures of meanings. Analogizing facial work to a mission achieves several ends. It helps to convey the organizational vision to others. Presumably, this language is strategically crafted to mobilize resources, but perhaps most significantly, positioning facial work in mission discourse infuses the ways that medical practitioners understand the significance of technical intervention. The three constitutive elements of missions emerge in interviewees' descriptions of their work with Operation Smile and coalesce to lend vital significance to facial work.

First, Operation Smile's work mimics a religious mission in that the activities are directly organized around a central task, namely the eradication of congenital facial anomalies. This is technical work, but Operation Smile also disseminates ideological formations. Positioning its efforts as not simply health care but rather akin to the activities of other kinds of missions situates facial work in the framework of salvation. In addition, the disfigurement imaginary, specifically the ways cleft is reduced to a kind of social death, functions ideologically, too. It's not simply that the organization conceptualizes facial disfigurement in particular ways, but that it implicitly encourages recipients to understand their lives in these terms, not unlike how biomedicine operates in its "home" contexts as well.

In this way, Operation Smile is a "troubled person industry," approaching its work as a mode of generosity toward people in need.[41] In an examination of programs related to deafness, psychologist Harlan Lane argues that a troubled person industry, like those organizations dominated by hearing professionals who provide services to the Deaf, "seeks total conformity of the client to the underlying construction of deafness as disability."[42] As opposed to the work of organizations premised on a disability rights model (like the United Kingdom's About Face) that calls into question fundamental tenets of the disfigurement imaginary, specifically that facial difference can be reduced to suffering,

Operation Smile provides technical intervention while co-constructing meanings with patients and others regarding the significance of facial anomalies. As is true across each site of facial work, the disfigurement imaginary operates to infuse repair with social and moral significance. In this framing, disfigurement is unambiguously tragic, sometimes the most catastrophic state of human existence, and the face is positioned as essential for everyday life, making intervention on human visages deeply essential. It may be a 45-minute, $250 operation, but it is imbued with the discursive force of "lifesaving" work.

Second, Operation Smile mimics the propagation function of other kinds of missions by vigorously sharing the "good news" of facial work. To be sure, evangelical Christian missions have worked for centuries toward the goal of "saving" indigenous people from the eternal damnation that comes with traditional, that is to say non-Christian, forms of spiritual practice. While Operation Smile is explicitly nonreligious, its work takes on sacred tones. In interviews with volunteers, medical mission work is described as a kind of Good Samaritan effort. Karen, an Operation Smile volunteer, explained it this way:

> I'm a doctor's wife. People are thinking why would you want to do this? Why would you want to go and live in that squalor, but it's not like I feel like I'm saving the world or what I'm doing is so important for the world. But it's important to me to I feel like I'm helping someone. It's addictive, and I want to go back and do it again and again.

In the same way that religious practice often positions asceticism or self-denial as a means for accessing spiritual insight or salvation, there is something to be gained by living in "squalor" for the sake of helping someone. While religion offers believers both a worldview and a set of rituals to order life, participating in mission work structures volunteers' lives in similar ways. Betsy, a nurse certified in plastic and reconstructive surgery who has participated in over forty missions, explained,

> We save the quality of the life. We enrich the quality of life. We give the life more purpose. We make such a positive effect. We change directions. We do this not only for the patients, but I've done over 40 missions, and I've referred to Operation Smile as the golden thread of my life tapestry.

The concept of the "golden thread" is an image sometimes invoked in Judaic-Christian traditions to describe the constant connection a divine being has to devotees. By describing her work in this way, Betsy characterizes Operation Smile as a method for facilitating spiritual connection in her life. Both volunteers and recipients deployed the sacred in describing medical missions. Betsy's story of a Bolivian girl with a facial angioma, a type of benign tumor, exposed how medical intervention becomes positioned as a hallowed encounter:

> The mother just looked at the girl and said, "Every day I prayed for a miracle, and God sent me you, and if it wasn't for you looking at me, and if it wasn't for the fact of your generosity, I don't know what I would have done. Our lives are changed forever." . . . If you ever want to play God, this is it. This is your chance.

This moment reveals how thoroughly sacred Operation Smile's work appears for those most deeply involved. The mother comprehended volunteers as an answer to her prayers, and volunteers understood the work of a mission as playing God—a role surgeons have long held.

Just as the religious mission approaches its work as imbued with grave consequences, most obviously salvation, Operation Smile volunteers described how medical intervention delivers patients from an uncertain end. When I asked Dr. Roberts why he focused his work toward facial repair versus other kinds of interventions, he replied,

> This is a disease that we have a cure for. There are a lot of diseases that we won't have a cure for in our lifetime. We have a cure for this. If we know that the disability is so large, why would we choose to ignore it? I would never try to oppose anyone who does HIV or malaria care or research. There are fundamental needs but I don't think one should stop the other from being pursued. To anyone who does not think that facial surgery is a big deal, I would invite them to see a mother receive her child after surgery, to see a father kiss a child, to see a boy back in school gaining confidence. Those are things that a lot of us take for granted, but a lot of people don't have the option of having [those experiences]. For all of this, there is an intervention . . . My belief is that if they were to see or to be in front of a face of suffering and had the option of changing that into

a world of opportunities in just forty five minutes which is all that surgical repair of a cleft takes, I would imagine that they would have a hard time saying no to changing the life of a child.

The idea implicit in this account is that surgery changes the life of the child and that without surgery, the nature of life is tenuous at best. Just as Christian missionaries can secure salvation by encouraging locals to "accept Jesus Christ as your Lord and Savior," medical missionaries can access vitality for children. Over and over again, volunteers pointed to what facets of life are not possible with facial difference. Dr. Tyson, a surgeon based at Shriners Hospital in Los Angeles, explained, "They can't smile. They can't kiss, and think about how we go through our life smiling and kissing." As Dr. Matthews remarked about the children who receive facial repair, "They would never get a job, never be able to feed their family. Their lives are dramatically different. You see people who have now been given an opportunity to in their world live a normal life. They don't become president of the bank or a beauty contest winner, but they can go out and do something."

Finally, Operation Smile's work takes place across geographic and cultural borders. Operation Smile traffics biomedicine between the "developed" and "developing" worlds, between the global North and the global South, between "America" and the "rest of the world," and between adults and children. Where Operation Smile is based versus where much of its work takes place diverges along lines of economic security, gender relations, war and conflict, environmental risk, access to health care, and exposure to disease. Who receives Operation Smile interventions and who conducts those interventions is defined by geopolitical disparities and uneven relations to privilege and cultural capital, as is also true for religious missions. Facial work beneficiaries are inherently "in need" of what Operation Smile missionaries have to give. Whether in the United States or in Afghanistan, the disfigurement imaginary continually positions those with facial difference as in desperate need of repair (just as religious missionary discourse understands the unsaved as in desperate need of salvation.).

Many mission volunteers conduct similar medical work in the United States as doctors, nurses, and speech therapists, but volunteers understand the work of Operation Smile as unique because the stigma of cleft varies by culture and the consequences of facial difference vary depending on where one is located. Thus, place figured prominently in volunteers' descriptions of recipients' preintervention experiences. Specifically, stories emphasized the interplay between culture and stigma. Karen, a speech pathologist who has traveled on fourteen missions to countries including Haiti, Ethiopia, and India, described the lives of children she has met:

> In Kenya, they [the family] kept her in a tent. She was the daughter of a Massai warrior. The person that brought her was her aunt, not even her mother. She brought her because she didn't want her to have the kind of life she had. She was sold when she was nine years old to a seventy-year-old for a cow, and she didn't want her not to have a voice. This little girl lives in a tent and never came out because she was so horrible looking in that society, and afterward she was able to come out. In another place, a little girl had a paper bag over her head because her family was so ashamed. In Morocco and Egypt, they wore a shawl over their face, so it wasn't so bad for them because they wore the shawl anyway.

This response ultimately pointed to the ways in which the experience of facial difference is particular to one's cultural location. Here, stigma was implicitly hierarchized, used to distinguish places from one another, and, by proxy, to convey the relative neediness of particular recipients. Extreme stigma, essentially the institutionalization of the disfigurement imaginary, like the kind Karen described, suggests that the significance of facial work is contingent on place. This idea was echoed over and over again by volunteers who see their work as both akin to and entirely distinct from the work they do as facial workers in the United States.

Operation Smile's Medical Coordinator Dr. Roberts first encountered Operation Smile as a seventeen-year-old local Panamanian translator for a 1980 mission. In our conversation, he described being amazed at how many children with facial clefts appeared at the Panama mission hoping for surgery. His story revealed the ways in which the incidence of facial difference is often undetectable because those who are affected may not enter public spaces with any regularity. The experience of seeing cleft lip and palate in such numbers was so shocking and the work of Operation Smile so transformative to Dr. Roberts that he quickly decided to pursue a degree in medicine. In this way, his story revealed how experiencing a mission first-hand led to his conversion to doctoring, generally, and to facial work, specifically. Using his own cross-cultural embeddedness in Panama and in the United States, he explained that facial difference causes suffering not only for the affected child but also for their families precisely because of distinct cultural worldviews.

> People try to find ways to explain, "Why them? Did I do something? Why am I deserving of this ill?" . . . People over the centuries have tried to figure out a way to explain. And there are such negative connotations for children with clefts. It was thought in the past that witches had their cats, which had the resemblance of a cleft, so that it [facial cleft] was directly linked to witchcraft or something evil. And even if you didn't do something bad yourself, your family must have done something bad to deserve this, so you try to imagine what it is like for parents who have a child born with a cleft. At this point they don't even know all the things they are going to have to deal with related to the care of these children.

While traditional religious missions are directly aimed at confronting indigenous beliefs in the occult, Operation Smile must negotiate with the very same worldviews given that these are the frameworks with which some patients and their families make sense of why facial cleft affects some and not others. Like other kinds of missions, cultural worldview becomes an object of intervention, in itself.

Historically, the religious mission, often implicitly and sometimes inadvertently, disseminated ideas about the relative value of cultural practices and "saved" locals from "native ways" including healing practices, rites of adulthood, and methods of infant care, even as the ubiquitous goal was religious conversion. Operation Smile conducts facial work but in doing that work across borders, workers inevitably intervene in circumstances directly tied the culture of the place where a mission occurs. Dr. Matthews, a pediatric anesthesiologist who has volunteered for over 16 years, told the story of a Bolivian woman repaired on a mission:

> I was in Bolivia two years ago . . . I take thousands of pictures. There were two Bolivian women . . . One had these scarves over her face, and

they had come down from the Andes mountains, and I went over to take a picture, and all of the sudden she lowered her thing and she indeed had a cleft lip . . . Someone came up to me and said, "Rich, we really need to fix this lady right now. Her husband just found out that her friend brought her down to get fixed, and she doesn't have her husband's permission." And I said, "What does that have to do with anything?" "Well if you don't get her fixed her husband is going to take her back to the mountains, and she'll never get fixed." We brought her in the operating room and thirty minutes later she was fixed. Then we had to send her to the women's shelter because her husband was going to come and probably split her lip in two just because he hadn't given permission for this surgery. So when you see stories like that, you realize you've made a huge difference in this woman's life.

To be sure, the "huge difference" produced by intervention was corporeal. The cleft was repaired, but equally significant is the fact that the woman was brought to a shelter for protection from an abusive marriage. Matthews's story implied that in addition to her disability, the woman was saved from a culturally determined power dynamic that felt foreign to him. To be sure, domestic abuse happens everywhere, but Matthews's description of this event emphasized the "lost in translation" moment. In this way, the relationship between mission volunteers and recipients is thoroughly infused with the politics of place.

Understanding how Operation Smile's medical missions resemble traditional religious missions is helpful for understanding the ideological and conceptual processes that happen alongside technical intervention. Facial work involves surgical repair, but as we have seen, it simultaneously drives ways of seeing facial difference. In relation to this site, the question remains: What are the consequences of structuring medical interventions on a mission model? In his book *Mission in Today's World* (2000), theologian and missionary Donal Dorr identifies five functions of contemporary missions. Missions facilitate 1) dialogue, 2) evangelization, 3) enculturation, 4) struggle for liberation, and 5) reconciliation. Rather than speculating about Operation Smile's adherence to these practices, I want to briefly describe what each of these functions might look like in the context of medical missions. In doing so, I raise questions about the promise and the problematics of missionary-style facial work.

Dorr asserts that missions are not simply about "doing" for others but are instead about listening and sharing. In the context of a medical mission, such conversation might take place via a consultation or in the downtime of recovery. Given that Operation Smile maintains relationships with patients and provides extensive services including counseling, it stands as a model for how international medical work *might* unfold in ethical ways. Dorr translates evangelization into "bringing the good news." For Operation Smile volunteers, bringing good news might be constituted through describing the hope and promise offered by technological intervention. Relatedly, enculturation involves the processes through which a culture embodies the good news. By surgically shaping children's faces, Operation Smile quite literally facilitates enculturation. As a part of some missions, local medical workers are trained to continue conducting facial work even after American volunteers have returned home. In this way, the culture of "first-world" medicine is transmitted. Certainly by offering free medical intervention, Operation Smile economically "liberates" recipients from certain constraints of poverty. But if the unspoken assumption of liberation is that those "saved" will become more like the missionary, medical missions may solidify existing inequitable economic, political, and cultural relations between the Global North and the Global South. Finally, reconciliation involves forgiveness and understanding. It is the work of acknowledging that a relationship is characterized by injustice and sometimes forged through violence.

In thinking through how dimensions of reconciliation play out in regard to Operation Smile, it seems important to distinguish reconciliation from reparation. While reconciliation relies on naming inequality, it is ultimately forged when that injustice is let go. By contrast, reparations involve the sustained acknowledgment of victimization and relative powerlessness through compensation. Reparation remembers who did what to whom. Medical missions offered in response to global inequality or the related guilt of privileged "first-worlders" may forge a sense of reconciliation that is accompanied by a kind of forgetting that perpetuates the structural inequalities at play.

The Christian missionary project has long been criticized as a venture that propagates colonialism.[43] Conversion sometimes comes at the cost of destroying local culture, perpetuating relative powerlessness in global economic structures, and rampant othering. But Operation Smile is not the Catholic Church. It does not deal in holy water, blessed beads, and devotional candles but rather in surgery, anesthesia, and radical shifts in subjectivity and status. It remains a question to what degree the mundane work of medical missions produces, perhaps inadvertently, similar outcomes as religious missions.

To be sure, Operation Smile trains local practitioners and not all volunteers come from the United States, but given that the majority of missionaries are white, educationally privileged Americans, and the majority of recipients are local to mission sites, mostly nonwhite, and overwhelmingly impoverished, we must ask whether mission practices intersect with the enduring legacy of colonialism and the white savior industrial complex. After seeing "Kony 2012," a viral video released by the nonprofit Invisible Children, an organization founded by white American college students to raise funds for war-torn Uganda, novelist and cultural critic Teju Cole took to Twitter to respond. He described the "white savior industrial complex" as the fastest growing industry in the United States. Philanthropic ventures, including but not limited to Invisible Children, led by white Westerners (or in the name of Western nations which are coded as white) fall under Cole's concept. The white savior, he explained, "support[s] brutal policies in the morning, founds charities in the afternoon, and receives awards in the evening."[44] In another Tweet, he elaborates, "The white savior industrial complex is not about justice. It is about having a big emotional experience that validates privilege."[45]

The very idea of the white savior industrial complex was met with both celebration and rage. Cole was alternately described as a truth teller and as a racist. In an *Atlantic* article, Cole rejects the criticism that his tweets were simply about calling out do-gooders and argues instead for rethinking the ethics of philanthropy:

> Let us begin our activism right here: with the money-driven villainy at the heart of American foreign policy. To do this would be to give up the illusion that the sentimental need to "make a difference" trumps all other considerations. What innocent heroes don't always understand is that they play a useful role for people who have much more cynical

motives. The White Savior Industrial Complex is a valve for releasing the unbearable pressures that build in a system built on pillage. We can participate in the economic destruction of Haiti over long years, but when the earthquake strikes it feels good to send $10 each to the rescue fund. I have no opposition, in principle, to such donations (I frequently make them myself), but we must do such things only with awareness of what else is involved. If we are going to interfere in the lives of others, a little due diligence is a minimum requirement.[46]

Ultimately, Cole implores Western (white) do-gooders to rethink doing good in two ways. First, own up to the motives that drive philanthropic interventions, so that personal catharsis does not subsume the real needs of others. Second, consider the structural underpinnings and historical legacies that together sustain the very infrastructure of the problems that capture our activist hearts. Cole does not ask us to stop doing good. He asks us to do good better.

Ultimately, thinking about how medical missions *are* like a religious mission is critically important in crafting ethical interventions. Specifically, we have to see the mission from all sides. At the most basic level, the mission requires someone going on a mission and someone receiving a mission. To be sure, receiving a medical intervention on behalf of a mission situates one in a relatively powerless position, but there are consequences for those that go on missions and for the societies that missionaries come from. Missions are directed at social problems in such a way as to minimize the complexity of an issue. A mission is bounded. There is a beginning and an end, a task to be completed, and a plan for completing it. Missions provide missionaries with the pleasure of helping, and in this way, the mission directly benefits the missionary. Yet the narrative of mission work emphasizes how good works benefit the needy while ignoring how missionaries are implicated in the underlying causes of the problems they aim to fix.

The mission of Operation Smile is enticing not only because it is described as so meaningful, but also because it seems so *easy*. The "Quick Facts" feature on the Operation Smile website seems to suggest that the "fix" for facial difference is simple relative to other health issues: "For $240 Operation Smile can change a child's life by giving the gift of a surgery . . . In as little as 45 minutes, one cleft lip surgery can

change a child's life forever."[47] While repair of the face may seem suspect at the precise moment in which children in the places Operation
Smile operates are dying of structural inequities, facial intervention is
positioned both as critical and as more simple. It is described as life-
changing, but at relatively little cost and time. Children are helped, but
this help does not require radical restructuring of economic relationships—as would need to happen, for example, to provide drugs to children suffering from HIV/AIDS. And while facial work is dispensed, no
solutions to the abject poverty, malnutrition, lack of prenatal care, and
toxic exposure that causes clefts in the first place are extended. In this
way, it is a downstream intervention that favors repair over prevention.
Children's lives are changed, and at the same time no political alliances
are dissolved or erected—as is needed, for example, to make Iraqi children safe from US-sponsored bombings. Children are given the gift of
a future, but not by reassessing policy, which keeps American borders
closed to those seeking entry for education or asylum.

I am not suggesting that Operation Smile missions should not proceed. In fact, as a feminist sociologist I deeply support any intervention
that makes it possible for young girls and boys to survive and thrive. As
a community engaged scholar and activist, I respect and applaud the
time volunteers invest in a venture they know to have a life- and world-
changing impact. At a personal level, I delight in the moments depicted
in Operation Smile infomercials capturing the moment in which a
young child, earlier pictured crying, smiles at her very first postsurgical mirror reflection. I celebrate the distribution of basic health care,
too. Yet in each site analyzed in this book, the overarching question is
not *should* this intervention exist, but rather what are the byproducts of
facial work proceeding as it does?

Each site of facial work conceptualizes disfigurement as socially
deadly and intervention, by extension, as a mechanism for facilitating
life, but in this site, facial work is also overlaid with another kind of lifesaving significance. In characterizing facial work as a mission, aesthetic
intervention is, by proxy, compared to the soul saving task of a spiritual
mission. To be sure, critics would claim that Operation Smile is a mul-
timillion-dollar organization and that describing facial work as a "mission" amounts to a branding strategy, nothing more. But is it the case
that "life" and "death" function merely as rhetorical devices deployed

with dramatic flourish toward strategic ends? Is the use of "vitality" throughout these sites simply metaphorical? Regardless of what facial workers intend, these patterns establish a subjective infrastructure that makes envisioning disfigurement and social death as inextricably linked. Refiguring facial work as a vital intervention is especially salient in this site because cleft lip and palate are not simply appearance disabilities but functional impairments that can lead to social death and bodily death.

Where Social Death Meets Biological Death

In practical terms, Operation Smile is in a unique position to convey how facial difference is not simply aesthetic but rather a functional impediment. While facial difference is regularly positioned as a socially deadly condition, particular congenital anomalies or facial traumas can produce other kinds of deadly effects. Especially in this site as compared to others examined in the book, the reconstructive, the aesthetic, and the vital dimensions of facial work map onto one another such that it is impossible to disentangle each element of intervention. It is true that the facial difference treated here carries deadly consequences in some cases, but what is interesting are the ways in which functional impediments and social stigma are routinely collapsed and each is positioned as equivalently deadly.

In our interview, Dr. Matthews explained how facial difference increases a child's likelihood of other threatening bodily harms, most specifically respiratory disease and infection:

> To try to feed a baby whose mouth and nose are connected is really complicated. In developing countries, you already have the complication of figuring out proper nutrition and on top of that the inability to feed properly and on top of that, because of the physical aspect, you're already more susceptible to upper respiratory infections. Your immune system is weakened. It's not just the cleft that you see. It's the function—the ability to prevail and develop just as anyone else would.

In his account, the "ability to prevail" was synonymous with survival, which is threatened if intervention does not occur. In this way, facial work not only wards off social death but also saves lives in the traditional sense. Similarly, Betsy, the mission volunteer quoted earlier, described how a cleft impacts basic oral functions and thus is a matter of life and death:

> If you have a problem with feeding or speaking, socially you are at a huge disadvantage. When you are eating if you have a cleft significant enough, food comes out of your nose. Because you don't have that palliative closing, when you swallow you put food in your mouth, food goes behind your vellum . . . And it goes right up your nose through your nasal cavity. When you talk you sound like this [makes garbled nasal noises that are unrecognizable as words]. You can't communicate, so it's hard to get through school. You can't get a job because people can't understand you, except for maybe your family . . . In a desperate third world country, you know Maslow's theory, you basically have to survive. Survival is about eating. If you can't get food in correctly, you're not going to make it. You're not going to have adequate nutrition.

Cleft is not simply an appearance or quality of life matter; rather, children with unrepaired facial cleft are "not going to make it." As Betsy noted, cleft inhibits proper nutrition; we eat to survive, and children who cannot eat will die. Interestingly, the ability to speak or communicate is positioned as vital, even though these processes are not typically conceived as essential for life. Here, Betsy conceptualized factors that potentially mediate stigma as ones that can decrease one's likelihood of dying. Communication is required for schooling, which is essential for employment, which is critical for survival.

The ways in which concerns about social death and bodily death converge to drive intervention are also demonstrated by volunteer Karen, who explained:

> The babies aren't thriving. They don't weigh enough because they can't get enough nutrition in . . . The way we're saving lives is initially, we're getting the baby to eat and to feed. We're keeping the baby from starving to death . . . Number one is survival . . . Number two is getting them to look a certain way so that they can be accepted by their family. A kid can be dejected and rejected by their family. The parents are so sad and

distraught about how their child looks. It's hard to smile at a baby that can't smile back. If a child can't make sounds, a lot of times parents won't make sounds back . . . We're saving the normality of life.

In these accounts, the function of the face is described in detail in order to demonstrate the ways that form and function are not separate and distinct. In the case of facial cleft specifically but also for other forms of facial difference, aesthetics and vital life processes map onto one another such that surgery is sometimes, quite literally, lifesaving. To be sure, each interviewee also expanded on the very notion of life. As Karen pointed out, first is nutrition, but second is "normality," which is in her account equally important to sustenance.

Nothing demonstrates the ways in which facial repair becomes understood as a vital intervention more than references to "throwaway babies." In interviewing Operation Smile volunteers, several told stories about children who, when born with facial difference, had been abandoned. Dr. Roberts explained,

In many countries children are left to die. There was a story of a Chinese man who found this baby in a box in a trash dump, and he brought this baby back to his wife, and ultimately his wife did not accept the baby, but the compassion of a man trying to save a creature who's been abandoned! So abandonment is certainly an option in many countries where you don't have the knowledge that a baby can be fixed or, perhaps not even the knowledge, but the option to have a baby fixed.

As an interviewer, such revelations were disturbing, but these were not uncommon stories. Dr. Tyson, a surgeon based at Shriner's Children's Hospital in Los Angeles, told of a similar experience:

This old man came in carrying this four month old baby . . . And we asked, "Is this your grandson?" And he said, "No I found this baby in the snow. I was just walking, and I found this baby in the snow. Someone just threw him away." He had a cleft.

The image of a baby born only to be abandoned because of difference is heartbreaking, but of course, the meanings of disability (and of

children) are themselves culturally bound. In fact, the same facial differences that are "fixed" via methods of routine surgery in economically privileged nations are potentially terminal in places characterized
by rampant poverty. Of course, there is nothing intrinsically different
about a baby born with cleft in Australia from one born in Kenya, for
example, but the response and thus the consequences to cleft vary dramatically. Betsy explained:

> Each culture looks at things differently . . . In Asia, the incidence of
> cleft lip is high, and then you look at the fact that they can have one
> child, and they prefer a boy . . . On three different occasions, we've taken
> deformed girls out of garbage cans. Think about what these parents
> go through . . . Asian families can have one child, and when they can,
> they prefer it to be a boy quite honestly, and then they get a deformed
> girl . . . There was a child who was born deformed, and the mother was
> quite sick during her pregnancy, and she delivered the baby. Given their
> resources the choice was to take care of the mother or the baby, and the
> baby was a deformed girl, so they gave the baby to the grandmother to
> get rid of, but the grandmother kept the baby and fed her by sucking on
> crackers and spitting the crackers into the baby's mouth to keep the baby
> alive just like a Robin bird . . . . Except for the grace of God any of us
> could be any of these places, and how would we survive?

This is a parable of sorts. The moral emphasizes both gratitude for having been born Western and, more importantly, the vital dimensions of
facial work. By emphasizing that a child born with a facial anomaly is
disposable, literally, repairing disfigurement takes on profound significance. Similarly, Dr. Matthews used horrific stories to allude to what life
untreated amounts to:

> Whether it's abandoned kids in China or these lost kids where these chil-
> dren are given up immediately and left on the street where people will
> pick them up and raise them . . . There was a girl in Bolivia one year who
> had been locked in the closet for sixteen years until her sister broke her
> out . . . Her parents had locked her in the closet because they were ashamed
> of her. Whether it's a facial burn or a severe facial defect, what little you
> can do to donate your time makes a world of difference in their lives.

If the preintervened upon body is one that is functionally unable to ingest nutrients or especially susceptible to deadly infection, then to describe repair of the cleft as "lifesaving" is not merely rhetorical. In this site, it is not simply social death, but rather vital life processes that are restored through this form of facial work. But when stigma drives parents to divert resources away from a child or abandon a baby to slowly die, we are bearing witness to a deadly condition, albeit one that is deadly in a unique way. Just as *Extreme Makeover* and facial feminization function to demonstrate how the distinction between cosmetic and reconstructive surgery is increasingly hard to define, Operation Smile illustrates how the line between social death and bodily death is blurred.

The disfigurement imaginary fortifies stigma of facial difference such that living humans are increasingly diagnosed as socially dead. What is especially horrific for us to consider is that *social death can function as a status that generates biological death.* When the bullying experienced at school or the shame of families hinders access to essential resources, the social death of facial difference gives way to biological death. The very fact that social death and biological death exist in an uneasy tension is significant. When biological death—because of function or because of stigma—looms as an outcome, it is easier to construct facial work as a vital intervention. In this site, children's lives hang in the balance. The mission metaphor is one way that Operation Smile mobilizes investment in its work, but there is an infinitely more glamorous approach to facial work at play here, too. Like mission-style facial work, it also deserves critical analysis.

Celebrity Aesthetics and the Disfigurement Imaginary

Philanthropic causes and charitable ventures have long used celebrities and entertainment culture to mobilize public sentiment and financial contributions. The annual Muscular Dystrophy Association Jerry Lewis Labor Day Telethon (1966–2011) relied on the name recognition afforded by Jerry Lewis and on performances by other noteworthy celebrities, including Gregory Peck, Paul Newman, Carol Burnett, John Lennon, Yoko Ono, and others. Throughout the 2000s, U2's Bono spent seemingly more time promoting (PRODUCT)RED, a licensing brand that generates funds for HIV eradication efforts, than recording the music that made him famous.[48] For many years, Oprah's Angel Network solicited donations through exhortations by Oprah herself for projects as wide-ranging as homebuilding in the wake of Hurricane Katrina to grants for charter schools. Increasingly, celebrities inspire not only donations aimed at alleviating social ills but also philanthropic consumption or purchasing consumer goods under the guise of supporting a "good" cause.[49]

Philanthropic organizations and even nongovernmental organizations have mobilized celebrities as spokespersons. For example, the United Nations has received attention for its collaborations with Angelina Jolie, a UN Goodwill Ambassador and Messenger of Peace, who has participated in over 40 field visits and worked as an advocate for refugees through forced displacement.[50] The United Nations Children's Fund (UNICEF) also relies on a cadre of celebrity Goodwill Ambassadors and Advocates including David Beckham, Katie Perry, Serena Williams, and Susan Sarandon to fundraise and speak on behalf of UNICEF's programs for children.

Fame thoroughly shapes the ongoing activities of the nonprofit industrial complex.[51] But it is not just that famous people speak on behalf of organizations or volunteer their time for particular efforts. Rather, a celebrity aesthetic permeates nonprofit and nongovernmental work through three distinct stylistic elements. First, a celebrity aesthetic emphasizes physical attractiveness and luxury consumer goods to lend value to a person, a place, or an activity. Second, a celebrity aesthetic relies upon emotionally riveting messaging and branding to mobilize visceral resonance. Third, a celebrity aesthetic deploys features of entertainment including high production value and mass media to garner attention. We live in a culture dominated by the celebrity aesthetic; to put its effect in sharp relief, consider how a celebrity aesthetic might vary from a scientific aesthetic in this context. Philanthropic ventures guided by a scientific aesthetic would likely emphasize research findings, for example predictive statistics, to establish the value of a cause. Likewise, a scientific aesthetic might deploy visual artifacts like graphs or even specialized, expert language in order to mobilize interest in and support for a venture. While celebrity-enabled philanthropy is not unique, I am particularly interested in the work of celebrities and the effects of celebrity aesthetics in relation to facial difference.

One of the more famous Operation Smile celebrity spokespersons is singer Jessica Simpson, who serves as Operation Smile's International Youth Ambassador. The pop star has released hit singles, starred in Hollywood comedies, hosted reality television shows, and even become a successful fashion designer. Throughout the 2000s, she regularly referenced her work with Operation Smile in promotional appearances and interviews. Simpson, infamous for her ditzy charm, was even invited to meet with Congress in March 2006 to speak on the organization's behalf. According to press releases appearing on the Operation Smile website, Simpson spent the day talking with senators, representatives, and congressional staffers.[52] Accompanying the press release was a photograph of Simpson—dressed in an elegant black suit, her blonde hair pulled into a perfect bun, her face expertly contoured and made-up. As usual, flashing cameras surrounded her. Her appearance is largely what drives the attention she receives.

News accounts describing celebrities' charitable efforts are striking on two fronts. First, the story of a celebrity spokesperson often supersedes reporting about Operation Smile's actual work. Second, charitable work is positioned alongside signifiers of celebrity status. Specifically, celebrities' exceptional appearances are described in detail. In an article entitled "Mariah Is Just Smiles Better," Mariah Carey's participation at a fundraiser is described: "Here's sexy singer Mariah Carey flashing her gnashers for Operation Smile . . . She looked stunning at the New York charity bash for kids with facial deformities."[53] The irony is that Carey's spectacular smile is juxtaposed with the faces of children, some of whom are not physiologically able to smile. News stories about celebrities consistently make reference to celebrities' access to glamour and luxury culture too. For example, a *Los Angeles Times* article about an Operation Smile fundraiser begins in this way: "Actress Roma Downey attends an unveiling party at the Lladro boutique in Beverly Hills."[54] Lladro, a Spanish high-end porcelain home décor company, produces small figurines that range in price from $250 to $1,000. Operation Smile acquires some cache (and donations) from its connection to celebrities, and celebrities' involvement with Operation Smile lends them a kind of down-to-earth credibility, while references to celebrity aesthetics keep their exceptionalism intact.

While Operation Smile's use of celebrities as spokespersons is not unusual, what makes the use of celebrities curious is the particular focus of the organization. The work of being a celebrity is, to a large degree, the work of being attractive. Celebrities function as the most visible points of reference for beauty culture. But unlike UNICEF or the Muscular Dystrophy Association, Operation Smile's work focuses on appearance disabilities and aesthetic stigma. In addition, celebrity aesthetics is defined by affluence, whereas the places missions take place are extraordinarily poor. The juxtaposition of celebrity aesthetics and mission-style facial work is at the very least odd, and at worst deeply problematic. Imagine a charity focused on alleviating world poverty, enlisting celebrity reporter Robin Leach to lead a tour of "Lifestyles of the Starving and Destitute" complete with televised images of slums and gruel meticulously described in Leach's immediately recognizable English brogue and broadcast into American homes.

Whether celebrities are engaged in entertainment—acting, singing, sports—or philanthropy, their exceptional ability to elicit an *emotional* experience is central to the work they do. In a sense, then, the charitable work of celebrities is not altogether different from their work as entertainers. And sometimes, it is not clear where the philanthropy begins and the entertainment ends. Given how these efforts are covered in weekly celebrity magazines and discussed in late-night talk show interviews, celebrity philanthropic work functions as a kind of entertainment, a genre that engages audiences if not to act then at least to increase their awareness of social problems. Portrayals of celebrities' philanthropic work carry the emotional resonance they do because they are bound up in production techniques that elicit specific responses. An interview on a late night talk show likely mobilizes curiosity, while a documentary-style infomercial shot like an evening news feature ignites a sense of alarm. Although each is stylistically distinct, both may be effective in garnering support.

Celebrity spokespersons' partnerships with Operation Smile extend beyond the celebrity bread and butter of promotion. Jessica Simpson, actress Roma Downey, NBA player John Salley, and mogul Donald Trump Jr. are among the celebrities who have participated in the hands-on work of the organization as support staff on a medical mission. For example, in 2005, Simpson joined an Operation Smile mission to Kenya, during which 280 children were treated. Simpson attests to the emotionally transformative experience: "My experience in Kenya with Operation Smile was incredible. To witness the truly miraculous transformations in the lives of so many desperate needy children was both powerful and personally rewarding."[55] The work of celebrities in this site—through participation on missions, fundraising, and publicly speaking about the organization—is unique from the work accomplished by medical volunteers, fundraisers, or student organizers. Celebrities can capitalize on the relationships they have with the public to mobilize emotion and glamorize work in the global bio-trenches, but nonprofits use celebrity aesthetics including television, print media, and popular music to evoke visceral responses in the service of strategic ends too.

Likely, you the reader have encountered Operation Smile infomercials. Infomercials are paid programming that airs during nonprime time slots—most often during early mornings, mid-afternoons, or late nights. Some Operation Smile infomercials feature Irish actress Roma Downey, most famous for her role on the CBS television series *Touched By an Angel* (1994–2003). Broadcasted infomercials are comprised of documentary-style featurettes with names like "Arnoldo's Story," "One Smile at a Time," and "A Smile Changes Everything." Each depicts the story of one child from one mission. In ways not dissimilar from *Extreme Makeover*, the story of each recipient is recounted. The costs of cleft lip and palate and the barriers to surgery, namely poverty, are described by Downey, who functions as an omnipotent narrator in a style not dissimilar from evening television news stories about global health crises. The message is simple and incredibly distressing too— without surgery, children are certain to face social death. Watching these infomercials is wrenching; I have never watched without crying. In fact, everyone to whom I have shown the infomercials has teared up. The catharsis precipitated by the footage is real, but infomercials provide us with an opportunity to think critically about our emotional register. What do we respond to and what spurs us to act?

Operation Smile infomercials resemble commercial television or films and employ common strategies for mobilizing emotional response. Featurettes have high production value. Newer infomercials are shot in a gritty style resembling a music video or the opening montage of a primetime drama. In an infomercial chronicling a mission to China, images of a barefoot girl walking through a neighborhood resembling Beijing hutongs (traditional courtyard houses) are inter-spersed with fast paced footage of doctors wheeling gurneys into a sur-gical suite, *ER*-style. Unlike in the original Roma Downey infomercials, these videos include fleeting footage of actual surgical procedures in ways similar to reality surgery television like *Extreme Makeover*. Popu-lar music, like Celine Dion's "A New Day Has Come" and Coldplay's "Fix You," plays throughout.

Infomercials feature families crying as they send their children into surgery, mothers hugging medical providers, and doctors carrying anes-thetized children back to their families. After surgery, children receive their "smile bags," which contain a mirror, and infomercials capture children seeing their faces for the very first time. This moment is shot as its own kind of extreme makeover "big reveal." The images captured are emotionally charged, but celebrity aesthetics is what makes the infomercials riveting. The actual mission involves waiting, paperwork, negotiation, disappointment, but the videos use emotionally evocative production techniques to ignite a response that viewers might not have if they were actually watching the events unfold in real time. As Cold-play's hit single crescendos and the pace of images increases, I notice the rapidity of my own pulse, my own quickness of breath. I am teary, overcome with desperation and confusion. These feelings are distinct and altogether different from the responses I have had to unmediated interactions with people subject to facial work.

Individual celebrity spokespersons and an overarching celebrity aes-thetic infuse Operation Smile's work and carry specific consequences. Celebrities' bodies have long been pictured next to bodies of the sick. Princess Diana's work in AIDS wards in the initial years of the HIV/AIDS crisis typifies the charitable work of high-profile celebrities. In photo-ops documenting celebrities' hospital visits, the presumably healthy and vibrant body of the celebrity is positioned next to the ill and dying patient. The contrast puts into sharp relief both what it means to be healthy and conversely what it means to be sick. Likewise, the juxta-position of celebrity faces, which reflect and constitute marketable ide-als of attractiveness, with faces demarcated by cleft lip or palate, confers a particular significance to facial difference. Because celebrity status is largely contingent on attractiveness, positioning celebrities along-side children defined as disfigured calls into question the ways facial difference precludes life chances, especially a child's ability to access the kind of future a celebrity's life displays.

Celebrities are integral to the intensification of the aestheticization of everyday life. Through celebrity endorsements of beauty products and "news" coverage regarding celebrities' beauty regimes, we are well acquainted with the services, goods, and personal effort required to look like a celebrity. Whether consumer culture created these needs or simply responded to our ever-increasing preoccupation with all bodily flaws, Americans are engaged in more body projects, self conscious efforts to cultivate one's body as a means of self-definition, than ever.[56] At the same time that our focus on beauty has increased, our tolerance for bodily flaws has declined.

Things deemed natural—attributed to aging or simply ignored twenty years ago—are now subject to an array of interventions. As feminist scholars interrogating men and women's relationships with our bodies have well demonstrated, celebrities play a central role in beauty culture.[57] Celebrities' bodies are images available for modeling, a standard or ideal demonstrating what the body might become, and as a result, celebrities are driving forces in making attractiveness take on the significance that it does. One consequence of juxtaposing celebrities with faces subject to facial work is that the imperative to repair is mobilized not only through the disfigurement imaginary but also through the emulation celebrities' appearances provoke. Celebrities' looks are the amalgamation of genetic fortune, the products and services of glamour culture, *and* aesthetic surgery. It may be highly desired, but the look of a celebrity is an extraordinary commodity and one that cannot be attained by the children subject to Operation Smile interventions. Disability, global poverty, and the production value of celebrities' images operate as barriers. Facial work will not leave children beautiful or glamorous but rather *unremarkable*, as we saw in chapter 4.

Here, celebrities work toward opposite ends. As Operation Smile spokespersons, they raise awareness and mobilize support for the reconstructive surgery used to repair and normalize faces. Simultaneously, as extraordinarily attractive celebrities, they intensify the aestheticization of everyday life. In effect, celebrities are a key part of the cultural landscape that makes disfigurement the tragedy it is often thought to be. In a sociohistorical moment where beauty becomes increasingly important, the costs of being defined as ugly intensify, too. When so much of the work of a celebrity is implicitly invested in the stigmatization of ugliness, their role in endorsing facial work is inherently vexed. It is also the case that high production value and popular media are effectively used to get people to care about facial work. What is less clear is if our responses to global problems gradually become contingent on the use of celebrity aesthetics, whether our affect is compromised—mobilized by skillful editing and recognizable lyrics but relatively unresponsive in the face of real-life difference.

Repaired, Reborn

During the 2013 Oscars, facial disfigurement made an appearance. Award-winning film and television actresses Rose Byrne and Melissa McCarthy presented Sharmeen Obaid-Chinoy and Daniel Junge with an Academy Award for their short documentary *Saving Face*, a Pakistani film that chronicles one surgeon's efforts using facial work to treat women's burns resulting from acid attacks. Acid violence has emerged as an especially horrific mode of gendered violence in South Asia. Women who turn down a marriage proposal or contest their husbands' desire to marry another woman face the risk of being attacked by perpetrators—men they know intimately and sometimes members of their husband's family. Islamabad is a place where beauty matters. Increasingly, Pakistani billboards feature faces not altogether dissimilar from those in American advertisements. Presumably the models are South Asian women, but their images replicate Western beauty ideals. It is also, perhaps not coincidentally, a place where 100 acts of acid violence are reported each year. Officials are never alerted to many others.

Obaid-Chinoy and Junge's Oscar acceptance speech functioned as a form of public education about acid violence, but given the context in which it occurred, the celebrity aesthetic was pervasive. Mid-speech, the camera feed switched from the podium to a close-up shot of Sandra Bullock, an actress regularly selected as one of the most beautiful people in the world by media outlets like *People* magazine. In some sites of facial work, celebrity aesthetics may foster stigmatization of difference (even as celebrities' work garners support for facial interventions). By contrast, *Saving Face* illustrates how an artifact like film and even cross-border intervention can transcend the traps of celebrity aesthetics and the limitations of mission-style facial work.

In an interview on NPR's Morning Edition, director Sharmeen Obaid-Chinoy explains, "This is a story of hope as much as it is a story of despair."[58] And the hope the film depicts is multifaceted. *Saving Face* features Dr. Mohammad Jawad, a surgeon born and raised in Karachi but who lives and works in London as a cosmetic surgeon, predominantly specializing in liposculpture and breast augmentation. To be sure, Dr. Mohammad Jawad's surgical fixes transform, and perhaps even save, Pakistani women's lives. But throughout the film, women also work alongside the Acid Survivors Foundation to lobby for acid crime legislation.

Rukhsana, an acid attack survivor, pleads with a group of Pakistani lawmakers: "Even our own people don't recognize us anymore. This is such an injustice to us. Someone must stop these brutal people who made us into the living dead . . . Your daughters are seeking justice from you."[59] In Pakistan, women themselves and those who come to their aid invoke notions of social death to describe life after acid violence. Marvi Memon, a female member of the Pakistan National Assembly, declares to fellow lawmakers: "It's better to die than to live this awful life." On May 10, 2011, Pakistan's Parliament unanimously passed the Acid Control and Acid Crime Prevention Bill, which established a new penalty for acid violence—a lifetime of incarceration—a social death of a different kind.

Throughout *Saving Face*, there are two kinds of reconstructive efforts at work—Dr. Jawad refigures survivor's faces, but the women concentrate on repairing Pakistani society. These two elements converge in Zakia's story. Zakia's face changes over the course of the film. Although her attack destroyed one eye and subsequent scar tissue has left her eye socket too atrophied to support a prosthetic eye, her burn injury is partially treated through grafts and partially concealed through a facial prosthesis. But the changes that happen for Zakia are due only in part to Jawad's work. Alongside medical intervention, Zakia boldly seeks justice. With the help of a female attorney, Zakia pursues a case against her husband for the attack.[60] He is the first man convicted under Pakistan's new law and is sentenced to serve two life sentences. The solution proffered throughout the film is not just facial work, but a legislative intervention in the institutionalization of disfiguring as a method of gendered violence. This is a radically different "fix" than what is offered to us through the disfigurement imaginary, which is intrinsically myopic—always preoccupied with normalizing individual difference. By situating disfigurement in a broader sociohistorical context, possibilities for intervention emerge that not only transform Zakia's life but potentially save the lives of Pakistani women who will come after her.

Saving Face has obtained critical acclaim, and as a result, promotion about the film is mired in Hollywood culture and celebrity aesthetics. And yet the content demonstrates how facial work can proceed alongside efforts that confront the particular stigma of facial difference. By the end of the film, Dr. Jawad is different too. When we first meet him, he aligns with celebrity aesthetics by describing the "gorgeous" work he does for English women, but in the final moments he offers a thoughtful reflection on his own relationship to facial work: "In a way, I'm saving my own face because I am a part of the society which has this disease." His is a structural account, one that recognizes the social embeddedness of acid violence and facial difference. Zakia too offers a new way of understanding facial work. She does not describe her life as "saved," but rather herself as "reborn." And this is an entirely different metaphor, albeit one with its own sacred significance. In pronouncing herself reborn, Zakia makes reference not only to physical repair but also to her emergent political agency. Facial work, in her view, has not bestowed her with a life or saved her from social death. She dispenses with the language of vitality in favor of a vocabulary that emphasizes self-determination and voice. One declares oneself born-again.

6

Facing Off

Debating Facial Work, Constructing a "Vital" Intervention

The patient got a new life and a new face, and she was a
silent hero of this historical moment. You need a face to face
the world.
—Maria Siemionow, *Face to Face: My Quest to Perform the
First Full Face Transplant* (2009)

On November 27, 2005, a team of French surgeons, led by Jean-Michel
Dubernard and Bernard Devauchelle, performed the world's first partial face transplant in Amiens, France. Face transplantation (FT) is an
experimental procedure in which a face is surgically removed from a
donor and replanted on a recipient's head for the treatment of facial
disfigurement, resulting from congenital conditions or trauma. News
coverage alleged that the recipient's dog had chewed off her lips, chin,
and nose in an effort to rouse her after a suicide attempt.[1] Initial stories announcing the transplant were followed with reports that the
recipient's results were so good that she had regained enough facial
functioning to resume smoking. This news was met with derision
from other surgeons, who suggested that the French team's choice of
patient was less than ideal.[2] The French surgical team had previously
transplanted a hand and forearm to a New Zealand man who had lost
his own in a chainsaw accident while serving time in prison. News
accounts criticized the team's patient selection protocol, implying that
such innovative techniques should be reserved for a nonsmoker or a

nonincarcerated person—in other words, someone "more deserving" or perhaps less culpable.[3]

On April 14, 2006, reports confirmed that a Chinese surgical team working at Xijing Hospital completed the world's second partial face transplant.[4] Two years prior a black bear had attacked this recipient, leaving open wounds and visible pink flesh in the place of a recognizable face. Press releases following the surgery displayed a man's face, albeit swollen and stitched, but relatively intact. In January 2007, Laurent Lantieri completed a third face transplant at another Paris hospital. This time the experimental procedure was used as a last-ditch intervention to treat neurofibromatosis, a condition that causes the growth of tumors on the face. This is the same condition Joseph Merrick, whose fictionalized life story is depicted in David Lynch's film *The Elephant Man* (1980), is thought to have experienced. The story of a man with a congenital condition is arguably less melodramatic than stories of "animals on the attack," but spectacular in its own right given the rarity and severity of the condition.

In the United States, advancement of the technology is dispersed across the country with different teams completing essential research and experimentation. Beginning in 1995, a research team based in the Plastic Surgery Department at the University of Louisville commenced extensive research establishing the critical technical, immunological, and ethical groundwork necessary to complete the procedure. Plastic surgeon Marie Siemionow from the Cleveland Clinic declared in 2005 (even before the first face transplant in France) to Katie Couric on NBC's *The Today Show* that she was in the process of identifying her first patient. Following Siemionow's appearance, periodic media outlets "announced" the Cleveland Clinic's intention to complete the first American transplant, and in 2008, Siemionow declared the United States' first FT a success.[5] Siemionow's patient later revealed her face on the *Oprah Winfrey Show* and told her story of being shot in the face by her husband. On April 9, 2009, Brigham and Women's Hospital in Boston followed with a partial transplant on a man whose injuries were acquired in an unusual accident in which he fell on the electrical tracks of the Boston subway. To date, additional transplants have been completed in the United States, Spain, and Turkey, but the procedure remains experimental, as surgical teams assess the capacity of FT to treat a range of facial conditions and innovate techniques for successful surgical outcomes.

The details of the recent transplants and the emerging science of FT make it an astounding development in aesthetic surgery. Not surprisingly, then, fantastic images pervade pop culture accounts. Some media accounts rely on fantasies fed by celebrity culture, as the first sentence of one news story about FT illustrates: "Have you ever wished that you had the good looks of Halle Berry or Ashton Kutcher or the hottest student in school?"[6] Similarly, the final page of a 2005 issue of *People* magazine contained a feature titled, "If you had to have a face transplant which famous face would you want?" Hollywood actresses responded with names of other starlets. These stories couch the technology in a celebrity aesthetic, with its emphasis on glamour and consumption. FT is treated as the newest, most innovative, albeit still in-development intervention that promises to make bodies beautiful. While those directly involved in developing the technology repeatedly rebuff the idea that FT will ever function as a cosmetic procedure, the story persists.[7] Other media accounts make reference to science fiction themes of wonderment or futuristic horror. Several recent newspaper articles reference the 1997 Hollywood action thriller *Face/Off*, in which a main character receives a face transplant in order to thwart a terrorist attack, and a 2005 episode of *Nip/Tuck* in which a botched face transplant results in rejection of the transplanted face, which has to then be removed.[8]

At the same time that FT is sensationalized, it is also celebrated as scientifically noteworthy. Dr. L. Scott Levin, chief of plastic and reconstructive surgery at Duke University Medical Center, has described the procedure as "the single most important area of reconstructive research."[9] Yet it is unclear what the future holds for FT. Experimentation may morph into a viable treatment option offered as standard of care, or FT may vanish from the scene entirely due to failure or ethical issues. FT is positioned strategically by proponents as a revolutionary intervention and by critics as too risky, and as such its ultimate trajectory is unknown—and thus deeply interesting analytically. As I write, the story of FT continues to unfold.

FT builds upon knowledge and skills from numerous scientific specialties including reconstructive surgery, transplantation surgery, and immunology. Simply put, FT emerged to improve upon traditional reconstructive methods. For faces with what is often called "severe facial disfigurement," reconstructive techniques such as free tissue transfer, which involves the relocation of tissue from one part of the body to another, are notoriously ineffective. These techniques require surgeries throughout the course of a lifetime, sometimes numbering into the hundreds, and the end results of reconstructive techniques offer modest results. For example, a face that has been severely burned is often repaired through a series of skin grafts. While this technique can facilitate some improvement in facial function and minimize the appearance of scarring, it can result in a face that resembles a conglomeration of skin grafts of varying colors and textures. In the case of injury, critical tissue like a nose may be missing or components of the face may be damaged beyond repair, making reconstruction particularly difficult to accomplish. Thus, FT was crafted to address the limitations of established reconstructive techniques and, ultimately, to produce better results with fewer surgeries.

Technically, FT is most akin to facial replantation in which a person's own facial tissue is reattached after trauma. The first case of facial replantation took place in India after a nine-year-old girl's face and scalp were torn off when a grass-cutting machine caught one of her braids. Her family packed the tissue on ice and traveled to the nearest hospital. After ten hours of microsurgery, the girl's face was reattached. The case made reconstructive surgery history, and opened up the possibility for the transplantation of a face from a donor to a recipient.[10] While replantation offers better results than other reconstructive techniques, it is only available in cases in which facial tissue remains in good condition. Thus, many kinds of trauma and congenital differences are not treatable through replantation.

FT also shares technical, ethical, and social histories with transplant medicine, specifically hand transplantation. In 1998, a French team also led by Jean-Michel Dubernard completed the world's first hand transplant, though credit for the world's first *successful* hand transplant belongs to a research team at the University of Louisville. In the French case, the transplanted tissue was eventually removed after the patient stopped following his immunosuppression regimen. Many experts understand hand transplantation and FT as analogous procedures. Both types of transplant are composite tissue allotransplants involving a number of tissues including muscle, nerves, blood vessels, arteries, veins, and skin.[11] Yet critics like bioethicist Francoise Baylis contend that "a face may be like a hand from the perspective of a surgeon interested in the technical problem of repair," but there are "morally significant differences."[12] As Baylis argues, that idea that the hand is just like a face only works as a technical analogy because in the event of rejection or failure, the stakes are appreciably different. A hand can be replaced with a prosthetic. A face cannot.[13] Analogizing face and hand transplantation highlights the technical similarities of the body matter, but the juxtaposition also points to the divergent meanings and significance accrued to each body part.

The history of sustained ethical debate in relation to transplant medicine is reflected in the story of FT, in that transplant protocols consistently raise unique and divisive questions. Because FT involves the transplant of a donor organ from a dead body onto a living recipient, FT relies on surgical research and the work of immunology. Like all kinds of transplantation, FT requires that recipients begin a lifelong regimen of immunosuppressive drugs in order to prevent rejection of the transplanted tissue. Debates about FT largely hinge on this fact—immunosuppressive drugs are toxic.[14] FT relies on the technologies of transplant medicine but also activates ongoing conversations within the field of transplantation specifically, and biomedicine more broadly.[15] With the advent of heart transplantation, bioethicists, medical professionals, and the public were forced to reconsider what constitutes life and death. For example, transplantation depends on the designation of brain death. When particular criteria are met, organs can be harvested for transplantation from the organ donor to the recipient. Undoubtedly, the emergence of a new death status, namely brain death, made lifesaving intervention possible. As such, the history of transplantation demonstrates that before innovations can become integrated into routine medical care, new ways of thinking about organic processes and human experience must emerge. Perhaps most significantly, our ways of thinking about what counts as death can evolve in relation to an intervention that promises to save lives. Thus within the field of transplantation, there is a well-established pattern of debate around unprecedented and complex bioethical questions. FT calls into question how we balance the benefits of intervention—in this case a new face—with physiological, psychological, and social risks. When identity crisis, public distrust, chronic illness, and even death are potential risks of intervention, the benefits must be significant in order to proceed.

The previous three chapters illustrate that one significant consequence of the disfigurement imaginary is that those labeled disfigured are positioned as socially dead. As my analysis of *Extreme Makeover* illustrates, characterizing faces as disfigured amplifies stigmatization such that appearance gets positioned as undermining critical facets of human life. Facial feminization surgery employs the disfigurement imaginary to characterize a particular aesthetic as fundamentally threatening to social interaction. Operation Smile routinely suggests that a universal dimension of human experience is undermined by facial difference. By framing the consequences of appearance in such stark terms, facial work becomes imbued with profound lifesaving significance. To be sure, the specter of social death inspires FT, and many of the primary benefits of FT are similar to those described in other sites. Yet the actual practices of facial transplantation also stand in stark contrast to the facial work described in the previous three chapters. FT is technically more complicated than the repair of a cleft palate, for example, and it is less routinized than the methods used on *Extreme Makeover* or in facial feminization surgery (FFS). Additionally, those potentially subject to FT experience the kinds of facial difference that result in the most profound social exclusion. Perhaps the most important difference is that FT raises unique questions about the benefits of aesthetic intervention in relation to other dimensions of bodily well-being. For FT to proceed, the costs of disfigurement must be weighed against the risks of compromised health—or even bodily death.

Ultimately FT illustrates the way the disfigurement imaginary not only structures the meanings associated with facial difference, but rather fundamentally shapes clinical practice. Each site of facial work demonstrates that when disfigurement is understood as socially deadly, facial work takes on lifesaving significance and moral authority. FT suggests something else altogether: that in the case of facial difference, bodily death might be increasingly understood as a reasonable risk for warding off particular kinds of social death.

Innovating Facial Work through the Disfigurement Imaginary

The work of innovating technologies is more mundane than spectacular science news coverage suggests. Often, the development of medical practices occurs within research universities, and as such the emphasis on respectability, protocol, and institutional politics (not to mention neoliberal profit-seeking) abounds. In the case of FT specifically and in most innovative procedures generally, what appears to be revolutionary science is built on a foundation of mundane scientific tinkering through routine practices like animal experimentation, intellectual labor through the development of bioethics protocols, and political maneuvering through institutional checks and balances, namely institutional review boards (IRBs). Understanding face transplantation outside of the sensationalized accounts offered in media required entering the sites in which face transplantation takes shape as a concrete medical intervention with real-life consequences. To this end, I conducted fieldwork at meetings of a US-based face transplant team and interviews with key team members to critically analyze how the work of technological innovation came to rest on the meanings of facial disfigurement.

The face transplant team I studied met at a 7 a.m. Monday morning meeting each week for almost three years. The meetings were held in a commonplace conference room in an ordinary building with an unremarkable name: Hospital Building One.[16] At the meetings I observed, those who attended varied, but four key members of the face transplant team emerged. A leading plastic surgery researcher, whose career thus far had been spent innovating a range of reconstructive techniques including hand transplantation, led the team. A philosopher served as the team's bioethicist, while a sociologist and a psychologist offered insights about the social psychological facets of FT. The team was also comprised of medical students along with additional clinicians and researchers, but these four comprised the hub around which the team's work was organized and carried out.

While the topic of the meetings might have been spectacular, the actual meetings were much like other research collaborations in which I participated in the context of university life. From the time I first attended a meeting in May 2006 until the team disbanded in July 2007, its work was focused almost entirely on disseminating research results and articulating an ethical approach to FT. The face transplant team's relationship with its institution, specifically hospital administration, is critically important for understanding the work of the team. Although the team had established scientific understandings and technical skills needed to complete a transplant, the institution had rejected requests from the team to serve as a site for *human* experimentation. There was to be no face transplant at the team's home institution, nor were any team members to participate in any transplant anywhere else in the world. In a strange way, then, the team's immediate goal was not to complete a face transplant; rather the central task was rhetorical—professional and lay publics needing convincing that FT could and in fact should proceed.

The work of the team took two related forms: collectively developing institutional and public arguments based on the team's research and collaboratively completing the mundane tasks of scholarly research, specifically writing articles for publication in peer-reviewed journals. As my fieldnotes demonstrate, the meetings of the FT team resembled other sites of academic research:

> As is typical, the director opens up his notebook, a bound journal, to review his notes on the manuscripts in process. One by one he goes through the team's writing projects. The team talks details. Who is writing what? Where are they sending it? Who is its intended audience? Can the stats be made more intelligible? But in the midst of these details, the team discusses *why* the team is writing the pieces they are writing. What purpose does each serve? The goal is clear—the team is establishing ethical arguments and extending knowledge for the purpose of facilitating FT.[17]

At any one time, the team worked on multiple scientific articles. Several were focused on putting medical specialties in conversation with one another. For example, the team submitted an overview of FT to a general plastic surgery journal with the aim of introducing the immunological information to professionals with the technical skills to complete face transplants. Other articles directly addressed the ethical questions raised by FT.

Much of the team's writing examined the psychosocial consequences of FT. The most crucial piece of research completed by the team was a survey, known within the group as the RISK questionnaire. The survey, developed largely by the psychologist who worked on the team, was aimed at empirically demonstrating the risks individuals were willing to incur in order to receive a face transplant. Critics' arguments against FT hinged on the supposition that the risks of FT surpassed the benefits. To combat this claim, the team decided to interrogate this operating assumption empirically by asking respondents a series of questions indicating the level of risk they would assume in order to receive a face transplant to repair facial disfigurement. In an interview, the head of the team described the results of that research:

Over the years, we've had over 300 people fill that [RISK survey] out. And that population that has filled it out are people who are missing their hand, i.e., somebody that could benefit from a hand transplant; people that are missing their larynx, i.e., somebody that could benefit from a larynx transplant; facially disfigured, i.e., somebody that could benefit from a face transplant; kidney transplant recipients, i.e., somebody that lived with the risks of immunosuppression. Also we had controls that are healthy individuals who do not have direct experience with either the risks or the benefits and plastic surgeons and transplant surgeons . . . In a nutshell, what came out of all that research over the years is that regardless of who you ask, everybody (and these are people without larynx, hands, with disfigured faces, on immunosuppression), everyone would risk absolutely the most to get a face transplant than any other procedure. Even the kidney transplant recipients would risk more to get a face transplant than the kidney that they already have and they are on immunosuppression . . . If I came to you and said that you needed a heart transplant otherwise you would die, but that you would have to take very toxic drugs for the rest of your life to ensure that the heart does not reject. You would probably tell me that yes, you would take those drugs to get a heart because the alternative is death. There is no debate about the risks vs. benefits. Whereas in hand or face transplantation, you can live a healthy life without a hand or with a disfigured face and so we as physicians are exposing you to the toxicity of immunosuppressive drugs and in exchange for that we're not saving your life we're just improving the quality of your life. That is the crux of all of our research, i.e., analyzing what risks people would be willing to expose themselves

to for the benefits of one of these non-lifesaving procedures. That is what
the RISK questionnaire addresses exactly . . . We try not to inject our
opinion but the opinion of 300 respondents to our questionnaires and
these are people with direct experience with the benefits and the risks of
immunosuppression. These are not our opinions. These are the opinions
of people with real-life experiences.

Several claims are made using the RISK research. First, those with
direct experience of the risks of immunosuppression agree that a face
transplant is worth the side effects of the drug regimen. This is tanta-
mount to arguing that the benefits outweigh the risks. By interpreting
the results in light of respondents' real-life experiences, the RISK survey
is given weight because it captures a kind of authority that critics, with
presumably no real-life experience, do not have. Second, and related,
those already negotiating chronic illness and disability understand
facial disfigurement as somehow worse than other kinds of bodily suffering. Getting a new face is positioned as more important than many
other kinds of interventions, including kidney transplantation, which
has saved the lives of some RISK respondents. The rhetorical force of
the RISK survey centers on the supposition that those with personal
experience are best positioned to assess which risks are reasonable for
the benefit of a new face in cases of severe disfigurement.

On the one hand, the head of the team characterized FT as nonvital,
remarking that FT "just" improves quality of life, but the RISK survey
results suggest that the work accomplished by FT is anything but just
another intervention. By conveying that any risk is justifiable for the
sake of facial recovery, the survey positions disfigurement as a uniquely
threatening bodily impairment. In this way, the team's work was twofold. The explicit aim of their work was to produce empirical research
to establish technical knowledge and an ethical framework required to
proceed with FT. Yet tacitly, their research relied on and actively constructed meanings attributed to facial disfigurement. While constructing "disfigurement" was not an explicit objective of the team, their work
implicitly relied on notions about how facial disfigurement devastates
human life. This case vividly demonstrates the subtle yet powerful
processes through which the disfigurement imaginary is socially constituted and facial difference emerges as a deadly condition. This is a

significant, albeit unintended, component of the work accomplished by the face transplant team.

In interviewing the four key team members, relationships between disfigurement, human suffering, and the significance of aesthetic intervention were continually negotiated. Consider the following excerpt from an interview with the team's director:

> The hand and the face are very unique parts of our anatomy . . . As you sit here and talk to me and as I respond to you, you are using your hands to express yourself to me . . . Not only do we use them for doing our daily activities, but we also use them for expressing ourselves. *That is uniquely human.* If you talk to the hand transplant recipients, and you ask them years after they've had their transplanted hands: what is the most important part of getting a hand transplant? All of them, the first thing they say are things that are more related to being a human being . . . "Now I can wear a wedding ring." That's something that doesn't have a lot of function. It's symbolic. "Now I can walk downtown holding my daughter's hands . . . " There are very emotional human aspects of having a hand . . . With the face, it's the same but times ten. Our faces, we use to communicate to the world around us, it is a window through which people see our emotions. The perfect example of that is to sit across from someone with severe facial disfigurement. It's not only that the person with the disfigurement feels uncomfortable but you, we, as human beings it is very difficult to sit across from someone who is severely facially disfigured . . . we feel uncomfortable. We don't know where to look. We feel uneasy. All of that emotion comes from the fact that we as human beings can't live without our faces. We take cues of communication from looking at people's faces. When that is robbed from somebody because of facial disfigurement, it only underlies how important the face is to making us human. We're social animals, without interacting with other human beings our quality of life is severely lessened. To be able to give somebody back normal human features is just a tremendous thing. One of the things that when we talk to people we were considering for face transplantation . . . we ask them, "What would you like to get out of getting a face transplant?" It's funny because the answer that I've heard many times—"I just want to be able to walk into a room and have nobody notice me." What does that mean? The face is so central

to them that when they walk into a room and everybody just changes because they see this horrible facial disfigurement. All these people want is to be not noticed—to just have a healthy looking face. The face is just a tremendous part of us as human beings. I would even venture to say with all the debate about risks versus benefits and that it's not lifesaving. I would say it *is* lifesaving . . . not just quality of life improving.

In the preceding excerpt, the face is characterized as an essential bodily part, a critical element of human social life. Face transplantation is described as a tremendous development in reconstructive surgery, not simply life-improving, but rather lifesaving. These claims are informed by an idea that circulated throughout the interview, namely, that facial disfigurement is "horrible." Underlying the importance attributed to the face and to face transplantation is the disfigurement imaginary—facial difference is conceptualized as deadly and as a threat to one's humanity.

Other interviews echoed elements of the disfigurement imaginary. When asked to respond to critics who suggest that efforts to develop FT should be redirected toward changing society's view of facial disfigurement, the team's bioethicist explained:

The argument goes like this: people who are facially disfigured suffer a lot of discrimination, but the problem is with the discriminators. The problem is not with the facially disfigured . . . It's the general public who discriminates that needs to do something about themselves . . . That's true . . . but suppose with face transplantation people could get a normal face and live better lives . . . There's certain people we could really help out from doing this, but we're not going to do it. We're going to wait twenty years, thirty years, forty years till society changes its opinion . . . In the meantime these people are going to live out their miserable life, behind closed doors, behind curtains, and they're going to die, but that's okay cause we're preparing for a better future in which people don't discriminate . . . That's using facially disfigured people as a means to an ends in a way you shouldn't do . . . We told ourselves anytime we get up to talk in public we will say, "The best solution here is for the public to change its attitude towards facially disfigured people . . . but in the meantime there's people who really suffer because they don't have a normal appearance and we think if you have the means to help these people you should use it. It's a medical benefit that we shouldn't withhold while we wait for society to change . . . " Politically it's very desirable, but it's unethical.

This response carefully considers the possibility of social change while at the same time affirming the promise of FT. It is also a highly empathetic reaction. Ultimately, the team's bioethicist expressed support for FT because he imagines that it will alleviate profound suffering. Specifically, he argued that waiting for social change while technologies are available to impact the present moment is an unethical response. Even though he imagined social change as a politically preferable response, he characterized such a response as unethical because it allows for the unnecessary continuation of suffering or, put another way, the prolongation of a "miserable life." The specter of death also haunts this explanation. While appearance-based discrimination is critiqued, social death is described as an almost unavoidable consequence of facial difference. Based on this logic, this team member advocated FT as a virtuous intervention to help those affected navigate around or away from stigma and social death.

Death also appears in the narrative of the team sociologist who described how he became compelled to work on the face transplant team:

A psychologist named Frances Cooke Macgregor . . . wr[ote] about disfigurement. She had a concept called "social death." She got me to thinking about how we've come up with different definitions of age. Age just doesn't mean chronological years anymore. Now we have an emotional age, a maturation age, a middle age. I started thinking similarly along the lines of death. We can have different kinds of death. We have the death that everybody grieves. We also have brain death. Why can't we have social death? . . . The stigma facing these folks, perhaps, is the strongest that still exists. It seems to be universal . . . It is the most damaging social disability that still exists . . . Reconstructive surgery does not bring them back to life. Face transplantation can do that.

This account is striking for three reasons. First, it reveals a working understanding of social death. Secondly, it explicitly positions facial disfigurement as like death, and finally, FT is described as a kind of life-saving intervention. This team member also articulates an intellectually nuanced and deeply empathetic understanding of the real costs of ableism. In the context of bioethical research about emerging forms of facial work, it makes sense that social death would be invoked as short-hand for stigma. Yet this way of understanding the relationship between social death and facial disfigurement operates in sharp contrast with the central analysis of this book, which critically unpacks "social death" as a discursive formation with embodied consequences.

Similarly, the team psychologist, in an effort to characterize the importance of FT, analogized disfigurement to cancer:

> The face is a primary organ of communication . . . Clearly, it doesn't entail the same level emergency or immediacy as medication to cause someone to recover from an ongoing stroke or heart attack, nor is it a cure for cancer. But facial disfigurements are a form of social cancer given that it's constantly intruding in your social relationships.

Though this explanation somehow positions disfigurement as not as "immediate" as other bodily conditions, it nonetheless relies on a link between disfigurement and death. Taken together, the interviews with team members captured a shared way of thinking and, by extension, talking about facial disfigurement.

Given that institutional rules prohibited the team from completing a FT, the rhetorical nature of the work they initiated is critically important to consider. The team routinely employed the disfigurement imaginary, and in effect they positioned facial difference as socially deadly. Because the disfigurement imaginary persists in various arenas of social life, it is not surprising to see those engaged in facial work reflect shared cultural notions about facial difference. In employing such perceptions of facial difference, surgeons and other professionals certainly reified the imaginary. But perhaps more importantly, positioning disfigurement as deadly lends a particular significance to intervention. Implicitly, aesthetic intervention is understood as a vital intervention. But what effects do these emergent meanings have? How does the disfigurement imaginary initiate a new, decidedly vital form of aesthetic intervention, and more specifically in relation to FT, how does the implicit diagnosis of social death make way for exposing patients to unique risks?

Just as transplant technology demanded a new way of understanding death and the invention of brain death facilitated the development of organ transplantation, FT is a case that explicitly demonstrates how positioning the lens of social death directly affects clinical practice. The preceding analysis reveals the routine interpretive work of one transplant team as they employed the disfigurement imaginary, but the question remains: How has the disfigurement imaginary infused the larger debate and the actual practice of FT? Importantly, the disfigurement imaginary transcended the collective understandings of this transplant team, and is, in fact, reflected in the ongoing deliberations in biomedicine. In moving the analysis toward a space where disciplinary consensus is sought, we can identify potential effects of such ways of thinking. Specifically, we can consider how the emergent associations between death and appearance extend beyond the idiosyncratic, representing a new way of approaching human appearance writ large.

Contested Risks and Benefits of Face Transplantation

In 2004, the *American Journal of Bioethics*, arguably the leading bioethics journal in the world, featured a series focused on the ethics of FT. The commentary, published before any surgical team attempted to complete a face transplant, was structured as a forum in which to consider the issue *prior to* clinical experimentation. According to the journal's website, "the mission of *The American Journal of Bioethics* and bioethics.net [*AJOB*'s complementary website] is to provide the clinical, legal, academic, scientific, religious and broad community-at-large with a rapid but comprehensive debate of issues in bioethics."[18] The debate was spurred by a target article, a piece that focuses on a single issue. In this case, the article, "On the Ethics of Facial Transplantation Research," written by a team at the University of Louisville and first-authored by bioethicist Osbourne Wiggins, argues that the ethical criteria developed for innovative transplant surgery had been satisfied and that it was time to pursue clinical experimentation.[19] An open commentary, a series of pieces written by scholars in response to the target article, followed. The entire debate consists of fifteen articles.[20] It is important to note that the second response, entitled "A Surgeon's Perspective on the Ethics of Face Transplantation," is coauthored by the French surgeons who, within the year following publication, completed the world's first partial face transplant. The AJOB website describes the commentary as "a conversation" about pressing bioethical issues.[21] But as bioethicist Tod Chambers suggested, the exchange was more than a conversation: "They [Wiggins et al.] view the publication of their essay in AJOB as an important illocutionary speech act that will permit them to begin performing the surgery."[22] Thus, hope of actually performing a transplant infuses the debate.

The *AJOB* commentaries represent a unique moment in the development of a technological innovation. While animal trials, testing of antirejection medication, and cadaver experimentation were successfully completed, in lieu of human experimentation the University of Louisville face transplant team initiated a conversation with transplant surgeons, bioethicists, philosophers, immunologists, and psychologists to debate "the issues," a strategy that preeminent bioethicist Arthur Caplan described as "prophylactic ethics."[23] In other words, the conversation was an attempt to demonstrate sincere ethical deliberation to circumvent public outrage and intraprofessional conflict that proponents worried would follow human experimentation. The Wiggins et al. target article came at a particularly contentious moment. In 2003, a Working Party of the Royal College of Surgeons of England, an independent body of surgeons, refused to endorse experimental FT, arguing that the requirements for ethical practice had yet to be met.[24]

As a key site of ethical deliberation, the *American Journal of Bioethics* issue can be analyzed as a cultural space wherein questions and critiques about FT are articulated and the terms of contestation come into formation. In this way, the *AJOB* special issue on FT is a source of data about the making of a new technology, specifically how the meanings attributed to bodies, bodily difference, and interventions are contested in the process of establishing a working framework for clinical practice. The contours of the *AJOB* debate illustrate the ways in which ideas about the face, and more specifically facial difference, are strategically deployed in an effort to shape the future of facial work. I position the journal issue as an object of sociological analysis in order to consider how the disfigurement imaginary operated throughout and how notions of social death were discussed alongside bodily death. Specifically, I analyzed the debate with two seemingly self-evident questions in mind: First, what *risks* associated with FT dominate the debate? Second, what unique *benefits* are attributed to FT? In articulating their stance on FT, contributors not only answer these simple questions but also reveal working assumptions about what kind of life is possible with facial difference *and* what an unremarkable face is worth.

Physiological Risks

Transplantation carries bodily risks. On this everyone agreed, but among the *AJOB* pieces, there were considerable discrepancies about what these risks entailed. Specifically, the rate of rejection emerged as the most contentious issue. In the world of transplant medicine, rejection is a specter to be prevented, feared, and managed. In a sense, transplantation medicine is as much about warding off threats of organ rejection as it is about transferring organs. Sociologically, claims about physiological risk and graft rejection are notable in part because they vary so widely both in numerical estimates and in the significance attributed to rejection. Bioethicist Carson Strong estimated that at best, one in five faces would be rejected within the first three years following surgery.[25] Similarly, Hastings Center bioethicist and public policy associate Karen Maschke and science writer Eric Trump cited the 2003 Royal College of Surgeons Report. In it, estimates suggest that 10 percent of grafts would be rejected in the first year and that 30 to 50 percent of patients would experience graft loss function within the first two to five years.[26] Yet in the target article, the Louisville team sidestepped concerns about rejection, arguing that FT is no more risky than other reconstructive techniques, which use a patient's own tissue.[27] Since the tissue comes from a donor as opposed to the patient (as is the case in skin graphing when tissue is harvested from another location on the patient's body), the Louisville team reasoned that one major surgical procedure, as compared to the numerous (sometimes upward of one hundred) surgeries often required with traditional reconstructive intervention, is overall a less risky approach. It is important to note that because these journal debates occurred *before* clinical trials, the rates of rejection participants cited were estimates rather than empirically derived percentages. No one could know exactly how the body would respond, and yet this was a critical detail in assessing the ethics of FT.

While claims about the actual risks of rejection varied across accounts, the significance critics attributed to rejection differed dramatically as well. Carson Strong argued that because FT involves transplantation of vascularized skin, subcutaneous fat, muscles, facial nerves, and bony facial structures, graft loss would result in major facial wounds.[28] Yet proponents posited that graft rejection would "merely" return the recipient to a state of disfigurement similar to the disfigurement preceding the intervention.[29] While proponents admitted that rejection of the new face is certainly a danger, it was not conceptualized as one that should prevent FT from occurring. Again given that there was no experimental evidence in order to base such claims, contributors imagined hugely variant consequences of rejection depending upon whether they either opposed or supported FT. Ultimately, varying accounts depicted FT as deeply threatening and acutely dangerous *or* as moderately risky and profoundly revolutionary. One fact remained consistent across accounts, however: Rejection is a real risk, and this fact raises the question of immunosuppression.

Immunosuppression or antirejection medication carries significant health risks, including infection and end-organ toxicity leading to diabetes and malignancies that can result in death. While contributors agreed that there are physical risks associated with immunosuppression, the significance attributed to these risks varies from account to account.[30] Though transplantation medicine provides a theoretical and experimental framework for thinking about how drug regimens affect the human body, the particulars of FT make identifying the risks of immunosuppression uniquely tricky. In other words, the specificity of transplantation matters in terms of calculating risks. Recipients of organs like kidneys are critically ill at the time of transplantation, but for potential FT recipients "severe disfigurement" does not compromise health in comparable ways. Viewed in this way, a question emerges as to whether the risks of immunosuppression apply in the case of FT, given that potential patients would presumably be healthier than most other transplant recipients on comparable drug regimens. The most sensible basis upon which to gauge the risk of immunosuppression in FT patients is research conducted on hand transplantation which explored complications related to tacrolimus and mycophenolate mofetil/predni-sone combination therapy, the drugs the Louisville team argued would most likely be used for FT. Yet the ways in which researchers used data on immunosuppression varied. Specifically, how critics approached FT as similar to or different from other kinds of transplantation impacted the ways in which they conceptualized the risks of immunosuppression.

On one side, critics argued that undoubtedly a face transplant would increase a recipient's quality of life, but that immunosuppression would threaten life itself. The patient may, in fact, be accepting a shorter life in favor of a better life.[31] Bioethicist Arthur Caplan assessed the risks as "staggering" in the most critical analysis that appeared in the issue, writing,

> It is not certain that the transplant will result in a functioning or even partially functional face. The drugs required to maintain a transplanted face are powerful, noxious, and potentially life-threatening. If the procedure should result in acute rejection, then the subject may die with the entire graft sloughing off his or her head. Even if that grim prospect does not occur, chronic rejection problems may be such that the recipient is exposed to doses of immunosuppression that lead to cancer, kidney failure, and other major problems. And this presumes the subject is compliant with the postsurgical regimen, a state that some patients find very difficult to achieve post-transplantation. Not only are the prospects of physiological complications and functional failures very real, but the first face transplant recipient will face enormous psychosocial challenges as well.[32]

Here, both the risks of rejection and immunosuppression function to position FT as an intervention that calls the very terms of risk/benefit assessment into question. In short, Caplan's critique rested on the assumption that no reconstructive intervention is worth the risk of death potentially associated with FT. In anticipation of this very criticism, the Louisville team suggested that risks associated with immunosuppression would be far less significant for face transplant recipients as compared with other kinds of transplantation, because facial disfigurement is less physically compromising than the chronic illnesses experienced by other transplant patients.[33]

Debates about the risks of rejection and immunosuppression are sociologically significant for two reasons. First, these debates demonstrate how facts are subject to deliberation and contestation, especially in relation to medical innovation. Second, and more importantly, the *AJOB* commentary illustrates that how risk is construed deeply affects the direction of clinical practice and the terms upon which ethical debate rests. In other words, a technology comes into formation depending on how risks are interpreted and represented in ethical debates, and at the same time, the contours of bioethics shift as new ways of thinking about risk emerge. Taken together, debates about the physiological risks of surgery, rates of rejection, and effects of immunosuppression deeply structured how FT was positioned as a risky or safe facial intervention. In some accounts, FT was imagined as a life threatening practice. Others treated these concerns as overblown. Yet all sides ultimately wrestled with one overarching question: Is aesthetic intervention that treats facial disfigurement a practice in which compromised health or, more specifically, death is an acceptable risk?

Psychological Risks

While transplantation always involves a multitude of risks, critics suggested that the transplantation of a human face elicits unique psychological risks.[34] While the debate about physical risks centered on graft rejection and side effects of immunosuppression, the debate about psychological risks focused on concerns about identity. In the *AJOB* exchange, then, FT was positioned as a technology with incredible power not only to reconstruct the face but also to undermine (and reconstruct) the very parameters of the self.

In keeping with their interest in proceeding with FT, the Louisville team's target article argued that the potential psychological risks of FT are similar, and thus not insurmountable, to those faced by solid-organ transplant recipients. These included "a desperation that creates unrealistic hopes, fears that his or her body will reject the transplant, guilt feelings about the death of the donor, difficulty conforming to the treatment regimen and its side-effects, and a sense of personal responsibility for the success of the procedure (Zdichavsky et al. 1999)."[35] Psychologist Nicola Rumsey, a contributing member of the Working Party of the

Royal College of Surgeons in England and a disfigurement specialist, concurred that the psychological risks of FT are similar to other kinds of transplantation.

> These include fears relating to the viability of the transplanted organ or limb, fear of the aftermath of rejection, the burden of adhering to complex postoperative medical and behavioral regimes and associated fears of personal responsibility for the success or failure of the transplant, coping with the side effects of immunosuppression, the difficulties of integrating the transplant into an existing body image, and identity, and emotional responses, including gratitude and guilt, in relation to the donor and family.[36]

Yet Rumsey also positioned the psychological risks of FT as unique because of the particular significance of the face and the psychological effects of facial disfigurement. Subsequently, she asked readers to consider the psychological costs recipients might endure while waiting for a facial tissue donation. Would life be put on hold in the meantime, inhibiting the development of necessary coping strategies?

Echoing the Louisville team, others rejected the idea that the psychological risks should operate as a barrier to FT, recommending that even in cases with "terrible" outcomes, the patient would be back to where she or he started rather than worse off. For example, bioethicist George Agich and plastic surgeon Marie Seimenow argued,

> The psychological consequences of graft rejection would undoubtedly be significant, but the significance relates to the fact that the patient would return to a situation of disfigurement that preceded the facial transplantation. The graft failure would return the patient to a state of disfigurement similar to the pre-transplant disfigurement.[37]

Interestingly, even those who favored experimentation conceded that FT is likely an experience with penetrating psychological consequences. As the Louisville team claimed, "What is unique to facial transplantation, however, is that facial appearance is intimately and profoundly associated with one's sense of personal and social identity."[38] Ironically, the very psychological transformation that some critics positioned as threatening operated as a justification for proceeding in proponents' accounts.

Proponents and critics alike acknowledged psychological impact, but there remained disagreement about whether shifts to recipient's identity constitute a risk. Proponents downplayed the effects of a new face, arguing that *all* transplants complicate a patient's identity. By contrast, others predicted that FT could lead to an identity crisis.[39] As Carson Strong warned, "Transplant patients might experience psychological distress over their new appearance, even if it is aesthetically more pleasing than the old one, arising in part from the introduction of a new appearance into preexisting social networks."[40] Ultimately, contributors conceptualized psychological risks in wide-ranging ways—from inconsequential disruption to existential catastrophe.

Social Risks

In addition to the physiological and psychological risks to potential FT recipients, several contributors addressed the "social risks" of FT. Social risks were broadly conceptualized as the effects of FT on society writ large. Some critics worried that media representations, including popular science news, would not accurately represent FT as a reconstructive technique and that sensationalism might result in a demand for cosmetic face transplants.[41] A response coauthored by French surgeon Francois Petit warned, "Care should be taken to not frighten or repulse the population given that this is a 'Frankenstein story.'"[42] The team emphasized that stories about FT should not function as entertainment, fearing that these kinds of stories exacerbate organ shortages. "FT is *not* a weapon of mass distraction," Petit's team concluded. Other teams expressed concern that science news featuring FT inevitably yet inadvertently sends the message that quality of life depends on radical intervention.[43]

Larger ethical concerns—including patient selection protocol, patient and donor confidentiality, and donation procedures—circulated throughout the *AJOB* issue, too. Most commentators agreed that premiere patients should be psychologically stable and cognizant of the physical and psychological risks. Put another way, those who demonstrate resilience and coping would, perhaps ironically, make the best candidates.[44] A contribution authored by a research team led by surgeon Peter Butler emphasized the need for thorough psychological assessment to determine which potential patients are "realistic," "determined," and "robust."[45] Their bioethical approach leads to a catch-22 wherein the distressed who most want FT are defined as "bad patients."[46] This moment speaks to the power differential always at play in sites of biomedical innovation. Medical expertise trumps self-determination, such that patients' own perceptions matter less than experts' opinions. The act of categorizing patients as "good" or "bad" and dispensing intervention according to these determinations is also significant in light of my larger question about the consequences of the disfigurement imaginary. What this moment in the *AJOB* debate vividly demonstrates is how doctors function as gatekeepers based on how *they* make sense of patients' lived experiences. In short, ways of thinking matter, corporeally and otherwise, and impact clinical practice in concrete ways.

In the target article, the Louisville team anticipated ethical quandaries and outlined a protocol for obtaining informed consent, even suggesting that a patient advocate usher candidates through the process. Because the Louisville team intended to use unaltered photographs in its published results, they conceded that scientific reporting might compromise patient and donor confidentiality. The Louisville team rejected standard bioethical protocol in an additional way, proposing that patients could not withdraw from clinical trials after treatment commenced.[47] Critics argued that despite the impossibility of assuring patient confidentiality, researchers should attempt to protect the donor's identity.[48]

These concerns about confidentiality pointed to a much larger question: How do researchers preserve ethical standards, specifically confidentiality, while publicly exposing and celebrating biomedical innovation? Ultimately, concerns about experimental protocol focused on avoiding practices that the public might perceive as grossly unethical, which could undermine biomedical expertise and future innovation.

Finally, risks to potential recipients' support systems—families, spouses, friends, and coworkers—fall under this rubric of "social risks." In particular, Carson Strong's response raised questions about how a new appearance might fundamentally alter the dynamics within a recipient's social networks, an idea echoed by several critics who imagined ways a patient's family might negatively respond to a transplanted face.[49] Others considered the postsurgery burden of caring for an FT recipient.[50] Within this larger conversation about family, critics posed multiple concerns about the effects on donors' families. Specifically, several pieces questioned the prospect of face donation given dominant Western death rituals, especially the tradition of open caskets and body viewing as part of funerary measures. How will families say goodbye when left with a faceless corpse?[51] In this sociocultural context, donors' families may understand the donation process as one that disfigures their loved ones in death even as it eradicates disfigurement in the living.[52] The grief process and its effects on face donation emerged in bioethicist John A. Robertson's response. Because we remember the deceased in terms of their faces (and not their kidneys or corneas), Robertson asked if donor families might believe that their loved one is living on.[53] In light of these questions and concerns, some contributors asked how a donor's "body integrity" could be preserved and/or restored.[54] Fears about the effects on donors' families acutely reflect the disfigurement imaginary, both in critics' concerns about the "disfiguring" effects of organ harvesting and the ways the face is reified as manifestly precious.

Through the *AJOB* debates, critics raised numerous concerns about the physiological, psychological, and social risks of FT, attempting to anticipate potential patient outcomes, consequences to scientific authority, and bioethical pitfalls. Yet the risks of any biotechnology are always weighed against the benefits in order to assess the significance of a medical intervention. Whether risks are deemed reasonable or not is always contingent on the condition at stake. For example, we accept minor side effects to treat everyday ailments. In cases of life-threatening diseases, we consent to greater risks. In everyday life, we take for granted that the seriousness of the consequences of treatment is relative to the severity of the condition. The inconsistency among how *AJOB* commentators conceptualized the risks of FT indicates discrepancies in how participants think about disfigurement specifically, and appearance writ large.

Very few of the risks mentioned in the *AJOB* debate are entirely unique to FT. Liver transplantation requires the use of immunosuppression. Cosmetic surgery is psychologically tricky, given that the effects may never approximate what a patient desires. Reproductive technologies ignite fear about how scientific innovation alters the nature and meaning of "life." The very fact that the risks are not especially unique suggests that the real, albeit implicit, significance of the *AJOB* debate centers less on the risks of FT and more on the benefits of facial work. Ultimately, how commentators positioned themselves as proponents or critics of FT was contingent on how participants framed both "disfigurement" and the promise of FT as simply reconstructive or, alternately, as lifesaving.

Making a Nonvital Intervention
"Lifesaving": The Benefits of FT

Throughout the *AJOB* debates, critics infer the risks of FT using scientific expertise, bioethics principles, and social psychological research. Without data from clinical experiments, these bodies of knowledge inform expectations and drive concerns about FT. Yet how contributors understand the potential benefits of FT is permeated by the disfigurement imaginary. For proponents especially, the idea that facial difference amounts to social death emerged over and over again. And yet FT was explicitly characterized as a "nonvital" procedure. Here, we see the terms of contestation. Clinical notions of life and death conflict with profoundly stigmatizing assumptions about what the experience of "disfigurement" is like. Ultimately, the designation of FT as "nonvital" (and thus "life-enhancing") is precisely what is at stake in articulating the benefits of FT.

Widely shared clinical criteria about what counts as death and thereby what interventions are lifesaving were deployed when talking about the significance of FT. At the same time, proponents used the disfigurement imaginary to push against what constitutes a vital intervention. Consider how the Louisville team juxtaposed FT with "vital" transplantation: "With the relatively recent advent of human hand transplantation, however, ethical reflection has shifted to the need to weigh the risks the patient assumes for the sake of receiving a donated organ that, unlike a heart or liver, is not necessary for his or her survival."[55] Rather than a transplant that facilitates survival, FT was described as necessary for "a person's self-image, social acceptability, and sense of normalcy."[56] The team even explicitly described FT as life-enhancing rather than lifesaving:

> While using transplanted tissues to reconstruct facial deformities would significantly improve a patient's quality of life, in most cases these procedures would not be life-saving in the strict sense of the word. This situation stands in contrast to life-saving treatments, like heart and liver transplants, in which the risk/benefit ratio is more readily conceptualized.[57]

Undoubtedly, FT is inherently different from the lifesaving treatments identified here, but even as FT is labeled nonvital, it is discursively positioned as something altogether different from life-enhancing interventions. By describing the procedures as not lifesaving in "the strict sense of the word," the team implied that FT *is* lifesaving in *some* sense of the word. By asserting that the risk/benefit ratio of heart and liver transplantation is easier to conceptualize, the team signaled that FT refigures the very ways we understand risks and benefits. In effect, FT was positioned as a vital intervention, albeit vital in a different way than heart or liver transplantation. Part and parcel to this meaning-making process, the debate about FT generated a reconfiguration of the object of intervention—disfigurement—as life threatening. In other words, disfigurement took shape as a life threatening condition in the very site positioned to repair human faces.

Consider how FT proponents George Agich and Marie Siemionow positioned the experience of facial difference here in order to argue for FT:

> Arthur Caplan has been widely quoted as saying, "What will you do if a face transplant fails? . . . I understand a disfigured face may be terrible to live with. But if a transplant should be rejected you're basically dying. That's a serious, high-stakes issue" (Allen 2003). This is clearly an overstatement, one that Caplan would not likely claim in a published article . . . We think that the inordinate suffering of patients with severe disfigurements should be recentered in the public ethical discussion.[58]

Agich and Seimenow's reference to Caplan's concerns about rejection was used in the service of positioning FT as an indispensible technology with a unique potential for alleviating "inordinate suffering." This reveals that it is not simply FT that is at stake in the *AJOB* debate, but rather the way facial disfigurement itself is conceptualized. As in the previous three chapters, social death operates as a lens through which facial difference is viewed. What makes this case different from the previous cases is that this intervention is controversial precisely because it may (or may not) result in actual clinical/biological death. Here, then, notions of social death are employed to position risks, including biological death of the organism, as acceptable in order to repair severe facial disfigurement.

Discussions of risk explicitly relied upon biomedical research and bioethics principles to justify claims. By contrast, contributors' imagined the benefits of FT largely through the disfigurement imaginary. Bioethicist E. Haavi Morreim's contribution included a story about a facially atypical taxi driver she randomly encountered. As opposed to social psychological research, the anecdote informs how she assessed as the benefits of FT:

> This is not the story of someone who would qualify for a face transplant. But it hints at the enormous difficulties facing people whose appearance is abnormal. What outsiders might categorize in dry academic terms as "quality of life" is for some of these people a very real assault on their personhood and their membership in society. Their problems will not be remedied by urging people to be more tolerant. Neither can we downgrade the idea of transplant because facial abnormalities are not life threatening. As autonomous adults we routinely do, and must be free to, undergo substantial risks to improve our quality of life and act on the many other values we hold dear. If general anesthesia is an ethically permissible risk for a cosmetic face lift, then so, surely, can significant medical risks be acceptable in hope of a significantly greater gain for those who are grievously disfigured.[59]

The very fact that within such a rigorous debate the disfigurement imaginary emerged over and over again attests to the ideological force of this way of thinking. In a space entirely devoted to questioning a surgical intervention on the face, ideas about the face—what its injuries mean and what its difference portends—went largely critically unquestioned. Not surprisingly, Morreim also invoked dimensions of social death, specifically compromised social interaction, and threats to one's human status to describe the possible benefits of FT.

Proponents of FT conceded that, technically, FT is not lifesaving. Morriem characterized facial disfigurement as "not life-threatening." Other contributors acknowledged that ultimately FT is an intervention aimed at improving quality of life. Yet their accounts implied that what FT accomplishes is different from what other life-improving interventions achieve. Thus, while critics employed established clinical notions of vital and nonvital to characterize FT as technically nonvital, they also suggested that FT is different than other interventions that are life-enhancing. Proponents argued that FT so alters central aspects of a patient's life that it makes living in society possible. This benefit is qualitatively different from the benefits afforded by interventions like lifesaving transplantations *and* by life-enhancing technologies such as face lifts. In short, proponents suggested that without FT potential patients might not be at risk of dying, but that they are at profound risk of social death. For some, even clinical death was defended as a reasonable risk to ward off social death. The links between the disfigurement imaginary and social death are made abundantly clear here. *Understanding disfigurement as so stigmatizing that it amounts to social death makes it possible to weigh the risks of intervention alongside the risks of living with disfigurement, and to conclude that the benefit of intervention is vital in its own way.* In the *AJOB* debate, a new kind of vitality is born.

The Time Is (Not) Now

While over the course of my research I was asked over and over again whether I was "for" or "against" the kinds of facial work I studied, this question does not exactly reflect the outcomes of bioethics deliberation. Consider that in the *AJOB* debate, contributors fractured. Some called for immediate experimentation. Others suggested further deliberation while ultimately endorsing the promise of FT. A few concluded that FT is inherently too risky and problematic. The University of Louisville team conveyed its position with a simple declaration: "There arrives a point in time when the procedure should simply be done. We submit that that time is now."[60] Surgeon Francois Petit and his coauthors were the closest to this position, writing, "Our position

is that FT could now be performed."[61] Others did not agree. Peter Butler and colleagues ultimately endorsed the procedure but called for
caution before experimentation: "There are a large number of ethical
issues that require consideration, and it is imperative that this occur
before any face transplants are carried out [emphasis added]."[62] In a
more scathing critique, Arthur Caplan contended that the Louisville
team had not satisfied the ethical standards of experimentation: "Any
experiment should not only be the subject of moral reflection and
deliberation prior to its initiation, but also must be able to successfully
engage the concerns and objections raised as part of that process. Has
this standard been met in the case of FT? I do not think so."[63] In contrast with endorsing immediate experimentation, these contributors
suggested that ethical concerns were not sufficiently resolved, but that
potentially FT is an ethically viable intervention.

These two positions stand in sharp contrast to commentators who
altogether rejected FT as a treatment for facial disfigurement. Social
psychologist and appearance researcher Nichola Rumsey concluded
that "the Louisville team feels that the time is right to undertake face
transplants. The headline benefits of a normal appearance and fully
functioning facial communication are certainly seductive, however,
the message in the small print is much less clear-cut . . . Surgical solutions rarely provide miracle cures for complex psychological issues."[64]
Feminist philosopher and bioethicist Sara Goering echoed Rumsey's
critique:

> But are their faces truly the source of their suffering? Our faces are inti-
> mately tied to our identities, and accepting oneself requires coming to
> terms with one's face . . . Suffering can be addressed in multiple ways,
> and we should be careful about offering services that frame the problem
> as primarily an individual deficit. Such a focus may exacerbate our ten-
> dency to misidentify sources of suffering.[65]

Rumsey and Goering are emblematic of perspectives that eschew medical intervention in favor of intensive psychological care at the individual level, and a radical restructuring of social norms that coalesce to
stigmatize facial difference at the societal level. In fact, the case of FT
vividly illustrates how critiques of intervention that favor social change,

described in greater depth in chapter 2, emerge in response to facial work. For example, in a 2005 issue of *Bioethics*, bioethicists Richard Huxtable and Julie Woodley employed noninterventionism to argue against FT: "The patient might be influenced or even coerced by our beauty-fixated society and as such there may be less invasive and certainly less risky means of improving both society's and disfigured individuals' reactions to facial disfigurement."[66]

In relation to how noninterventionism operates in response to normalizing interventions, the case of FT is unique too. Noninterventionist critiques of FT premised the vulnerability of individuals subject to intervention as the very reason not to intervene. While vulnerability is certainly critical in assessing the ethics of medical practice, the intervention at stake often aims to address the very vulnerability critics point to. These facts make calls for nonintervention particularly curious and unwieldy. In the case of facial work, references to suffering are bound up with noninterventionism, and potential patients are imagined as psychologically fragile, desperately hopeful, potentially unreliable, and unfoundedly optimistic. Carson Strong's contribution to the *AJOB* debate demonstrated such logic: "Potential recipients are likely to be psychologically vulnerable because of their disfigurement. Affective factors may compromise their ability to weigh risks and benefits autonomously and to have realistic expectations about the success of the transplant."[67] In essence, Strong argued that because potential patients might want the procedure too much, they are incapable of providing informed consent. Psychologist Nicola Rumsey employed a similar logic, arguing, "These [most distressed about their disfigurement] are the people most likely to seek a face transplant, yet they are also the more psychologically vulnerable and less well equipped to deal with the rigors of complex surgery, uncertain outcomes, and demanding postoperative treatment regimens."[68] Here, desire for intervention became the criteria upon which to argue against intervention. It is ironic, indeed, that suffering is simultaneously the grounds upon which critics based arguments against FT and proponents made arguments for FT. Potential patients are "disfigured" and vulnerable, thus they are not able to consent to the surgery, and nonconsensual surgery is unethical, but consent is not possible because candidates are disfigured. This is logically untenable. In addition, noninterventionism in this case replicates a disparity in how facially typical and facially variant patients are treated. The agency generally attributed to patients is absent here. When is suffering precisely the grounds upon which informed consent can be given? In a health care system structured on free market models of consumption, why does a patient's desire for face transplantation preclude him or her from being an "ideal candidate"? Why, in the case of facial work, is desire for consumption suddenly indefensible? Ultimately, the pressing question about whether human experimentation should proceed was bound up with the disfigurement imaginary, not only for those arguing for FT but also for those arguing against it.

The Medical Midway: Hawking Meanings of Technologies in the Making

Proponents of FT, as a technology in the making, are centrally focused on strategic claims-making processes.[69] As the everyday work of a face transplant team and the *AJOB* debates revealed, the disfigurement imaginary is deployed to influence ways of thinking about facial difference and by proxy FT.[70] As with *Extreme Makeover* participants, the social, economic, intimate, emotional, and bodily lives of potential FT recipients are diagnosed as fundamentally compromised. As with facial feminization patients, social interaction for those likely eligible for FT is made to seem impossible. And as with Operation Smile recipients, facial difference is positioned as at odds with so-called universal human features. Ultimately, whether we are "for" or "against" FT depends on the degree to which we subscribe to the disfigurement imaginary. If the face is reduced to appearance (and appearance is conceptualized as nonessential), then it is not reasonable to incur the risks of immunosuppression and death to repair it. If, on the other hand, the face is, as bioethicist John A. Robertson wrote, "the external manifestation of our persons (our souls?)," then "reasonable" risks of intervention might very well include death.[71]

FT is taking shape not simply as a biotechnological intervention, but as an artifact that raises questions about how we conceptualize life and death.[72] In the spaces where the future of FT is negotiated, it is both differentiated from other vital or lifesaving interventions *and* characterized as more transformative than any other nonvital intervention. In effect, FT is positioned unequivocally not as life-enhancing but rather as a lifesaving intervention, albeit lifesaving in a new sense of the term. Implicitly, new notions of death are innovated.

In the final essay published in the *AJOB* issue, "Medical Ethicists, Human Curiosities, and the New Media Midway," bioethicist Steven H. Miles analyzed the FT debate (which he described as a "medical docusoap").[73] He argued that the very work of deciphering biomedical ethics is guided by a deeply problematic principle. According to Miles, bioethics is not "allowed to reflect publicly on why particular subjects or framings of the issues have been chosen."[74] His insight is especially helpful toward understanding the larger consequences of the disfigurement imaginary. The work of the FT teams and the *AJOB* debates reflect how the disfigurement imaginary operates to reify facial difference as a life threatening and socially deadly condition. The nature of disfigurement becomes taken for granted. Viewing disfigurement as socially deadly is a critical rhetorical move in garnering support for an intervention like FT that carries the risk of clinical death. This framing is clearly strategic, but this way of thinking is also conceptually noteworthy because it transposes lifesaving significance onto an aesthetic intervention.

We might consider bioethical stances in relation to emerging biomedical interventions along a continuum—at one end lies unqualified support, and at the other lies absolute denunciation. The voices brought to light through this analysis operate in the space between these extremes, supporting FT if (and only if) certain conditions are met, and under specified conditions. But the question about whether to do or not to do a face transplant fundamentally ignores the framings that structure this very question. Bioethics organizes knowledge claims according to binary oppositions that rely on definite boundaries between self and other, mind and body, subject and object, health and disease, and life and death.[75] FT precipitates a reevaluation of what counts as life and death. Can one "live" with a disfigured face or not? Are we to take social death as seriously as biological death? Strategic claims in favor of FT call into question the binary between life and death without engaging the consequences of rethinking life and death as unambiguous categories.

The long-term effects of those Monday morning meetings in Hospital Building One are not tangible. No consensus emerged in the

AJOB debates either—no protocols were formulated, no funding was attained, no institutional partnerships were formed. Yet the meanings that emerge here are incredibly momentous. FT opens up a Pandora's box both in terms of technological possibility and bioethical questions. Biotechnologies that improve the quality of life while threatening life itself will continue to emerge. FT does not ward off clinical death. Yet the power of the disfigurement imaginary is perhaps nowhere more apparent than in relation to FT; facial work is defended as a kind of lifesaving work that staves off social death. While the consequences of understanding facial difference and facial work in this way are relevant to FT, these ways of thinking potentially have broader consequences for aesthetic surgery and, more specifically, the status of appearance.

FT raises metaethical questions.[76] Metaethical questions have implications beyond the immediacy of a new intervention. FT provokes such questions about how we conceptualize death and what counts as a lifesaving measure. What we experience and label "life" and "death" changes in response to biotechnologies that do not easily fit within existing ways of understanding risk and benefit.[77] FT is one of these biotechnologies.

There is another story of transplantation that elicited public fascination and raised similarly weighty ethical questions. Heart transplantation was a revolutionary technological innovation, but the technology required a redefinition of life and death. Subsequently, both experts and lay publics reimagined what it meant to be alive and what kind of existence constituted death. Consider that over the last 30 years, death has been radically reconceptualized to make the field of organ transplantation possible and the practice of organ donation viable. Doctors must think about death differently in order to harvest and transplant organs from one person to another, and how we experience life and death in everyday life has changed, too. The very notion of brain death makes it possible for families to think of loved ones on life support as in fact *not* living—as dead—and more specifically, as organ donors.

FT troubles how we conceptualize lifesaving and life-enhancing work. If disfigurement is merely unfortunate or even tragic, it is not ethically justifiable to pursue FT, given its myriad risks. But if disfigurement is life threatening as the disfigurement imaginary presumes that it is, then FT promises to be a revolutionary mode of repair, a tremendous innovation in reconstructive surgery, a *vital* intervention. Precisely because FT raises such fundamental metaethical issues, it is important to critically analyze how we are thinking and talking about it. Situating disfigurement as socially deadly and framing interventions which traditionally have been life-enhancing as lifesaving makes a particular future possible for FT, but it simultaneously transforms broader understandings of life and death.

The future of face transplantation, if it is guided by the disfigurement imaginary, also potentially reconfigures the stakes of appearance. In a moment in which being beautiful is so valued, having an abject face is incredibly stigmatized. The debates about FT and the meaning attributed to facial work point to a momentous social transformation. For particular bodily configurations, specifically facial difference, aesthetic intervention is gradually becoming defined as lifesaving work. If disfigurement equals social death, then facial work is a vital intervention. As we watch the face transplant story unfold, one overarching question arises: What are the consequences of this conflation of appearance and life, disfigurement and death?

7

At Face Value

The process of coming to terms with facial injury or deformity—what I have called "changing faces"—is ultimately
about showing to the world that your face alone is in no way
indicative of your real worth as a human being. Just because
you have been unlucky enough to suffer facial damage is no
reason to suppose that you are less of a person.
—James Partridge, *Changing Faces: The Challenge of Facial
Disfigurement* (1990)

While writing this book, I noticed a small blemish on my face. My complexion is not one that could be described as "clear." In fact, every day
I spend time monitoring my skin, applying acne treatment, lathering
on sunscreen, and, honestly, picking and prodding in exactly the way
the dermatologist tells you not to. But unlike other blemishes, this spot
was warm to the touch, extraordinarily sensitive, and over several days
it tripled in size. Some years earlier, I'd watched a scrape on my brother's
abdomen swell exponentially until he was put on an intravenous antibiotic regimen. The diagnosis was MRSA. Methicillin-resistant Staphylo-
coccus aureus is bacteria most often spread through skin-to-skin contact,
but it is notoriously treatment resistant. MRSA is one of the "superbugs"
that the Centers for Disease Control and Prevention increasingly warns
us about. The red spot on my face, warm to the touch, growing in size,
and increasingly painful, appeared to be MRSA. The general practitioner
who looked it over suggested that we lance it right there, in the office.

"He wants to cut my face," I thought. Outwardly, I remained stoic
(my tried and true strategy for advocating for myself in doctor-patient
interactions), but inwardly, I panicked.

That day, the doctor did not lance the infection. Probably because of my work on this very project, I asked if there was any other alternative and insisted that if my face needed to be cut, I wanted to talk to a "plastic" surgeon first. I took a powerful antibiotic. The infection waned, and as of this writing, I have not had any surgery on my face. From one vantage point, these events are ironic; the sociologist of aesthetic intervention turns toward the very specialty she studies and critiques. But as I see it, my desire to consult with an aesthetic surgeon speaks to my awareness of the technical skills upon which the field is built and my understanding of and complicity with the ever-increasing significance of appearance.

Throughout this book, my intent has not been to demonize the skilled surgeon or mock the hopeful patient, to definitively criticize aesthetic intervention or to naively celebrate medical innovation. Rather, my central aim has been to ask questions about ways of thinking that equate appearance difference with social death, that refigure aesthetic surgery as a vital intervention, and that even position nonintervention as a politically preferable solution in lieu of facial work. The degree to which the disfigurement imaginary has been reified as the lens through which particular forms of facial difference are viewed impacts which interventions are taken for granted and which are called into question. Facial work, like that practiced by Operation Smile, is universally accepted in ways that extreme makeovers and FFS are not. Some faces are resolutely positioned as "really" disfigured and thus in need, while other forms of intervention still carry some elective connotations. To be sure, repair of cleft lip and palate facilitates physiological functioning, but functioning is not the linchpin upon which calls for nonintervention subside. Noninterventionism is palpable in the case of FT, even as those faces are surely most in need of intervention relative to functioning. Even though the disfigurement imaginary is most evident in relation to FT, innovation seems to animate a kind of anxiety that trumps functioning, with the effect of inhibiting emergent interventions from becoming taken for granted.

Throughout this book, the processes through which facial work takes shape as a seemingly unavoidable method of coping are described and analyzed. One final factor that inspires noninterventionism is worth noting here. The children upon whom Operation Smile operates are innocent by the very fact of their youth, and they are uniquely vulnerable, poor, and disenfranchised relative to neoliberal operations of global economics and politics. By comparison, the faces that circulate in the narrative of *Extreme Makeover* belong to those whose very participation is premised on their inability to cope. While their faces do not look altogether different from those of the audience, extreme makeover candidates are presented as desperate, inappropriately so. Facial feminization is marketed to trans women, a group who remain the object of widespread cultural mockery and, in some cases, loathing. Face transplantation is aimed at repairing severe disfigurement—cases in which public personhood is significantly compromised because of appearance. The common thread amongst these cases is that potential recipients are positioned as socially dead, albeit for different reasons. Only the interventions aimed at especially vulnerable children seem to be immune from noninterventionism.

How is it that the children of Operation Smile unequivocally deserve intervention and the "psychopathological", the "transsexual", and the "severely disfigured" do not? It is not simply that functionality works to justify some forms of normalization and invalidate others; or that the degree of disfigurement operates as the key determinant of what intervention goes unchallenged. Rather, the most devalued, the most stigmatized, and the most abject are positioned as not deserving. As I describe in chapter 2, noninterventionism rests on valuing social change more than the change an intervention might produce in a single human life. When intervention is aimed at a life that is fundamentally devalued, its promise is more likely to be dismissed in favor of broad-scale progress, even if nonintervention extends individual suffering. In some cases a single life seems to matter, and in other cases it does not. Ultimately, the push for nonintervention rests on privileging some lives at real costs to others.

Clearly, we need to restructure how we look at bodies and assign them differential value, redefine what constitutes the normal body, and interrogate how people are expected to navigate bodily differences. Radical social change is needed, but it is deep social revisioning that may be long and hard in the making. And what shall be done in the meantime? What of the first FT recipient, Isabelle Dinoire, who has a life made possible, in part, by receiving a new face? What of the woman who approached me at the International Foundation for Gender Education describing how her life was infinitely better after facial feminization surgery? What of Thanh Ngan, whose crying face occupies the

Operation Smile homepage? What of *Extreme Makeover*'s Ray Krone, the "snaggle-tooth killer," whose makeover was part and parcel to his pursuit of a new life after ten years wrongly incarcerated? It is the either/ or that is so problematic. Privileging social change over intervention is untenable because it impedes the possibility of changing lives *now*. While premising "life itself" on facial work carries insidious consequences, rejecting facial work when the social change needed may not come in Dinoire, Ngan, or Krone's lifetimes seems equally unethical.

Noninterventionism also imagines biomedicine as separate and apart from society, as if intervention can come in the form of *either* medicine *or* social change, but not both. As we have seen, the practices of biomedicine are inherently social, and as such, biomedicine itself might play its own role in driving the kinds of social change noninterventionism desires. Consider the case of obstetric fistula, a childbirth injury preventable through access to emergency obstetric care. Physiologically speaking, obstetric fistula describes a hole that develops between the vagina and bladder or the vagina and rectum. The immediate cause is protracted obstructed labor, and the immediate consequence is social ostracization. But as feminist scholars and nongovernmental medical organizations have pointed out, gender inequality and poverty are root causes for obstetric fistula too.[1] Global efforts to decrease the rates of obstetric fistula emphasize quality maternal health care; women's agency, including access to birth control and ability to delay the age of pregnancy; and the need to combat stigma. There is no doubt that obstetric fistula represents the embodiment of highly problematic social arrangements.

Surgery on obstetric fistula offers a biomedical repair. Following intervention, the constant leaking of urine and feces ceases, and women are less susceptible to infection. Social change, specifically increased awareness of obstetric fistula, makes biomedical intervention increasingly accessible, but so too does medicine potentially inspire social change. Put another way, biomedicalization does not function solely as a depoliticizing force.[2] Women who no longer have to constantly manage the symptoms of obstetric fistula are better situated to do the work of challenging the structures that produce both a maternal health context susceptible to dangerous childbirth and the stigma faced by women who are deemed "too dirty" to live in community. Noninterventionism ignores the possibility that we might envision ways to harness biomedical intervention in the service of a more just world.

Instead of subscribing to noninterventionism, I critically interrogate facial work in order to consider how these practices could work otherwise—specifically, *better*. Most importantly, aesthetic intervention could operate outside of a vocabulary of social death. Aesthetic interventions that aid basic physiological functions could be reconceived as a human rights issue. Our everyday ways of seeing and categorizing humans as abled or disabled and representing people as disfigured or ugly in popular culture could more regularly be called into question, in order to undermine the notion that painful, expensive, and risky repair is absolutely necessary. The ways the disfigurement imaginary shapes doctor–patient interaction might be challenged, opening up the possibility for "choosing" intervention in a less coercive context.

This book is less about positing a set of guidelines for practice and more about "open[ing] up the discourses in which people—both professionals and potential patients—are able to think about how their actions affect themselves and their communities."[3] This style of critique is about shifting the question away from classifying a proposed solution as good or bad, useful or not, safe or risky. The more robust question is *not* whether one supports face transplantation or Operation Smile or facial feminization, but rather, given that these interventions *are* unfolding, how might we transform these practices in the service of just and better living?

Yet rejecting noninterventionism is not synonymous with innocently endorsing facial work. To conclude this book, I ask: What are the problematics of forging ahead with facial work as it is currently embedded in notions of salvation and vitality? Three major consequences of the practices described in these pages are particularly important to consider. The first directly applies to those people with lived experiences of being labeled "disfigured." The remaining two consequences have more far reaching effects.

First, facial work informed by the disfigurement imaginary positions aesthetic intervention as lifesaving work. By characterizing those with facial difference as socially dead, the humanity of potential patients is called into question. Ultimately, then, the disfigurement imaginary has both stigmatizing—and, more startlingly, dehumanizing—effects on those defined as facially atypical.

This analysis of facial work also reveals the transforming significance of appearance and new meanings of aesthetic surgery writ large. As everyday life is rapidly infused with aesthetic language and techniques focused on appearance are increasingly deployed to navigate the life course, shifting meanings of aesthetic intervention also impact so-called normals in two startling ways. A second consequence to consider is that ultimately, aesthetic intervention is increasingly premised on a mythical past and a false sense of the reality of embodiment.

Facial repair is often a response to bodily trauma. Specifically, facial work is directed toward repairing or "restoring" the body to a pretraumatic state or as close as techniques allow. But what happens to our bodily histories when we focus our efforts on achieving an unmarked body, when "marks" are unavoidable effects of living?

The third consequence of facial work is that it proliferates a distinct aesthetic goal—unremarkability or the desire to be visually taken for granted. There is no doubt that beauty is (made to be) compelling. But in the case of facial work, surgery will almost never produce what is culturally conceptualized as attractive. Instead, the desired outcome of facial work is to produce a face that goes unnoticed in order to decrease the stigma of facial difference. When beauty *and* unremarkability motivate interventions, the pressure to medically monitor and continually alter appearance is magnified. While facial work unfolds in relation to medical contexts dominated by the imperative to repair and a social climate so hostile to facial difference that being atypical is positioned as deadly, the effects of facial work potentially extend far beyond the bodies it surgically shapes. Ultimately, the story of facial work reveals not only the specific stigma associated with facial difference, but also the intensifying importance of appearance more broadly.

Lifesaving, Human-Making?

Bodily interventions from Botox injections to limb-lengthening, from dental veneers to hair transplantation, from electroconvulsive therapy to facial work rely on and mobilize hope. These procedures promise that through biomedical technologies, life can be better. Yet when disfigurement is characterized as deadly, the meaning of facial work transforms such that it increasingly is understood as a lifesaving, not simply an enhancing, intervention. Being perceived as living and being understood as human are highly contingent statuses. For example, classifying the cellular cluster that forms from the merging of an ovum and a sperm cell as a *nonhuman* fetus or a *human* baby is essentially a distinction about where "life" begins. Within US reproductive rights organizing, for example, this political debate is so weighty because a human is an organism entitled to rights and recognition. Historically, a nonhuman is not entitled to legal protections. Ultimately, where we decide *life* begins is bound up with what we understand as person or human. Being human is to be alive; nonliving humans are not quite human but rather bodies or bodily material. The ways in which one's status as living and one's status as human are bound up together should make us look very critically at the equation of disfigurement with social death. By implication, one's very human status is called into question.

As we have seen throughout this book, it is precisely the unique features of the face—specifically its role in human social interaction—that makes it possible to construct disfigurement as a uniquely weighty difference. The work of sociologist and symbolic interactionist Georg Simmel exemplifies the aura attributed to the face. In one very brief but profound essay, "The Aesthetic Significance of the Face," Simmel considers the human face:

> The essential accomplishment of the mind may be said to be its transformation of the multiplicity of the elements of the world into a series of unities . . . The organism, with the intimate relation of its parts and the involvement of the parts in the unity of the life process, is only once removed from mind itself . . . Of all the parts of the human body, the face has the highest degree of this kind of inner unity. The primary evidence of this fact is that a change which is limited, actually or apparently, to one element of the face—a curl of the lips, an upturning of the nose, a way of looking, a frown—immediately modifies its entire character and expression. Aesthetically, there is no other part of the body whose wholeness can as easily be destroyed by the disfigurement of only one of its elements.[4]

Here, Simmel suggests that the information gleaned from a face is critical to our sense of reality. Society—or, put another way, human social life—depends upon human faces. Understanding faces in quite this way makes disfigurement, even for Simmel, a threat to one's human status. His premise reflects a shared sensibility about facial difference. What we see here is that the sacredness attributed to the face feeds the idea that the end result of disfigurement is social death. When we confer social death to particular bodies, we implicitly dehumanize those very bodies. Disfigurement is conceived of as an embodied state incontrovertibly outside of the "symbolic order."[5] Just as the experience of encountering a dead body devastates our notion that to be human is to be alive, disfigurement seemingly functions to undermine one's humanity.

Changing Faces, a UK-based organization that aims to educate the public about disfigurement, speaks directly to the dehumanization experienced by those who are facially atypical:

> Seeing someone who looks different, who may have scars, no hair, a birthmark or an unusual appearance due to a missing ear or fingers may at first be a shock or surprise. Although it is normal to wonder, "What is that?" or to take a second look these are reactions that someone with a disfigurement experiences every day. Sometimes curiosity and surprise can lead people to focus on the difference or, conversely, avoiding eye contact or normal conversation.[6]

"What is that?" is a distinctly different question than "Who is that?" To ask "what" something is conveys a category crisis. The pronoun "who" is a stand in for human beings, while the pronoun "what" is a catch-all for everything else.

It is equally revealing that one suggestion offered to parents of children who ask such a question is to respond, "Her name is Lauren. She has a patch of red skin on her face. She was born with it. Shall we find out more about what she likes to do? Let's read her story on the website." This response is grounded in an effort to humanize by naming and narrating what the child sees as not human. Given this tendency to see disfigurement as not simply a discrediting condition but a dehumanizing condition, the climactic scene of David Lynch's film *The Elephant Man* is quite telling. The film, which is a dramatization of the life of Joseph Merrick, a man with neurofibromatosis, culminates in Merrick's character (played by John Hurt) screaming at a crowd who has chased him through a train station to stare at his facial difference, "I am not an animal. I am a human being." The scene is so powerful because it so blatantly speaks to the ways in which the ableism directed at particular disabilities, including facial difference, threatens human status and results in a kind of nonperson standing. Nonpersons are "standard categories of persons who are sometimes treated in their presence as if they were not there."[7] As Erving Goffman anticipated, nonperson status, in other words profound dehumanization, is the logical extension of social death.

As a material practice, facial work repairs the human face, but as a meaningful practice informed by the disfigurement imaginary, it relies upon notions of social death such that intervention takes on vital significance. Facial work invokes life and death, and by extension notions of human and nonhuman. While medicine is not exclusively responsible for the dehumanization experienced by those perceived as visually different, the inherent effect of the disfigurement imaginary is that patients subject to facial work are potentially deeply dehumanized in the very process designed to facilitate healing. Thus, choosing facial work is deeply embedded in a coercive discursive structure, which continually fortifies the notion that attaining human status depends upon medical intervention. Positioning interventions as humanizing is potentially insidious for this very reason. If a technology or a practice possesses the power to make one human, is there a way of opting out? If humanity hangs in the balance, repair is deeply coercive because there is no other available way to live. Facial work calls into question how we conceptualize life and death. Yet what is at stake is *not* our heartbeat, our respiration, or our sustenance. In this case, what is at stake is the face, which depending on one's perspective might be *just* a face, or it might be everything. If facial work is positioned as what makes humanness possible, this is profound for those defined as disfigured. What stigma weighs heavier than one that calls into question one's status as human?

Ultimately, too, it is important to consider the broader stakes of constructing disfigurement and facial work in this way. When disfigurement can be medically intervened upon but this intervention is painful, expensive, or embryonic, understanding humans as socially dead expedites intervention. Notions of death must evolve in order to make way for new innovations. This is not science fiction. Rather, it is an established pattern within contemporary biomedical practice that has consequences not only for those subject to the specific intervention at hand, but also for all of us. Every human being experiences critical moments in which designations about what counts as life and what counts as death matter. In the raging war over reproductive technologies like abortion and contraception, what life *is* informs the rhetoric but also subsequently the policy that makes certain interventions legally and financially accessible. At the end of life, as well, where and how we are situated in relation to brain death, clinical death, and even social death has profound consequences for the kinds of medical interventions we are likely to experience. While the very process of medical innovation may depend on such meaning-making maneuvers, the designation of social death or the prospect of being deemed nonhuman carries a rhetorical and social power that cannot be overstated. Perhaps, then, we should deploy these classifications with great caution.

The Erasure of Human Living and Difference

In the case of facial trauma, an animal attack or a car accident for example, repair harkens back to (and relies on) a notion of the face as it existed before trauma. Facial work becomes a way to return the face to its preinjury state or some close proximity. In the case of congenital anomalies, a cleft palate for example, the reference point for facial work is slightly different. Since there is no face that preexists the difference, facial work intervenes upon the atypical effects of congenital development, establishing a semblance of "normalcy." Ultimately, though, there is no surgery that comprehensively restores the face to a prior form or expunges all signs of difference. For all that facial work accomplishes, it does not produce an appearance that looks entirely unburned, unmauled, or unmarked. And yet facial work (along with other aesthetic interventions) is sold, consumed, researched, anticipated, and enacted as if it recovers and fully normalizes the face.

The experiences that mark our bodies are evidence of our lived humanity. In the case of fetal development, congenital anomalies reveal that we are born imperfect, and thus our ideas of perfection are not, in fact, reflective of reality. Visual effects of injury or illness are evidence of the inherently unpredictable and risky nature of life. Even as human life varies dramatically by place and is inscribed with privilege and inequalities, one inescapable fact that unites the human experience is that all humans are potentially subject to biological realities and life events that affect the ways our bodies look and function. Facial work aims to be a kind of surgical, technical, and cultural *erasure*, in which life experience and statuses are expunged in favor of the face that does not display injury or difference. This is true of other forms of aesthetic surgery too, which attempt to produce a younger or slimmer or whiter body. In all of these cases, aesthetic intervention aspires to eradicate the parts of our history and experience that make themselves known via our bodies. But this impetus toward erasure has consequences.

Bioethicist Arthur Frank vividly describes how the bodily evidence of injury ignites empathy: "Scars do hit us like a brick, as they connect immediate persons to imagined forms of suffering and thus render that suffering tangible."[8] The problem with bodily interventions that erase the very process of living is that we need access to a range of human experiences in order to develop modes of handling those experiences. Encountering burn injury or facial atypicality, for example, makes us better equipped to handle the unexpected in our own embodied lives and to support those we love when children are born with differences, illnesses are diagnosed, or the unimagined and unanticipated comes to fruition. If we do not encounter difference, we have no embodied frame of reference for developing personal and social coping strategies. Disability and trauma, injury and illness are not going anywhere, and yet we rush to obscure the very experiences that yield deep insight into how to live with the difficult or unexpected.

Our bodies, marked as they are with scars and difference, injury and anomaly, tell the stories of where we have been and what we have encountered. Erasing these embodied stories obscures part of what makes us who we are. Yet there is transformative potential of being with or living alongside that which we have a tendency to fix or turn away from. In 2002, the National Portrait Gallery in London debuted a series of portraits by the artist Mark Gilbert. The paintings represented disfigured faces before, after, and during facial work. Saving Faces, a UK-based organization focused on combatting facial stigma, commissioned the works. The people depicted in Gilbert's portraits described being painted as cathartic.[9] Specifically, it was the experience of being captured precisely because of, rather than in spite of, disfigurement that elicited such an emotional, and presumably healing, response. Could the experience of being treated as aesthetically valued because of one's face, and all its difference, function as a mode of repair in and of itself? Is Gilbert's artistic practice of carefully observing and painstakingly representing facial atypicality an alternative method of facial work?

Visual artist Laura Ferguson's work also attests to the power of living and being just as she is. In an article entitled "Towards a New Aesthetics of the Body," Ferguson explains,

> As an artist, I understand that fixing, healing, transforming an abnormal body into a more normal one, is what gives doctors satisfaction, a sense of accomplishment—that it is their form of creative expression. But the result is that there is no alternative paradigm offered to patients, no acknowledgment that an unusual body might be okay the way it is—that there doesn't have to be a "fix." I realize that the idea of deformity having its own beauty, without the need of fixing or altering, is a radical one. But I believe in an alternative vision of aesthetics in medicine, one that gives more value to process, to empathetic connection, than to fixing or curing. Art is a good place to look for an alternative aesthetic: a place where the less-than-perfect body can be shown to have its own kind of beauty, grace, sensuality, originality.[10]

Ferguson's self-portraits capture the beauty of her own body. It is a body marked and devalued, in particular contexts, by scoliosis.[11] In reflecting on her work, Ferguson does not suggest that fixing be dismissed altogether, but she does call for a new aesthetics in medicine, one that leaves open the possibility of alternative beauties. Imagine a body desired for its originality, for the ways in which life and biology have made themselves visible on the body. Imagine a face longed for because it embodies a vision of the self that includes trauma and difference. Taking in difference rather than turning away from it, recognizing the viability of atypicality rather than rushing to normalize it, is a precious and perhaps even vital practice because it is only through "being with" that new modes of coping and living can emerge. The work of Gilbert and Ferguson and the everyday practices of witnessing, accepting, and celebrating difference contest the fundamental assumptions of the disfigurement imaginary, namely that social death is the inevitable outcome of disfigurement.

In 2012, MAC Cosmetics announced a new cover girl. Iris Apfel is an it-girl of sorts. She is a New York insider, a fashion maven, a tastemaker and trendsetter, and a power broker in the world of design. Apfel is also in her nineties. This new face of MAC Cosmetics is striking, albeit in a way that stands in sharp contrast to the "faces" of most other cosmetic companies. Apfel's face is etched with deep wrinkles. Its tone is uneven. It lacks firmness and elasticity. The MAC spreads featuring Iris Apfel, though, do not obscure any of these facial features. Instead, her face is prominently displayed. She directly faces the camera. Her eyes stare intently at the lens, and her lips boldly feature MAC's signature classic red lipstick. She looks as if she could take on the world, perhaps because she has, for almost a century. In the world of glossy advertising production, MAC could have Photoshopped Apfel to appear young— eradicated the deep forehead wrinkle that is undoubtedly a result of countless hours of intense thinking and observation, or obscured the variations of skin tone that suggest years in the sun likely as a result of traveling the world. Instead, the MAC ads feature a ninety-year-old Apfel and the face marked from living those ninety years. Not in spite of, but rather because of, all of those wrinkles, Apfel shines. The pressure to erase the embodied marks of living and to normalize human anomalies is real. But resisting or perhaps even delaying facial work opens up the possibilities for new methods of living, even in an aestheticized twenty-first century.

The Perpetual Work of Being Not Ugly

So much scholarly attention has focused on efforts invested in making the body beautiful, but what of making the body *not ugly*? Given the inordinate amount of research on cosmetic surgery and beauty in the last several decades, it is interesting that "ugliness," for lack of a better term, is comparatively unaccounted for. There are a few exceptions. In cultural critics Helen Deustch and Felicity Nussbaum's *"Defects": Engendering the Modern Body* (2000), "ugliness as an aesthetic category" is taken up along with other anomalous bodies. Their book explores the cultural work accomplished by monstrosity in the eighteenth century in the service of understanding modern notions of difference, particularly sexual difference. While the text injects ugliness and disfigurement into the intellectual conversation, it is largely a historical account. Similarly, disability scholar Susan M. Schweik's *The Ugly Laws: Disability in Public* (2009) considers the legislative history of disability in the United States. Schweik takes up the set of ordinances collectively known as "the ugly laws," which regulated the public appearance of those with visable disabilities, particularly in urban spaces. As Schweik demonstrates through skillful cultural analysis, "The ugly laws were motivated not simply by appearance politics but by the need to control the economics of the underclass and group behavior within it."[12] This historical account of the social control of disabilities conveys that ways in which appearance, specifically ugliness, is always bound up with notions of health and illness, mental competency, moral fortitude, and fit citizenship. There remains much to be said about how ugliness operates in the contemporary sociohistorical moment and how ugliness, in addition to beauty, motivates aesthetic intervention.

The collective fantasy fed by celebrity aesthetics and consumer culture is that our bodies might be made beautiful, which is ultimately a desire to heighten our value and status. Attempts to identify what is beautiful routinely find that beauty represents an aesthetic outlier. Ironically, like disfigurement, to be beautiful is to be *not* average. Numerically speaking, disfigurement and beauty are both relatively unusual. While we may hold onto the fantasy about what it might be like to be beautiful, there is another impulse that drives aesthetic intervention, though this one so often goes unnamed. It is the hope that we will be good enough, and that those facets of our appearance that make us different and situate us dangerously close to the margins might be amended. Facial work is an intervention aimed at making faces defined as disfigured not ugly, but all faces—the variant and the normal—are subject to attempts at erasing ugliness. The work of making not ugly stands in sharp contrast to making the body beautiful. Rather than inscribing the most desirable attributes onto the body, as is the goal in cosmetic surgery, the work of making the body not ugly attempts to mediate features that situate us precariously close to stigma or social death. As opposed to a fantasy about standing out, the desire to be not ugly is motivated by the hope of blending in, about embodying an aesthetic so unremarkable that no one notices us at all.

Some everyday aesthetic practices may be guided by the desire to be beautiful, but many are unambiguously aimed at erasing "ugly" features.

For example, eyebrows that grow together meeting over the bridge of our noses are plucked, waxed, and lasered in attempts to avoid a "unibrow." Concealer, pressed powder, and bronzer do more than highlight bone structure and define faces into more beautiful structures. Makeup is a tool for hiding pores, obscuring lines, and evening skin tone. Teeth are whitened, with bleach and flashes of light, sometimes in an effort to create a gorgeous smile, but just as often whitening is aimed at altering the appearance of yellowing or graying teeth. Hair is cut and colored, straightened and relaxed not purely in an attempt to be beautifully tressed, but also in an attempt to make our hair less ugly—less frizzy, less gray, less blah—than it would "naturally" be.

Sometimes better is not more beautiful. Sometimes better is less ugly.

Beauty and ugliness exist, then, in an uneasy tension, each informing the other.[13] Beauty and ugliness stand in sharp contrast to one another; however, both depend on the other for their respective significance. Beauty and ugliness are also contextually bound. We know beauty when we see it, partially because we have some looming, culturally inscribed sense of what is ugly. But there is much to be learned by analytically separating out attempts toward producing beauty and techniques aimed toward obfuscating ugliness. Our desire to be beautiful is driven by cultural discourses and practices related to youth, able-bodiness, gender, race, class, and heterosexuality, and this desire is continually forged through commercial culture, through material and experiential consumption. Yet notions of exceptionalism and rarity also inform the desire to be beautiful. Most of us know that there is only so much that we can do.

In contrast, the work of making the body not ugly is a never-ending project. It is a Sisyphean task. The stone will not stay atop the mountain. Aging, bodily injury, and aesthetic fashions are not fixed, and thus the work of not being ugly is an ongoing and impossible project. We may be finished for today, but tomorrow is another day complete with another set of problems—solar damage, car wrecks, emergent standards of bodily care. The specter of disfigurement specifically, and ugliness more generally, is so overwhelming because it is always there, threatening to affect our bodies with every passing day, with every risk encountered. Relative to our everyday lives, the feat of being not ugly looms large, and the ways in which the specter of ugliness inspires consumption (including consumer debt), self-loathing, and postmodern sensibilities must be queried in the same way that the fantasy of beauty has been dismantled.

The question of ugliness matters for us all, but it particularly matters for those with bodies defined as ugly by our collective norms of bodily appearance. We know that we are not all equally beautiful, but we are also not all equally unremarkable. We all wrestle with ugliness, but as this inquiry into the work of repairing the face demonstrates, this struggle is disproportionately stacked against those perceived as facially variant. The stakes are higher because the possibility of attaining unremarkability is much lower. In this way, the disfigurement imaginary, along with the fear of ugliness it inspires, looms not only for those with facial difference but also for anyone pursuing bodily interventions focused on repair and avoiding. Images of beauty culture drive cosmetic industries, but specters of ugliness drive aesthetic intervention, too. Ultimately, our fixation on appearance, the interventions we pursue, and the stigma we impart to a range of bodies derives from our extraordinary obsession with beauty *and* its polar opposite.

So What?

As a teacher, I regularly pose the "So what?" question. Whether in a social problems or a feminist theory course, students acquire the language of my discipline—systematic imperative and hegemony, matrix of domination and symbolic violence, social fact and cultural norms—and come to articulate a more nuanced account of why inequalities persist. In so many college classrooms, critical thinking is evidenced by sophisticated analysis, theoretical innovation, or critique of a dominant perspective. In the end, though, we are all left asking the same questions: So what do we *do* with these ideas? How can we use this language in the service of changing the dynamics we now understand?

The ideas presented in this book call for the "So what?" question, too. What does it matter, practically speaking, if social death is the register that is increasingly used to talk about facial injury, atypical appearance, facial disabilities, and even the faces of those who fall toward the devalued end of the appearance spectrum? The disfigurement imaginary is a discursive formation, but its effects are real and palpable. This way of seeing signals a fortification of stigma, which amplifies the imperative to repair. While this constellation of meanings implicitly serves strategic purposes, specifically imposing a vital significance onto reconstructive intervention, it comes with human consequences.

Ultimately, this book is about naming processes at work in contemporary reconstructive surgery and revealing how assumptions guide real interventions. Other scholars have taken on similar projects in relation to normalizing procedures. For example, Suzanne Kessler's groundbreaking work *Lessons from the Intersexed* (1998) ignited a field of study that queried how gender norms inspire interventions on infants who are diagnosed as sexually anomalous at birth. Specifically, expectations about penis size and the presumed centrality of penetration to adult men's sexuality lead to genital surgery in infants whose phallus is deemed "micro." The surgical management of infants with disorders of sex development is now regularly criticized as premature and potentially damaging long-term.[14] This is not to say that medical intervention is eschewed entirely.[15] Rather bioethicists, medical sociologists, and intersex activists have successfully pushed pediatric surgeons and endocrinologists to disentangle cultural ideas about gender and medical interventions on genitals so that surgery might reflect a patient's long-term desires rather than social norms regarding sex.

Consider, also, the evolving framework for transgendering interventions. The surgical procedures historically termed sex reassignment surgery (SRS) are increasingly described as gender affirming/confirming surgery (GAS)/(GCS). The techniques have not changed, but the language, and by extension the culture of intervention, is transforming. The first acronym is steeped in notions of normalization, and the term "reassignment" implies that one's presurgical body is valid, albeit subject to alteration. The second acronym denotes that one's identity and body is subject to self-determination, that intervention is a tool used by the patient as part of a process of self-articulation. The differences between the two terms are significant. The first reifies the sex/gender binary and implies the validity of essentialism. By proxy, the medical model retains authority over the process of making one's body one's own. The second situates the patient as the expert who possesses the power to self-define and employ biomedical technologies to materialize one's identity.[16] Ultimately, what these two cases demonstrate is how intervention may proceed, and even be offered as the standard of care, without subjecting individuals' bodies to stigmatizing narratives.

Cosmetic interventions like we see with *Extreme Makeover*, facial feminization, medical mission work, and face transplantation might proceed outside of the disfigurement imaginary. Patients need not be treated as essentially socially dead. Dispensing with the disfigurement imaginary disrupts the changing significance of facial work. If disfigurement is not deadly, then facial work cannot function as a vital intervention. As a field, aesthetic surgery has a vested interest in amplifying the importance of reconstructive intervention. The work of saving lives yields a very particular kind of status, but as the previous cases indicate, the discursive formations that undergird medical practices can evolve and change in response to critical analyses that demonstrate the latent effects of stigma.

Talking back to medicine may not be a sufficient response, but it is a necessary one.

While this book explores how the disfigurement imaginary operates via sites of facial work, the assumptions implicit in the disfigurement imaginary abound not only within medicine, but also in everyday life. Notions of social death emerge outside of the surgical suite. In the years that I have been at work on this project, people have regularly asked me to describe what kinds of faces are subject to facial work. Sometimes I describe a case like Lucy Grealy's or the effects of burn injury. It is not uncommon for a person to respond, "I would die." The subtle but enduring patterns of the disfigurement imaginary are reflected in commonplace language, which in turn impacts how facial atypicality is thought about and treated. The ideas explored here demonstrate vividly how routine accomplishments stem from and result in ever-changing perceptions.

One tangible intervention, then, involves shifting the social dynamics that fortify the disfigurement imaginary. The UK-based organization Changing Faces offers resources to facilitate coping for those who are perceived as disfigured, but its Face Equality campaign focuses on raising public awareness about appearance disabilities.[17] It is worth thinking about specific strategies that could be employed outside of the medical sphere to combat ableism and the assumptions that facial atypicality is akin to some kind of death. As demonstrated throughout this book, subtle but consistent interaction patterns fortify the disfigurement imaginary. Of course, medicine operates in tandem with other social institutions, including mass media, education, and civic society, and reflects broader stereotypes and hierarchies of everyday life. What happens within medical spaces does not remain within the confines of the doctor's office or clinic, the hospital or the research laboratory. News about technologies shapes the ways people relate to their bodies, and ways of understanding the body infuse the popular imagination, shaping how we see (and react to) disease and disability. It is equally true that what happens in popular culture and in everyday life works its way into the hospital and research laboratory. The assumptions about what life with facial difference means are negotiated via aesthetic surgery, but given the reciprocal relationship between medicine and society, the assumptions that shape medical intervention can be acted upon outside of the actual sphere of aesthetic surgery.

Here I redirect the "So what" question toward my own analysis and offer some thoughts about what challenging the disfigurement imaginary in everyday life might look like.

1. We can disrupt the fix-it response by not assuming that everyone with facial difference is interested in pursuing facial work. We might interrogate questions or ways of thinking that are premised on "what is wrong" or "needs fixing." We might treat the process of seeking facial work with the kind of discretion and respect for individual privacy that we afford many other forms of medical intervention from weight loss surgery to preventative mastectomy.

2. We can work to disassociate facial difference with suffering by remembering, and reminding others, that what we look like is only one facet of our lived experience. Doing so requires that we embrace inquisitiveness about one another's full humanity and that we employ empathy rather than an attitude of pity.

3. Owning our discomfort or unfamiliarity with experiences *and* doing the self-reflective work of unpacking ableist stereotypes and facially typical privileges are central to combating the unconscious cognitive patterns that materialize through ways of talking, and via social interaction.

4. We can challenge ableism, including stigma toward those with appearance disabilities, in the ways we confront racism, heterosexism,

xenophobia, classism, and all other forms of oppression. Contesting microaggressions toward those with disabilities, refusing to collude in disparaging those with disabilities in contexts wherein the presumption is that everyone is able-bodied, and naming and confronting policies that dis-able difference are all part of this process.

5. The fix-it imperative is not limited to sites of facial work. Rather, the entire beauty industry is premised on selling products and services under the guise that intervention on appearance has broadly impactful consequences. While undereye cream may minimize the appearance of "tired" eyes, it is unlikely to reduce stress or generate the kind of carefree affect featured in so many commercials. We might disrupt this broader fix-it imperative by naming and rejecting the conflation of changes in appearance with improvements in other spheres of our lives.

6. Relatedly, we can undermine the power of beauty industries by buying fewer products and services. Additionally, we can serve as consumer watchdogs by responding to marketing that suggests that our human worth is reducible to what we look like. It is also the case that many of us rely on products from moisturizers with SPF protection to toothpaste with whitening agents, and as such, it is unlikely that we will go beauty-product free. That being said, support companies that market products in ways that affirm human variability, that reject hegemonic beauty norms, and that operate outside of rhetoric that inspires body loathing.

7. The empirical evidence demonstrates that appearance matters in concrete ways, from impacting earning potential to quality of parenting received. Thus, appearance functions as a vector of inequality similar to that of race and ethnicity, sex and gender, sexuality, age, disability, and citizenship. Structural interventions are needed to challenge the effects of appearance in schools and the workplace, for example. This process might begin though by contesting moments (for example, in hiring) when appearance blatantly operates as a litmus test for individual value and worth.

8. We can also challenge the ways medical expertise operates to define subjective elements of human experience. Central to this effort is to identify how regularly notions of normalcy operate to inspire medical intervention. Act as a critical patient advocate for yourself and others by questioning the assumptions and dynamics that shape doctor-patient interactions, like the dismissal of integrative medicine or the push to make an immediate decision about a treatment path.

9. All of us might protest stereotypic representations of facial difference. When appearance variability is used as a characterization device to elicit dislike, fear, or pity, respond. Talk back to culture industries. Engage in conversations about the ways this plot device feeds stigma and is eerily familiar to racialized and ethnocentric tropes that have fortified enduring patterns of racism and xenophobia.

10. Supporting the efforts of organizations like the Changing Faces, Let's Face It, About Face USA, Facing Forward Inc., and About Face Canada is another concrete strategy for challenging the disfigurement imaginary.[18] These organizations offer incredibly well-crafted resources that invite us to reflect on the associations we have about facial atypicality and concrete strategies for navigating our responses to our own and others' bodies. Consider making a financial donation to support education efforts aimed at challenging appearance-based stigma, or use their materials to create some programming about appearance-based discrimination on your campus or in your local community.

11. Finally, we can think critically about how much of our identity and self-worth is bound up with what we look like. Complimenting others' appearance and even discussing the strategies we use to manage our appearance fortifies aestheticization. If we want to disrupt the intensifying significance of appearance, then we must stop affirming its importance in our everyday conversations with others and with ourselves.

This list is certainly not comprehensive, but my hope is that it ignites more thought and conversation about our respective roles in "disfiguring" one another.

Face in Context

In the end, I am reluctant to offer a framework that differentiates between the ethical and necessary moments of intervention and the unethical and gratuitous. Instead, I am acutely aware of how intervention varies according to context. The specificities and stories of the faces involved matter, and procedures that are technically identical carry different meanings depending on who the patient is and how a practitioner understands the stakes of facial difference. But I also understand that the desire to appear unremarkable is profound. Despite my critical take on facial work, I am hesitant to definitively reject what so many hope for. Ultimately, I find that the empathetic profacial work or the analytic antifacial work positions are inadequate, because each requires that we universalize bodily experience.

If there are any facts of life, they are that all humans breathe, consume, and excrete, though even these functions are mediated socially and technologically.[19] Language, geopolitical locations, familial context, and personal narrative vary, but *all* humans are embodied. This is universally true, but even in the face of the only universal, there is no there there. Even the universal experience of breathing varies dramatically. Some breathe with the aid of ventilators or masks. Some breathe through transplanted lungs. Others breathe air saturated with pollens. Some are allergic, and others are not. Bodily experience varies so dramatically that even those embodied experiences shared by all humans are experienced differently. This is the paradox of bodily experience and the source of tension that makes a politics of bodily intervention so complicated. The fact is, the only thing common to all beings designated as "human" is that we inhabit a certain kind of body, and yet bodily experience differs profoundly between human creatures. Culture, ability, aesthetics, and trauma imprint the human body, marking and making each one in ways entirely different from the other. Embodiment is absolutely universal and yet incomprehensibly unique.

Faces may be common to all humans, and appearance matters, regardless of the culture we find ourselves in. There are functional impediments associated with disfigurement, and those who appear atypical routinely encounter stigma. But the meanings associated with facial difference vary across time and place, as do the experiences of living with a face that does not correspond to social expectations about what faces are, how they should function, and what they should look like. It is precisely because of this variation that we must a resist the disfigurement imaginary, which is ultimately a universalizing narrative about facial appearance. It is a story that positions some people as hardly (worth) living at all. In reality, despite of or perhaps because of difference, humans live.

Losing Face

A Postscript

When my face gets fixed, then I'll start living.
—Lucy Grealy, *Autobiography of a Face* (1994)

Academics are so often asked why we study what we study. Some of us have clearly delineated narratives. We situate moments from our lives or facets of our identities in logical order, suggesting that we could think of nothing else besides what we research and write about. Others of us retroactively construct stories that will be compelling to editors, colleagues, students, or strangers at dinner parties. Too few of us anticipate the political problematic of our projects, but some of us do craft explanations that we hope will garner forgiveness for persons and communities our work objectifies and overlooks. My own response to this question has radically evolved over the years as I have written this book. In recent years, my answer has been far more intellectual than personal. Honestly, though, throughout these years, I have expected to recall a memory or to see my own biography in such a way that would explain—*why faces?*

As a child, I anticipated the stories my uncle would tell about working in a burn unit as a physical therapist. What I remember in particular are the details of how children came to be burned. A pot of scalding oil heated to fry doughnuts was overturned. The naked body of a screaming child was submerged in a bathtub of blistering water as a punishment. There was a fireworks accident, a house fire and flammable pajamas, industrial chemicals gone wrong. Sometimes, stories were told as the adults lingered at the dining room table. Their jobs were much more commonplace, and the details offered a voyeuristic glimpse into what it was like to do lifesaving work. Other times, Uncle Aaron played Aesop, turning to the children and explicitly offering a moral: Don't play with bottle rockets or gasoline or the unmarked containers in the garage, EVER. But I learned other things from these stories. Some parents are really bad people, bad things happen to good people, and perhaps most significantly, sometimes the effects of a single bad thing remain long after the bad thing itself is actually over. I also wondered if these bad things could happen to me.

Uncle Aaron's stories focused on children because when he was not physically treating burns, he was founding a camp for children who had been burned. For as long as I can remember, I heard all about "burn camp," but it was years into this work before I thought about the relationship between those burn camp stories and my work as a sociologist. I decided I had to go to burn camp. I did not want to study burn camp in the same way I studied face transplantation or Operation Smile. These cases were the empirical basis from which I theorized the power of experts, specifically surgeons, in establishing modes of living for people subject to the interventions they offered. I approached burn camp as an opportunity to interrogate two facets of my own expertise.

First, burn camp is essentially the kind of effort that I have spent my professional life touting. It provides safe space, opportunities for self-definition, and joy through means other than medical intervention. It is a *social* intervention, ultimately inspired by the understanding that medicine cannot help us comprehensively recover. While in the process of critiquing science and medicine, I often advocate about the promises of social reengineering. Going to burn camp provided me with an opportunity to directly confront this claim. Secondly, I chose to relinquish my role as a researcher of others and to use the opportunity to volunteer in the service of considering more deeply my own relationship to this theoretical story. I regularly encounter the critique that the voices of people subject to the facial work I describe here are missing. I defend this choice, arguing that my work critically interrogates those that have extraordinary power in shaping others' lives, namely doctors. Unlike other incredibly skilled scholars, my intervention is not about providing a space wherein silence is remedied per se.[1] Instead, my work is more akin to a public reckoning of sorts. Here, the critical potential lies in the promise of diligently taking expertise apart in the hopes of bringing to light the ineffable ideological assumptions guiding the tangible work of aesthetic surgery.

Yet I remain dissatisfied. Why assess the power of medicine if not to dismantle its effects on the lives subject to that power? Isn't opening up new possibilities for living and healing the goal of questioning medical interventions, and doesn't that effort matter most to those for whom interventions are directed? While my account potentially impacts the experiences of those who are often defined as "disfigured," I only limitedly wrestle with the subjective experience of facial difference.

Much has been written about writing and teaching what we are not, and while I agree that white people must talk racism, and men need to teach feminism, and privileged academicians can and should study poverty, I remain acutely aware that as a visually unremarkable woman, it is critical that I wrestle with my own position in relation to my topic. Experts, be they surgeons or scholars, whose work is conceptualized as an intervention—bodily or theoretical—must make claims about the effects of said intervention. These claims often rely on speaking *on behalf of* those the intervention would most deeply affect. Stories and observations are used to claim expertise, as if hearing another's experience is the same as embodying that experience. Speaking on behalf of, even if it is acknowledged as such, always involves claiming something not one's own *as* one's own. One cannot write a book about facial "disfigurement" unless one continually insists that one knows something about facial difference, and I do know some things. But going to burn camp was the means through which I thought I could decipher what my research on expertise could not tell me.

So for the first time in August of 2010, I packed a duffle bag and went to camp. For ten days, I slept and ate and talked in the woods of Northern Virginia with firefighters and rehabilitation therapists and an extraordinary school counselor, but most significantly, I listened to children who ranged in ages from six to 18, whose injuries spanned from relatively minor burns accrued through kitchen accidents to third-degree burns covering every bodily surface inflicted by a parent for reasons that even if we knew, we could never understand. In the process, I was forced to encounter my own limitations, especially my fear and anxiety that I would not be very good at camp.

Many philosophies guide the burn camp programs that exist throughout the United States. One approach takes as the founding premise that children who have been burned should be given opportunities to live, even if for only one week a year, as if they had never been burned. These camps have schedules that maximize summer camp fun—swimming, horseback riding, arts and crafts, and evening campfires. A different approach acknowledges that ignoring the very experience upon which children are invited to camp does not do any favors for the children who participate. Being burned is the very reason children are there. What emerges is a shared sensibility that *the idea of* naming the glaringly obvious is often more scary than actually just doing it. At camps premised on this later philosophy, there may not be programming explicitly focused on talking about burns, but there doesn't need to be. The kids take care of that all on their own.

Midafternoon on a Sunday, I waited at the camp gate along with the other counselors. We had spent the preceding three days reviewing the schedule, learning very basic burn facts, and team-building via a ropes course. Now, we stood waiting for two buses filled with this year's campers. If I have learned anything from my embeddedness in academe, it is the capacity to appear stony even in the face of immense anxiety, fear, and sadness. We may have undergone a cultural turn premised on a fierce critique of detached positivism, but postmodernism has done little to challenge the crushing indifference and abstraction that pervade university life. As part of our work, we think; but perhaps more importantly, we *look* thoughtful. This serves as an incredible coping strategy to disavow emotion, and it was this skill that I used as I coolly waited. Who would these kids be? What did we have in common? Would they like me?

Like so many things we fear, it happened fast. The buses came one right after the other, and I along with two other counselors found the six- and seven-year-old kids we were charged with, and together we walked to the cabin that would serve as home base for the week. The kids did what most adults have forgotten how to do—they sized each other up and then decided that whatever assumptions they were making about each other didn't matter anyway. A couple shared their names, but before we had completed introductions, one girl asked another, "How did you get burned?" She responded with her story, and when she paused, the first girl turned to a third and repeated her question—"How did you get burned?" One by one, the girls shared the facts. And as soon as it had begun, it was over. There were more important things to discuss . . . like who got the top bunk.

The contemporary viability of Max Weber's concept "life chances" comes into sharp relief at burn camp. It is absolutely the case that we do not all have equal opportunities to be burned. Race and class converge to wreak bodily trauma for those of us who are most fragile to begin with. Kids who grow up in public housing projects with booming drug economies are susceptible to being chemically burned, as one child was when a dealer established his market share by throwing acid onto his competitor. The child had been sitting on the rival's lap. Working piecemeal to forge family life means that suitable supervision is not always possible. Children get hungry, and when they try their best to self-soothe, they sometimes spill boiling water. It is also the case that recovery from burn injury is deeply structured by access to resources. Even with Medicaid, little girls who need pressure garments—startlingly tight elasticized rehabilitation devices—to facilitate healing will not receive the newest and incredibly promising compression garments lined with silicone. One child's scars will heal differently than another due to access to innovative medical care, and children's life chances will be fundamentally affected given the relative visibility of their trauma.

Burn camp is the best week of the year for many of the kids who come every year from the time of their initial injury until the time they age out. And not for the reasons you might expect. Laying in sleeping bags directly under the night sky, a seven-year-old whispered to me, "I wish on that star. I want to stay here forever." It wasn't the kind of declaration bursting from Christmas morning excitement, but rather an exclamation of desperation and deep sadness. The third-degree burns that scarred her were not healing well. This was probably attributable to the fact that she was not taken to the hospital immediately after being accidently burned when a pot of boiling water spilled. Instead, she was wrapped in bandages and charged with the most insidious game of make-believe—pretend it doesn't hurt. Not until sometime later, when upon removing her bandages and seeing that in her words, "My skin just melted off," did she get the burn unit treatment she desperately needed. In the year after burn camp, I wondered about her, but when I returned the following year I discovered that she never made it to the burn camp bus, even though her name was on the roster. I never found out why. Her burns were indelibly shaped by class and race. Both factors converged to make her mother understandably afraid to report her daughter's injury. Just like the burns of upper-class and working-class kids heal differently, so too do black and poor women experience greater rates of state surveillance when their children experience accidents.[2]

For other kids, burn camp may be the only space in which they are really seen for more than their injuries. Gangly adolescent girls in bikinis jump off a diving board into a swimming pool and experience what may be the most ubiquitous rite of passage for teenage girls in this historical moment—objectification by boys their age. To be sure, their scars are on full display, but in the context of the burn camp swimming pool these are far less significant than the body they got between now and this time last year. Kids talk to other kids with faces displaying severe burns and lacking facial features, but more importantly, kids look each other in the eye. Nicknames like "Pretty Boy" get distributed, not with the mean-heartedness endemic to middle-school life but rather as a term of endearment. The kids tease one boy: "He is so particular about his shoes. He ironed his shirts before he came." His body also displays grafts taken from here and there. It's not that the other kids pretend this isn't the case. It's just that they don't care.

The children I met have cultivated their own kind of expertise. They are experts at naming, and living through difference. Like the six- and seven-year-old girls I first encountered at burn camp, I saw kids routinely acknowledge the fact of each other's burns. Sometimes, they remarked: "His burns are different from mine," "She was younger than me when she got burned," or "I used to wear pressure garments like that." One could—and most of us do—pretend that nothing is wrong. But we might, as these kid experts do, acknowledge that things are wrong, and it is not the end of the world. These kids were experts at boldly acknowledging the fact of their burns, but beyond naming their difference, these kids had a range of strategies for living through difference.

Being an expert at living through difference is not the same as living in spite of difference.

For many years, I have worked with teenage girls through a grass-roots program Act Like a Grrrl based in Nashville, Tennessee, cultivating feminist consciousness and life skills including goal-setting, self-care, and community-building. I brought this experience to burn camp, and I spent hours with burn campers crafting vision boards—collages comprised of images and words that symbolized their futures. Kids filled posters with pictures of cars and houses, vacation destinations, and families cut from advertisements. Letter by letter, campers took apart headlines from newspapers and glossy magazines to spell out words: College, Success, and Love. Not a single camper alluded to a surgery or a technology that would transform or erase their burn injury. Even those campers with the most visible facial burns cut and glue-sticked their way to a vision of what ages 22 and 37 could be like. They planned on living, even as they understood that their burns would be a part of that future. Some (though not all of them) would choose to be unburned, but rather than obsessing over what could have been, they recognize what is. Instead of resorting to magical thinking about what life without their burns would be like, they imagine a future with their bodies as they are.

In the place of a narrative of bodily trauma (like the disfigurement imaginary) that suggests that life is over, following their lead we might proliferate notions of being alive that allow us to claim vitality *and* suffering simultaneously. On the day before camp concluded, I met with each group of campers. We talked about gratitude and the subtle but enduring power of identifying what we appreciate, especially in our most hopeless moments.[3] Our last activity together was to write thank-you notes. Given the thousands of volunteer hours, the substantial financial contributions, and the boundless encouragement of counselors and fellow campers that together make burn camp what it is, there was much for which to be thankful. That year and the following, I found myself hustling to find more paper and envelopes. During the first year, around 60 campers wrote over 600 notes. In them, they described hard things like loneliness at school and fear about finding a girlfriend, but their notes also

contained appreciation for efforts that made life better. To other campers, they expressed gratitude for deep friendships built on their shared
experience, and they promised to be friends forever. To camp staff, they
wrote notes about what meals they looked forward to, their appreciation
for having learned how to swim, and gratitude for personal photo albums
containing camp pictures. They did not disavow painful things; nor were
they subsumed by sadness. Hope and anticipation lived alongside grief.

The children I met know something else, too. Living through difference is not necessarily forged through attempts to fix or erase that difference. "What can we do to make the scars go away?" we ask. To that
question, I imagine one of the precocious teenagers matter-of-factly
responding, "Oh yes, I tried that. In some ways, it worked, and in other
ways, it didn't. But this is what I look like now." As desperately as we
dream of healing and as fiercely as we hold onto possibility, we sometimes desire what we cannot effect in the material world. Our bodies
are not infinitely recoverable, and while the world's leading surgeons
seem to struggle to overcome the laws of physiology, kids are figuring
out other methods for coping. They find ways to live.

The expertise of medicine neglects this fact. Instead, the disfigurement imaginary dominates; from this vantage point, facial difference
causes social death. But the kids I met are living, breathing testaments
to the contrary. For them, bodily injury contours their lives, but it does
not prevent living. Especially for children whose burns are the most
visible—the ones whose faces are burned—no surgery will make their
injury disappear. And yet, they go on. They live. In spaces carved out
for them just as they are, they live. Together with their kid peers and a
motley crew of adults who neither pity nor treat them as people to be
saved from social death, they live.

These facts exist alongside some others. Desperate hope for repair
and utter despair over technical limitations persist. Trauma is sometimes so beyond our frame of reference that we struggle to find the
words to talk about what an injury means. Communities, families, and
intimate partners sometimes cannot look directly at a face marked by
difference. It is no wonder that facial difference is conceived as deeply
threatening or as deadly. But as burn camp kids live, they demonstrate
that this is only one way to understand difference.

There are alternatives, and hope.

APPENDIX

Methods, Methodologies, and Epistemologies

Ugly people are just beautiful people with horrible facial
deformities.
—bathroom graffiti in the Villager, a dive bar in Nashville, TN

We bury strange things in landfills—syringes dripping insulin, toenail
clippings, old credit cards, and sometimes dead bodies. Of course, there
are mundane things, too—junk mail, orange peelings, cotton balls, and
expired coupons. If we tried to separate our trash into clear categories,
we would be hard-pressed to do so. Unlike the paper, plastic, metal, and
glass of our recycling, our trash is not nearly so discrete: Are cotton balls
paper? What if they are saturated with human blood? Then are cotton
balls medical waste? Without a doubt, landfills are a mess: a jumble of
refuse including human waste, food waste, chemical waste, paper waste,
and so on. The landfill is an excavation nightmare, but taking each piece
of garbage into account is incredibly revealing. Everything in a landfill
tells us something about who we are.[1]

Likewise, this project is empirically messy. This work is based on four
cases, and in my analysis of each I draw on multiple sources of data.
While on its own, each piece demonstrates something about the significance of facial repair, taken together the data explored here allows for
"thick analyses."[2] In excavating the practice of facial work, I employ multiple methods—ethnography, interviewing, content analysis—and rely
on varying kinds of data—television shows, interviews, fieldnotes, professional journals, organizational websites. My approach to analysis was
informed by strategies of grounded theory and situational analysis.[3] From

one perspective, then, this book bastardizes carefully conceived methods. From another perspective, this approach—perhaps best termed multi-sited ethnography—approaches methodologies as a set of tools rather than as stringent procedures.[4] As Michel Foucault has proposed, "'All my books . . . are little tool boxes. If people want to open them, to use a particular sentence, a particular idea, a particular analysis like a screwdriver or a spanner . . . so much the better!"[5] This cobbling together of methodological approaches is one approach to analyzing what are four disparate cases.

For my chapter on *Extreme Makeover*, analysis is based on observations collected while viewing 30 episodes chosen at random. Through fieldnotes, I chronicle the show as it unfolds for television viewers, emphasizing the narrative turns upon which each episode relies. In short, I trace the narrative arc embedded in each episode and query patterns to interrogate what kind of storytelling the show accomplishes—specifically, how the series positions disfigurement and aesthetic intervention. Additional data was gathered from the official *Extreme Makeover* website, including the materials applicants had to complete prior to participating along with before and after pictures of candidates.

I base my analysis of facial feminization surgery on fieldnotes collected at seminars held during two of the largest transgender conferences in the world—Southern Comfort and the International Foundation for Gender Education Conference. Transgender conferences are unique quasi-public spaces. Many who attend and present programs self-identify as trans*, but my focus centered on each of the US-based facial feminization surgeons who dominated the specialty at the time of observation. My fieldnotes exclusively capture how surgeons discuss and market facial feminization. In addition, I analyze the materials—pamphlets, journal articles, and promotional materials—distributed to attendees during these seminars. Importantly, except for the moment in which my own appearance drew attention, conference attendees are deliberately missing from my analytic focus. My introduction to FFS came by way of a dear friend who was surgeon-shopping and who sometimes asked me to bring my sociological lens to bear as she weighed pros and cons. Social scientists have a long history of exploiting trans people as research subjects in the service of broader theoretical projects.[6] As a researcher and as a human deeply invested in queer politics, specifically the sacredness of self-determination and queer space, my work relies exclusively on the surgeons' words rather than on the personal experience of pursuring medical intervention.

My exploration of Operation Smile is based on content analysis of 132 articles gathered from English international and national newspapers chronicling the organization's work around the world between 2005 and 2007, years in which the prominence of the organization grew dramatically. While news media works to convey "the facts," media also does the work of transmitting cultural hopes and fears about new medical—and in this case philanthropic—interventions. Media coverage makes its way outside of medical sites too, and for this reason, content analysis of media captures the ways the disfigurement imaginary makes its way outside of medical sites shaping popular imaginations. In addition, I analyzed how the organization represents its work on its website, specifically through annual reports and promotional materials, and in popular media through television infomercials. Interviews with Operation Smile employees and volunteers provided rich detail about the mission experience. While it was my original intention to ethnographically capture a mission, limited financial resources and other professional obligations prevented that work from taking place. In my conversations with mission volunteers, I was aware that with my lack of medical training and inability to speak a language other than English would likely mean that I would be in the way of those doing the pressing work.

Telling a critical story of face transplantation requires recording the sites in which face transplantation is taking shape. This means entering the university-medical-technological complex and becoming acquainted with the key figures working toward solidifying this technology in the making. In my chapter on face transplantation, I rely on fieldwork conducted at meetings of a US-based face transplant team, along with interviews with key team members to critically analyze how, in this case, the work of technological innovation rests on the discursive negotiations of the meanings of facial disfigurement. In addition, I employ content analysis of a 2004 issue of the *American Journal of Bioethics*, in which medical researchers, surgeons, bioethicists, and psychologists considered and debated the issue of face transplantation. Through content analysis of the *AJOB* exchange, I highlight the terms of contestation.

My thoughts about burn camp emerge from an altogether different approach that most closely resembles autoethnography. I sought out the opportunity to attend burn camp as a volunteer without any intention of writing about the experience. Originally it was not clear to me that burn camp was directly related to my research, since it is not a site of facial work per se. Instead, I saw volunteering as an opportunity to do my part in an effort that operates directly at odds with the disfigurement imaginary, but I took notes while I was there, as I and perhaps all qualitative social scientists are prone to do. My experiences with the kids and my conversations with other counselors, many of whom are engaged in medical intervention work when not volunteering at camp, inform my postscript.

Research guided from critical perspectives, like my own, looks very different than what might emerge from positivist methodologies. First and foremost, I work from the assumption that all knowledge is partial or situated.[7] No single group will be able to tell the "truth" about facial disfigurement. Nor could a single site sufficiently represent facial work. Rather, I use each site to create a story of repair that represents multiple standpoints and perspectives that may complement, contradict, or complicate one another.[8] While some sociologists might critique such a project for not attempting to create a generalizable social science account, work inspired by feminism and postmodern methodologies recognizes the "crisis of representation" or the problematics of constructing an account that claims absolute authority.[9] There is, by contrast, a deeply rich and analytically powerful story to be told by looking for similarities across what initially appears to be a set of disparate sites. In analyzing reality makeover television alongside cutting-edge surgical techniques, we can identify the cultural narratives that drive both sites of intervention.

At the same time, I acknowledge the power a scholarly representation might have over other versions of the story. In the end, I offer my version as a complex, multilayered, albeit partial theory about facial repair. This is important to note, because this project was made possible by the generosity of those who agreed to be interviewed. Scholarly representation is a guilty enterprise. Stories are shared; perspectives are offered. Then the sociologist sifts through these words for meanings and resituates these viewpoints in a theoretical logic. Likely, those who find their words on these pages see facial work differently. Rather than eschewing those different accounts, I understand that there are multiple ways of understanding the processes I describe here. This is one true story, but certainly not the only one.

Thinking through the politics of research involves not only naming the meta-level concerns about knowledge production, but also discerning the ways research itself propagates social inequalities and exclusion. The first drafts of this book contained a number of photographs. Some exposed the faces of the people described in these pages, to put facial difference into sharp relief. Others depicted before and after images to give readers a sense of what exactly facial work accomplishes. Ultimately, I made the editorial decision to remove all photographs from the text. One of the things that this book hopes to demonstrate is the way that bodies can be subject to intense stigma. Displaying faces calls forth the dynamic of the historic sideshow. This kind of objectification too often works to justify the status quo treatment of those on display. Instead, my hope is that readers can consider the ideas presented here without having their unconscious stigma and internalized disfigurement imaginaries ignited by images of difference.

As a critical social scientist, I critique modes of intervention aimed at disfigurement, but I also recognize certain facts about facial work. Repair of the human face literally saves lives. For example, children with cleft palates are often unable to adequately nurse or drink from a bottle without surgery. In addition, those at whom the intervention is aimed often desire repair. In critically interrogating facial work I do not mean to suggest that intervention is intrinsically bad, that repair should not exist as a mode of coping, or that those experts who engage in this work are inherently suspect. Rather, I critique facial work in order to disentangle the consequences of the disfigurement imaginary. Critical theories of the world, from feminist science studies to disability studies, query the politics of knowledge.[10] Sometimes, the point is not simply to understand but to transform social relations. In addition, these areas of inquiry have traditionally celebrated self-determination and theorized inequalities from a subject position etched with the effects of power and devaluation. As a consequence, writing what we are not remains a suspect practice.

And so there is no way around the question of my own face.

I am not disfigured in many senses of the word. My own face is what most would call unremarkable. It is, for the most part, seen and unnoticed by others, but I have been called ugly more than once. It was the word used against me when I stopped to help a woman whose boyfriend accosted her on a college campus, screaming and shaking her. It was the word used by a girlfriend on our way home on a night that started good and ended badly, and it is also the word that my mother regrets using when, as a teenager, I would leave the house dressed provocatively or unconventionally. Leaving aside the question of why ugliness works as the ultimate insult for women especially, I *can* claim to know and understand what it means to be devastated by another's insistence that what I look like is not good enough, and even repellant. And I can claim to know what it means to hear those words and to take them in, to have the experience of seeing one's self inexorably determined by the worst things you have ever heard about yourself. I think that most of us know the feeling of momentarily glancing in the mirror only to be disgusted with our own reflection. But as Margo Jefferson, in a *New York Times* review of Lucy Grealy's *Autobiography of a Face* writes, "Suffering is exact. Each kind has its own weight and measure. Fearing you are ugly is not the same as knowing you are."

Despite my own tenuous relationship with ugliness, I cannot and do not make claims about "knowing" disfigurement in any profoundly personal way. And yet, I speak of it because I know facial difference in some very real ways. I know disfigurement as a cultural specter in the ways that we all do. Many claim that they have never seen someone who might be described as disfigured. But regardless of whether or not we encounter disfigurement in everyday life, we certainly encounter bodily difference in popular culture, literature, visual art, science, and news media. We are, as of this writing in 2013, still seeing injured veterans return to the United States from Iraq and Afghanistan. We encounter disfigurement, and I would argue, routinely produce disfigurement as part of our war work.

I also know disfigurement as a work object. In her account of fetal surgery, sociologist Monica Casper describes the work object as "any material entity around which people make meaning and organize their work practices."[11] Through this project, disfigurement has taken shape for me as a work object of medical intervention, and I have empirically investigated the ways in which disfigurement takes shape in hospital corridors, in philanthropic literature, in bioethics debates, in news media, in surgeons' seminars, and in popular culture. I do know something about the ways disfigurement is imbued with significance in sites that aim to fix faces defined as different.

Finally, I know facially disfigurement also as a politically tricky and ethically weighty subject. How we speak of disfigurement is constitutive of the ways we think about, respond to, manage, and represent disfigurement, and so I am cautious about how I speak of facial differ-ence in this work. Disability scholars vividly demonstrate how tropes about disability infuse discursive formations and, subsequently, social practices.[12] Given this insight, it is critically important to point to the ideological assumption embedded in word choice. The very word "dis-figurement" connotes a form of embodiment that is negative or asun-der. While it is empirically useful to use the language employed by those I study, namely surgeons, it is equally important to undermine the politics of language by alternating the term "disfigurement" with words and phrases like facial difference, facial atypicality, and facial uniqueness.

A recent publication released by Changing Faces notes,

The word "disfigurement" is used in this booklet to describe the aes-thetic effects of a mark, scar, asymmetry or paralysis to the face or body. *Changing Faces* uses the word as a noun, (for example, "a child who has a disfigurement"), but avoids its use as an adjective, (for example, not "a disfigured child" but "a child with/who has a disfigurement"; not "a dis-figured face" but instead, "a facial disfigurement"). We recognise that the word "disfigurement" is not particularly positive and some people may not want to use it to describe their condition or appearance, preferring other words like "visible difference," "unusual appearance" or the actual name of their condition. These words are used on occasion. *Changing Faces* encourages the real cause of a person's disfigurement to be spelled out, (for example, a person with/who has a cleft lip, Bell's Palsy, burn inju-ries, cancer, acne, etc.) because this is an informative way of describing a person's medical condition. The charity continues to use the word "disfig-urement" as it is a succinct, generic term widely understood by the gen-eral public and enshrined in British law in the Disability Discrimination Act (DDA) 1995, which legally protects people who have disfigurements against discrimination.[13]

In talking through the tensions around language, Changing Faces echoes other disability rights organizations that encourage the use of person-first language. Yet the organization also acknowledges that the choice to use "not particularly positive" language is strategic. The term "disfigurement" allows Changing Faces to speak of a collective experience and to convey their work to potential stakeholders, including the state. My own process of writing on this topic required wrestling with similar tensions, and in many ways, my own linguistic choices echo those of Changing Faces. My sense and my hope is that more affirming language will emerge in the coming years.

When speaking of bodily difference, it is also important to resist the trope of tragedy that so often surrounds disability and disfigurement.[14] It is critically important to dispel the monolithic story of suffering and the imperative to overcome that often infuses stories and even scholarly analysis about disability. But then *what of suffering*? Though politically problematic to acknowledge, can we not agree that there is real suffering that is experienced and attributable to our bodies? In asking this question, I do not mean to suggest that disfigurement is reducible to suffering, as is presumed when one views facial difference through the disfigurement imaginary. But the fact remains that suffering is experienced by all of us as a very condition of embodiment. Yet this suffering is not wholly constitutive of our human experience.[15]

There is the possibility of speaking of the suffering that comes with facial difference without producing a totalizing narrative of disfigurement. If we are to acknowledge suffering, which we must do if we seek to capture and represent a broad range of human experiences, stories of suffering must be articulated in transformative ways. They must not be told in order to confirm that what we are already doing and how we are already thinking is all that can be done and thought. When we acknowledge suffering, we can self-reflexively consider if the stories we tell about suffering activate particular patterns of response, relationships, and thought. We can ask if the ways we describe human experiences reify suffering. This is ultimately what the disfigurement imaginary does, because its way of viewing disability is couched in terms of pity and an imperative to repair. In resisting the idea that facial work is good or bad, my intention has been to craft a critical account of intervention without criticizing the desire that some might have for these interventions, precisely because of the suffering that is a result from living in a sociohistorical context that overvalues appearance and aesthetic intervention.

NOTES

NOTES TO THE INTRODUCTION

1. Peiss (2011) provides a historical account of the processes through which consumption of beauty products and services transformed over time into an overarching "beauty culture" in the United States. Specifically, Peiss highlights the role of women in establishing beauty regimens as women increasingly entered public life beginning in the Victorian era.
2. Taussig 2012, 5.
3. American Society of Plastic Surgeons 2010.
4. Dohnt and Tiggemann 2006.
5. Psychologists Kenneth and Mamie Clark's (1939) famous doll experiments demonstrate a correlation between racial identification as black and lower self-image. Specifically, the Clarks showed how both white and black children attributed positive traits to white dolls and negative traits to black dolls. Kiri Davis's (2005) recreation of the experiments captured in her film *A Girl Like Me* illustrates how self-image is racialized, such that that black girls disproportionately self-report feeling unattractive.

NOTES TO CHAPTER 1

1. The word "disfigurement" is a thoroughly problematic term. Understood through a disability studies lens, the label reifies social stigma. At the same time, I use the term strategically throughout this book to socially and semantically situate the faces in the institutional contexts I analyze here. This term is widely used in the medical sites this book explores. Rather than taking the term for granted, I analyze the construction of "disfigurement" as an operative category that shapes social meanings of and responses to atypical faces in various contexts. As such, I regularly mark the term by placing it inside quotations to signal that its meaning should not be taken for granted. I discuss the tensions implicit in use of the term more thoroughly in chapter 2 and the appendix. In order to contest the power of such language, I alternate the term "disfigurement" with other words including facial difference, visual difference, facial atypicality, visual uniqueness, and atypical appearance. The facial appearances referenced throughout this book might be different than what is understood as the norm, but one central idea explored here is that language reinscribing social norms implicitly devalues difference. For more discussion of subversive language to talk about facial difference, see Garland-Thomson 2009.
2. Grealy 1994, 154.
3. Grealy 1994, 152.
4. Grealy 1994, 7.
5. Grealy 1994, 155.
6. Lehmann-Haupt 2002.

7. The reviews discussed here are those reprinted on the cover and in the front matter of the 1994 edition of the memoir.

8. Braidotti 1996; Kemp 2004.

9. Veiling functions as one method for concealing the face, but this, of course, is a culturally specific practice and one that is increasingly suspect in a post-9/11 world.

10. Over the last decade disability studies and feminist theory, in particular feminist science studies, have theorized the "the natural" as a cultural and political construction (Barnes 1998). Hinging this analysis on a material body part is an attempt to theoretically challenge "the nonfleshiness of social constructionism" (Rosengarten 2005). See Shabot 2006 for a discussion of "grotesque" body metaphors that challenge disembodied analysis.

11. See Evans and Lee 2002 for a discussion of making sociology of the body "real."

12. Robertson 2004, 32.

13. See Turner 1996 and 2001 for a gorgeous framing of how to sociologically think about the body and disability.

14. Weber 1978.

15. As sociologist Chris Shilling, drawing on Pierre Bourdieu, writes about the body, "Physical capital is most usually converted into economic capital (money, goods, and services), cultural capital (e.g. educational qualifications), and social capital (interpersonal networks that allow individuals to draw on the help/resources of others), and is key to the reproduction of social inequalities (Bourdieu, 1978, 1984, 1986)" (Shilling 2004, 474). Conceptualizing facial appearance as a kind of capital makes it possible to understand beauty and ugliness as social statuses that are relational and differentially valued.

16. Langlois et al. 2000.

17. For a sociological discussion of uglyism, see Synott 1989; 1990; 2008.

18. Sociological examinations of appearance tend to focus either on beauty culture or subcultural body modification, leaving the question of unattractiveness or facial atypicality relatively unexamined through a sociological lens. Several outstanding sociological examinations of appearance driven cosmetic surgery include Elliott (2008), Gimlin (2010), and Pitts-Taylor (2007). Featherstone (2000) provides an overview of the sociology of body modification.

19. Clarke and Fujimura 1992.

20. Foucault 1973.

21. Hsu and Lincoln 2007, 23.

22. Hughes 1998.

23. Centers for Disease Control 2012.

24. World Health Organization 2001.

25. Frank 2004.

26. Callahan 2004; Kent 2000; Rumsey and Harcourt 2004.

27. Wasserman and Allen 1985.

28. Barden et al. 1989.

29. Wald and Knutson 2000.

30. Stevenage and McKay 1999.

31. Landsdown et al. 1997.

32. Rumsey and Harcourt 2004, 84.

33. Macgregor 1990.
34. Macgregor 1974, xxiii.
35. *New York Times* 2002.
36. Kemp 2004, 73.
37. Clarke et al. 2003.
38. Clarke et al. 2010.
39. Bishop (2011) includes an extensive discussion of the politics and ethics surrounding brain death criteria.
40. Timmermans 1998; 1999.
41. Berger 1972.
42. Martin 1995; 1999.

NOTES TO CHAPTER 2

1. While stigma and dramaturgy retain sociological currency, Goffman's notions of face and face-work are surprisingly absent in recent sociological surveys of his theoretical contributions (Burns 1991; Smith 1999; West 1996).
2. Goffman 1967, 5.
3. Goffman's notion of face follows a theoretical lineage in symbolic interactionism wherein sociality is conceptualized through metaphors of the body, specifically the visual processes of seeing another human or one's self. Charles Cooley's (1902) theory of the "looking glass self" established a framework for thinking about the relationship between the self, and by implication the body, and others. For Cooley, the looking glass self describes a process wherein individuals constitute a self through other's responses, opinions, and feedback. It is a process that relies on reflection, through which individuals incorporate a sense of self thoroughly determined through others via social interaction. Goffman's theory of face-work is an extension of this very premise, and provides a more elaborated way of thinking about how self and society are formed in concert.
4. Goffman 1967, 5.
5. Goffman 1967, 12.
6. Manning 1992.
7. Goffman's concepts of face and face-work are taken up in linguistics, specifically in politeness theory. Brown and Levinson's classic work on politeness (1987) relies on Goffman's concepts of face and face-work, specifically in their articulation of face threatening acts (FTAs). Rather than emphasizing face-work as an ongoing practice central to the creation of social reality, they understand face-work as a strategy deployed by individuals in the service of politeness. Francesca Bargiela-Chiappini (2003) argues that Brown and Levinson dilute Goffman's concepts and that face and face-work are not simply methods of politeness, but tools for creating social order. Other linguists and communication researchers continue to engage Goffman's work in studying interpersonal communication dynamics (Heisler et al. 2003; Holtgraves 1992; Merkin 2006a, 2006b), and scholars have also employed face and face-work to examine such varied phenomena as divination (Wyllie 1970), pornography (MacCannell 1989), presidential billboards (Kusa 2005), and health care professionals' management of risk (Myers 2003). Yet these extensions of Goffman tend to frame face-work as simply a communicative process rather than a reality-generating practice.
8. Blumer 1969; Mead 1934.

9. Goffman 1967, 7. Others have explored the sociology of the body implicit in Goffman's work. See Gardner and Gronfein 2006; Waskul and Vannini 2006.

10. Cisgender describes individuals whose gender identification, assignment at birth, and physiology coalesces according to normative gender expectations.

11. Casper 1998.

12. Here Goffman draws extensively on Emile Durkheim (1965), for whom ritual refers to the sets of practices imbued with sacred meaning that societies engage in toward the creation of solidarity.

13. Trevino 2003.

14. In a 2001 *Annual Review of Sociology* essay "Conceptualizing Stigma," Bruce G. Link and Jo C. Phelan write, "The stigma concept is applied to literally scores of circumstances ranging from urinary incontinence (Sheldon & Caldwell 1994) to exotic dancing (Lewis 1998) to leprosy (Opala & Boillot 1996), cancer (Fife & Wright 2000), and mental illness (Angermeyer & Matschinger 1994, Corrigan & Penn 1999, Phelan et al. 2000). It is used to explain some of the social vagaries of being unemployed (Walsgrove 1987), to show how welfare stigma can lead to the perpetuation of welfare use (Page 1984), and to provide an understanding of situations faced by wheelchair users (Cahill & Eggleston 1995), stepparents (Coleman et al. 1996), debtors (Davis 1998), and mothers who are lesbian (Causey & Duran-Aydintug 1997)" (364).

15. Goffman 1963, 5.

16. For a consideration about how one response to stigma, namely staring, can be reclaimed by individuals, see Garland-Thomson 2006 and 2009.

17. Janet Shim (2010) explores how the biomedicalization of difference with regards to research on cardiovascular risks both reflects and reproduces racial, class, and gender inequalities.

18. Clarke et al. 2010a, 29; emphasis in original. In the original, Clarke et al. identify the ways biomedicalization maintains racial and class inequalities resulting in "stratified biomedicalization," wherein practices of biomedicalization fortify social inequities.

19. Althusser 1971. Chrys Ingraham explores the ways in which ideas about heterosexuality structure gendered relations. She describes the heterosexual imaginary as "that way of thinking which conceals the operation of heterosexuality in structuring gender and closes off any critical analysis of heterosexuality as an organizing institution" (1994, 203–04).

20. See Rose 2007.

21. Spellman 2002, 1.

22. Greco 2012.

23. Given the ways in which "before" and "after" pictures are routinely consumed through ways of seeing that implicitly and explicitly reify stigma, this book does not contain any such images. Instead, I invite readers to notice when the feeling of wanting to see the faces described arises and to ask what undergirds that desire. Would before and after pictures generate a critical insight, and if so, at what cost?

24. Spelman 2002, 6.

25. Shildrick 2002.

26. Kristeva 1982.

27. Kaw 1998; Kessler 1998. For more on the term "disorders of sex development" and its relationship to the classification intersex, see Intersex Society of North America 2006.

28. Davis 1995.

29. Davis 1997.

30. Ravard and Stiker 2001.
31. Canguilhem 1991.
32. Foucault 1999.
33. Clark and Myser 1996.
34. Frank 2004, 18.
35. Shilling 2003.
36. Frank 2004, 24.
37. Frank 2004, 25.
38. Garland-Thomson 2005, 1579.
39. Morrison 2013.
40. The *Telegraph* 2012.
41. *On the Media* 2012.
42. Auger 2000.
43. Kalish 1966.
44. Sudnow 1967, 74.
45. Timmermans 1998.
46. The clinical guidelines for brain death vary among clinical contexts within the United States (Bishop 2011).
47. Ad Hoc Committee of the Harvard Medical School 1968.
48. Whitelaw 1986.
49. Zussman 1992.
50. Lawton 2002.
51. Timmerman 1998, 66.
52. Sweeting and Gilhooly 1997; 1991.
53. Quill 2005.
54. Garland-Thomson 1994; 2002.
55. DeVries and Subedi 1998; Kuhse and Singer 2006.
56. In recent years, science studies scholar and sociologist Bruno Latour (2004) has explored the pontential of a normative sociology of science and medicine that aims to stake claims about pressing issues of the day. This represents a new epistemological stance that seeks to dispense with the perceptions that science and technology studies or sociology of medicine are essentially relativistic fields of study.
57. Rosengarten 2005.
58. See Kessler 1998 and Sullivan 2004 for emblematic examples of noninterventionist arguments. Chapter 6 disentangles how noninterventionism structured bioethics debates about face transplantation too.
59. In chapter 6, I demonstrate how critics of face transplantation make a noninterventionist argument in sites of bioethics deliberation.
60. Shildrick 2005, 9.

NOTES TO CHAPTER 3

1. Reality television is a genre of television that chronicles unscripted situations experienced by ordinary people, though celebrities increasingly participate in programs modeled on similar premises.
2. See Boyd 2007 for a discussion of the production of identity via reality television.

3. In later episodes, the "mini extreme makeover" was introduced. The "mini" quality of these makeovers was striking in conjunction with the "extreme" nature of other makeovers. In these very short segments, usually no more than five minutes, candidates are restyled using nonsurgical techniques like fashion styling, haircuts and coloring, and teeth whitening. These segments mirror other television makeovers like those featured on *Queer Eye for the Straight Guy*, the *Oprah Winfrey Show*, or the *Today* show.

4. Weber 2005.

5. ABC Television Network 2007.

6. In the time since ABC aired its controversial reality show, "extreme makeover" has entered the American vernacular. Cars, dogs, and presidential contenders are all getting "extreme makeovers." See Baker 2007, Hinchliffe 2007, Marcus 2007.

7. See Elber 2002, Petrozzello 2002. Shows like *Extreme Makeover* offer participants resources, financial and otherwise, to overcome personal limitations that inhibit one's ability to alter one's appearance. Historically, bodily variance was understood in supernatural terms; one's moral standing, one's virtuousness, one's elect status was imagined to be reflected by one's body (Daston and Park 1998). Disabilities and chronic illness, disfiguring conditions and bodily trauma were conceptualized as indicative of moral failings and thus, in a sense, deserved. Virulent public response to the show seems to indicate a lingering sensibility that our bodies reveal moral transgressions or laudable asceticism. For example, the discourse around body weight, which posits obesity as the result of a lack of willpower, clearly relies on such moralism (Bordo 1993). The sense is that we deserve the bodies we have, and by extension, makeovers interfere in what seems natural and fair. Interestingly, the public response to *Extreme Makeover: Home Edition* is strikingly opposite; suggesting that offering someone the opportunity to improve their class status is much more acceptable than facilitating bodily transformation. See Palmer 2004 for a discussion of class transformation through makeover television.

8. James 2002, E8.

9. Oldenburg 2003.

10. In the summer of 2007, a British television network announced that they were looking for "disfigured" persons to participate in a show in which they would receive cosmetic intervention (Templeton 2007). The idea of intervening in disfigurement with radical means seemed to generally be accepted, but critics seemed to agree that broadcasting such content was crass. *Beauty and the Beast: The Ugly Face of Prejudice* (2011–2012), a documentary-style program, was eventually broadcast on the United Kingdom's Channel 4.

11. Examples of such language can be identified in almost every episode analyzed. See Garland-Thomson 1997 for a culture history of "freakery."

12. Haiken 2000, Sullivan 2004.

13. Blum 2003, Pitts-Taylor 2007.

14. Crawley 2006.

15. Thompson 2003, B4.

16. McGee 2005.

17. McGee 2005.

18. Wallusis 1998.

19. Corvino 2004, 56.

20. Huff 2006.

21. CBS's *The Amazing Race* has won the Reality-Competition Award every year between 2003 and 2009. Makeover shows have won in the Reality Category as well. ABC's *Extreme Makeover: Home Edition* was the 2005 and 2006 winner, and Bravo's *Queer Eye for the Straight Guy* was the 2004 winner.

22. Holmes and Jermyn 2004.

23. For a discussion of the pedagogical functions of reality television, see Lane and Giles 2009. For a broader discussion of body pedagogics, see Shilling 2007.

24. While FOX's *The Swan* was similar to *Extreme Makeover* in the sense that both pushed the boundaries for what makeovers had previously attempted on TV, *Extreme Makeover* stood apart from *The Swan* for several reasons. *The Swan* aired for two seasons on FOX. *Extreme Makeover* lasted for three seasons and part of a fourth. *Extreme Makeover* continued to reach audiences via syndication on the Style network, too. In addition, *The Swan*'s gimmicky concept included forcing participants to participate in a beauty pageant post-makeover. Because *Extreme Makeover* purported simply to chronicle the process of transformation, it garnered a degree of respectability not afforded to *The Swan*.

25. Tait 2007.

26. Huff 2006.

27. Crawley 2006.

28. Clarke et al. 2003.

29. Clarke et al. 2010b, 41.

30. See Foucault 1988 for a discussion of technologies of the self.

31. Holmes and Jermyn 2004, 5.

32. ABC Television Network 2006.

33. All questions are excerpted from the *Extreme Makeover* Application. See ABC Television Network 2006.

34. Deery 2006, 166.

35. The only exceptions are two "Battle of the Bulge" episodes, in which three participants must lose weight in order to earn their makeovers.

36. Reality television might also be characterized as democratic given the ways it sometimes encourages audience participation. Often the audience shapes the outcome—through voting for the winner, for example. Sometimes audience members communicate with participants through blogs and online chat sessions. Audience members are also given the opportunity to apply to participate in upcoming seasons (Andrejevic 2003).

37. Andrejevic 2003, 6.

38. Watts 2009.

39. Evanier 2010.

40. Crawley 2006.

41. Dovey 2000.

42. Stevens 2009.

43. In essence, the very pain patients hope to resolve through surgery consumption may be reproduced because in effect, the cosmetic surgery industry relies on that very pain for its survival and expansion (Corvino 2004).

44. Casper 2014.

45. Weber 2005, 1.

46. Sullivan 2004.
47. McGee 2005.
48. Deery 2006; Weber 2005.
49. Deery 2006, Weber 2005.
50. Weber 2005, 1.
51. Casper 1998.

NOTES TO CHAPTER 4

1. Roth 2005.
2. Murray 2011; Smiley 2009.
3. Murray 2011 suggests that temperature creates multiple problems for silicone. In the *New York Times* story, a woman reports that when exposed to freezing temperatures, silicone enhanced facial features harden dramatically.
4. Given the serious medical complications associated with the cosmetic use of free-floating silicone, it is unlikely to be approved by the FDA for medical use. See Luscombe 2003.
5. Martinez-Jimenez et al. 2006.
6. I use transgender and trans* to refer to a range of gender identities. Put another way, transgender describes gender identities that challenge hegemonic understandings of the relationships between bodies (specifically sex characteristics) and gender identity. Trans* designates radical inclusivity; it functions as a way to describe transgender indenties alongside other nonbinary expressions including gender queer, genderless, masculine of center, and Two Spirit indentities. Transgender and trans* are emergent and contested terms. The meaning of each word depends on context. A queer politic that values self-identification informs my approach to trans* related language. My analytic focus is on FFS surgeons' language rather than FFS patients' self-identifications, and is thus inherently problematic. The words surgeons use to identify their patient population may not be the terms patients use to self-identify.
7. Trans women in this context refers to female identified transgender people.
8. Other surgeons practice techniques akin to facial feminization surgery, but the four I discuss in this chapter treat facial feminization as a distinct and intelligible practice.
9. Etcoff 1999.
10. A dremel is a high-speed rotary tool used for grinding, drilling, and sanding.
11. By contrast, trans men often achieve masculinization of the face through hormone supplementation, though facial masculinization surgery is emerging as a distinct intervention. See Ousterhout 2011.
12. Garber 1997, 105.
13. Raymond 1979.
14. Given that much of Gilman's book is focused on facial aesthetic surgery, it is curious that there is no discussion of facial feminization.
15. Ines et al. 2006; Peterson and Dickey 1995.
16. For an expanded discussion of the politics of querying trans genitals, see Talley 2011.
17. Kessler and McKenna 1978; Serano 2007.
18. Harry Benjamin was a sexologist who pioneered "treatment" of transsexualism beginning around 1950. Benjamin established contemporary methods of transitioning, specifically the use of hormones and surgery, and his work informs the Harry Benjamin Standards of Care. The Standards function as a treatment protocol, and many surgeons will not provide

surgery to patients who have not satisfied the path prescribed in the document. Surgeons often require that patients receive "permission" from their therapists before receiving surgery. The Standards have undergone five revisions and updates since they were first released in 1979. The organization recently changed its name to the World Professional Association for Transgender Health (WPATH).

19. See WPATH 2011.

20. Elroi Windsor's (2011) comparative analysis of cisgender and trans-identified surgery consumers demonstrates the inequities and transphobia built into medical care. Whereas treatment protocols for trans patients are often situated within discourses of care and patient well-being, the persistent disparity between regulations for gendered body inter-ventions like breast implants for cisgender women and trans women demonstrate a kind of institutionalized paternalism. Windsor explores the social psychological costs of this disparity and potential policy implications.

21. HBIGDA 2001, 21. Each of these procedures is used in feminizing the face.

22. Tsroadmap.com is an Internet resource providing information on transitioning from male-to-female. James cites her annual traffic at around 4 million visitors per year.

23. James 2006.

24. Each of the surgeons I observed is male. This should not necessarily be surprising given that men disproportionately pursue plastic surgery specialties, but it does make for interesting, and sometimes concerning, gendered dynamics between surgeons and trans women patients. Specifically, male facial feminization surgeons often offer their personal opinions about appearance, and sometimes interactions between surgeon and patients take on sexualized overtones. While it is beyond the scope of this book, future research might query these patterns through a feminist lens.

25. Fieldnotes April 14, 2007.

26. Fieldnotes April 14, 2007.

27. Conway 2000.

28. I use pseudonyms when quoting from my fieldnotes.

29. Fieldnotes April 14, 2007.

30. Longmore 1997.

31. Fieldnotes April 13, 2007.

32. Fieldnotes September 22, 2006.

33. Bartky 2003; Blum 2003; Pitts-Taylor 2007; Sullivan 2004; Talley 2012.

34. Dull and West 2002, 137.

35. Bordo 2000.

36. Becking et al. 2007.

37. Becking et al. 2007, 558.

38. Becking et al. 2007, 563–64.

39. Feminist science studies demonstrates how formal and informal theories of sex difference structure science. Distinct notions of masculinity and femininity are both reflected by and constituted through scientific research. See Bleier 1986 and Fausto-Sterling 1992.

40. The importance of this single pamphlet must be contextualized. First and foremost, Dr. Ousterhout is often attributed with originating facial feminization methods. His account of FFS is the first published in a peer-reviewed medical journal (1987). In addition given the fact that there are a limited number of FFS surgeons, there are limited sources of information about FFS that originate from medical providers. Ousterhout's pamphlet is

routinely distributed at trans conferences and is regularly mentioned on websites in which trans women chronicle their experiences and discuss possible interventions.

41. Text is in all capital letters in the original.
42. Gould 1981; Oudshoorn 1994; Schiebinger 1989.
43. Fieldnotes September 22, 2006.
44. Fieldnotes April 13, 2007.
45. Fieldnotes September 22, 2006.
46. Kessler 1990.
47. Lorber 1993.
48. Laqueur 1990.
49. Fieldnotes April 13, 2007.
50. Fieldnotes September 22, 2006.
51. Fieldnotes September 22, 2006.
52. West and Zimmerman 1987, 126.
53. Schippers 2007, 89–90.
54. Shapiro 2010, 158.
55. Fieldnotes April 13, 2007.
56. Fieldnotes April 13, 2007.
57. Fieldnotes September 22, 2006.
58. Fieldnotes April 13, 2007.
59. Gilman 2001.
60. Davis 2003.
61. Kaw 1998.
62. Ginsberg 1996.
63. West and Zimmerman 1987, 145.
64. Lorber 1993, 578.
65. Shapiro 2010, 165.
66. I cite these names because both cases received relatively large amounts of publicity, especially in queer media outlets, but tragically, these are not isolated instances of transphobic violence. In 2002, Gwen Araujo, a 17-year-old trans women, was brutally beaten with a frying pan and barbell before being strangled by four men. In February of 2008, transphobia motivated the Bronx stabbing death of Sanesha Stewart.
67. Harrison et al. 2012.
68. FFS surgeons' narratives premise not passing as the core problem for trans women. Similarly, scholarship on transgender subjectivities regularly emphasizes discordance within the self rather than a culture of transphobia. Yet Raewyn Connell (2012) asks us to rethink trans women's lives through a lens of social justice paying special attention to vulnerability, poverty, and violence—social patterns that undermine agency and political efficacy—rather than obsessively focusing on supposed contradictions between identity and embodiment.
69. Boswell 1995.
70. Queer critiques highlight the symbolic violence effected when passing is positioned as the ultimate trans pursuit. Ultimately, the expectation of passing undermines self-determination and exacerbates the costs associated with not passing.
71. Ousterhout 1994.
72. Connell 2009,108.
73. Fieldnotes September 22, 2006.

74. Fieldnotes April 13, 2007.
75. Fieldnotes April 14, 2007.
76. Fieldnotes September 22, 2006.

NOTES TO CHAPTER 5

1. Gates Foundation 2013.
2. Centers for Disease Control and Prevention 2013.
3. World Health Organization 2006.
4. Farmer 1996.
5. Operation Smile 2007a.
6. Dixon et al. 2011.
7. Shaw et al. 1995.
8. Elahi et al. 2004.
9. Farmer et al. 2006.
10. Missions have taken place in Bolivia, Brazil, Cambodia, China, Colombia, Ecuador, Egypt, Ethiopia, Gaza Strip/West Bank, Honduras, India, Jordan, Kenya, Mexico, Morocco, Nicaragua, Panama, Paraguay, Peru, Philippines, Russia, Thailand, Venezuela, and Vietnam.
11. Operation Smile 2010.
12. McQueen et al. 2007.
13. See Lacey et al. 2012 for an in-depth discussion of philanthropic tourism, altruism, and the problematics of othering.
14. Operation Smile 2007b.
15. Clarke et al. 2010.
16. De Arellano 2007.
17. The feature I describe here was observed in November 2007. While the specific children featured changed over the course of the following several years, the site continues to feature similar imagery.
18. Garland-Thomson 2009.
19. Longmore 1997.
20. Operation Smile 2013.
21. Argus 2007.
22. Champion 2006.
23. Bolpur 2006.
24. *Irish Times* 2007.
25. Halloran 2006.
26. *Africa News* 2007.
27. *Business World* 2007.
28. *Irish Times* 2007.
29. *Business World* 2007; Condren 2007.
30. The word "smile" figures in the organization's name, and perhaps not coincidently in the name of another organization, Smile Train, which touts itself as the "the world's leading cleft charity."
31. *Africa News* 2007; Doke 2007.
32. Franco-Diyco 2006.
33. Birnbaum 2005. Another similar example includes "Operation Smile South Africa, whose mission is to give 'the gift of a smile'" (Argus 2007).

34. *Business World* 2007.
35. *Africa News* 2007.
36. Condren 2007.
37. Higgs 2008.
38. Russell 1994, 123.
39. Ekman 1992.
40. Montgomery 1999, 2.
41. Gusfield 1989.
42. Lane 1997, 158.
43. Neill 1966.
44. Cole 2012.
45. Cole 2012.
46. Cole 2012.
47. Operation Smile 2007a.
48. Product Red 2007. Harry Browne (2013) considers Bono's work as a celebrity philanthropist and demonstrates how his efforts are complicit with neoliberal policies.
49. Talley and Casper 2010.
50. UN Refugee Agency 2013.
51. The nonprofit industrial complex is a phrase coined by radical women of color activist organization INCITE to describe both the institutionalization of nonprofit work into corporatized systems of revenue generation and the depoliticization that results from the management of tax exempt 501(c)(3) status. See Incite! 2007.
52. Operation Smile 2006.
53. *Daily Star* 2006.
54. *Los Angeles Times* 2006.
55. Look to the Stars 2007.
56. Brumberg 1998.
57. Bordo 1993.
58. National Public Radio 2012.
59. Following the release of the documentary, news stories broke that Ruksana was pursuing legal action against the filmmakers for what she says are outstanding unfulfilled promises for appearing the film. The filmmakers contest that any agreements were broken (*Express Tribune* 2012).
60. Recent work suggests that facial work without corresponding justice is insufficient (Zia 2013).

NOTES TO CHAPTER 6

1. Bernard and Smith 2006.
2. Osterweil 2006.
3. While news coverage conveyed surprise at patient selection for initial FT procedures, the history of biomedical innovation is ripe with examples wherein individuals with devalued social statuses are used for experimentation. Presumably, this is a strategy to manage public backlash in the face of unknown risk. The selection of socially devalued persons is not altogether different from the use of vulnerable populations (e.g., enslaved women, incarcerated individuals) as nonconsenting research subjects. See Dudley 2012 and Hornblum 1997 for histories of exploitation within medicine.

4. Macartney 2006.
5. Glaister 2005.
6. McLaughlin 2003.
7. Bowen 1999. This is a common theme in popular media coverage about experimental surgery. Popular science news imagines a future wherein cutting edge technologies have become routinized, while experts repeatedly insist that these are specialized techniques not intended for widespread use. Monica Casper (1998) explores this trend in her work on fetal surgery.
8. Hanlon 2005; LaFerla and Singer 2005.
9. Mason 2005.
10. Thomas et al. 1998.
11. Baylis 2004.
12. Baylis 2004, 30.
13. Facial prosthetic devices exist. Patients sometimes find prosthesis aesthetically effective but functionally cumbersome given that eating, drinking, and communication may be more difficult while wearing the device. Film critic Robert Ebert debuted a facial prosthesis on PBS in January 2011 after much of his jaw was removed to treat thyroid cancer. Ebert's silicone prosthesis was two years in the making, and while state of the art, it appeared mask-like and, as Ebert conceded, did not "fool anyone" (Shahid 2011).
14. Just how toxic these drugs are is highly contested. While some critics of FT equate these drugs to a death sentence, others, including the University of Louisville team, argue that the risk is grossly overstated since most information about the drugs is based on research with people suffering from serious illnesses like kidney failure. The team argues that the drugs are not intrinsically toxic but rather that the drugs in combination with a preexisting conditions yield serious side effects.
15. Fox and Swazey 1974.
16. I use pseudonyms to refer to team members, institutional sites, and research tools like surveys in an effort to protect confidentiality. Several of the researchers I interviewed are public figures identified by name in news accounts about FT, and as such, they expressed no concerns about confidentiality. I conceal their identities because this analysis is about the discursive work accomplished in relation to FT rather than the particular scientists involved in the process of innovation. In this case, confidentiality is a strategy for shifting the focus from individual personalities and toward the work of innovating facial work.
17. Fieldnotes April 16, 2007.
18. American Journal of Bioethics 2004.
19. Wiggins et al. (2004) relied on the work of transplant surgeon Dr. Francis Moore to justify their appeal for human experimentation. The team identified four ethical guidelines in Moore's work that should be considered in the process of transplant innovation. First, surgeons are to consider the scientific foundations of an innovative procedure. Wiggins et al. reasoned that solid organ and hand transplants provided sufficient information about technique and immunosuppression regimen such that equipoise—the moment wherein the uncertainty posed by the innovation can only be resolved by proceeding—had been reached. Second, according to Moore, the transplant team's "field strength" should be considered. The team at the University of Louisville—which was comprised by reconstructive surgeons, head and neck surgeons, transplant surgeons, immunologists, psychologists, psychiatrists, ethicists, university IRB members, and organ procurers—concluded that

their collective expertise positioned them as the ideal team for initial experimentation. Third, Moore queried the ethical climate of the institution. To this point, Wiggens et al. argued that the motivation of their home institution was not self-aggrandizement, but rather patient benefit. Fourth, according to the team, Moore encouraged public discussion and professional evaluation. In an attempt to initiate discussion, the Louisville team hosted the first International Symposium on Composite Tissue Allotransplantation in November of 1997 and in May of 2000 the second International Symposium on Composite Tissue Allotransplantation to share the initial hand transplantation results. In addition, the team participated in public discussion concerning FT at the Dana Center of London Science Museum. While the Louisville team employed Moore's framework to demonstrate their ethical approach to human experimentation, even their use of Moore is criticized in the *AJOB* issue. For example, Agich and Siemionow (2004) argued that the team misrepresented Moore by claiming that he encouraged public dissemination of experimental results. Their response bordered on the accusatory: "Is this commitment to publicity simply a misreading of Moore or does it reflect deeper program commitments that deserve ethical scrutiny?" (25). It is interesting to note that Siemionow courted the media following her participation in a 2008 FT, even publishing a memoir *Face to Face: My Quest to Perform the First Full Face Transplant* (2009).

20. The analysis that follows is based on content analysis of the FT *AJOB* issue. Contributors sometimes cite published work that appeared elsewhere. These works are not part of the formal content analysis, but how *AJOB* contributors employed external works shapes my understanding of the debate.

21. According to the *AJOB* website, the journal attempts to structure the writing and review process in accords with this spirit of public debate: "*AJOB* does not leave the reader in the passive mode of reading. Unique JournalX technology lets the peer commentators respond to each other and to the Target article during their writing process. Then bioethics.net opens the conversation with additional Open Peer Commentary articles and online Letters to the Editor. Live conversations fill out the discussion of each Target Article. With the American Journal of Bioethics, Taylor & Francis Group and Penn have implemented a publishing system that is truly worthy of bioethics, a way in which scholarship about bioethics can reach the widest and most intellectually broad audience, magnifying the rigor, intimacy and interdisciplinary value of the discipline" (American Journal of Bioethics 2004).

22. Chambers 2004, 21.

23. Caplan 2004, 18.

24. RCS Working Party 2003.

25. Strong 2004.

26. Maschke and Trump 2004.

27. Wiggins et al. 2004.

28. Strong 2004.

29. Agich and Siemionow 2004.

30. Ankeny and Kerridge 2004.

31. Petit et al. 2004.

32. Caplan 2004, 18–19.

33. Wiggins et al. 2004.

34. The work of Margaret Lock (2001), Lesley A. Sharp (2006), and Linda Hogle (1999) demonstrates that psychological risk has long been positioned as a risk of transplant surgery.

AJOB contributors suggest that the face elicits *unique* psychological risks. In this way, critics imply again that something about intervention on the face is different than on other body parts.

35. Wiggins et al. 2004, 5.
36. Rumsey 2004, 22.
37. Agich and Siemionow 2004, 26.
38. Wiggins et al. 2004, 5.
39. Baylis 2004.
40. Strong 2004, 13.
41. Rumsey 2004; Wiggins et al. 2004.
42. Petit et al. 2004, 15.
43. Rumsey 2004; Wiggins et al. 2004.
44. Wiggins et al. 2004.
45. Butler et al. 2004.
46. See Powell 2006 for greater discussion of "bad patients."
47. Wiggins et al. 2004.
48. Agich and Siemionow 2004; Miles 2004; Rumsey 2004.
49. Agich and Siemionow 2004; Strong 2004; Wiggins et al. 2004.
50. Rumsey 2004.
51. Agich and Siemionow 2004.
52. Caplan 2004; Rumsey 2004; Strong 2004.
53. Robertson 2004.
54. Petit et al. 2004.
55. Wiggins et al. 2004, 1.
56. Wiggins et al. 2004, 1.
57. Wiggins 2004, 3.
58. Agich and Siemionow 2004, 26.
59. Morreim 2004, 28.
60. Wiggins et al. 2004, 11.
61. Petit et al. 2004, 15.
62. Petit et al. 2004, 17.
63. Caplan 2004,18.
64. Rumsey 2004, 24.
65. Goering 2004, 34.
66. Huxtable and Woodley 2005, 507.
67. Strong 2004, 13.
68. Rumsey 2004, 23.
69. Aronson 1984.
70. Latour 1987.
71. Robertson 2004, 32.
72. Within science and technology studies, specifically actor network theory, analysis regularly considers the ways artifacts function as actors. Latour's (1987) explication of the "roles" technologies play in the making of science pays careful attention to the ways in which nonhuman actors are produced through and subsequently shape human action. In this site, FT operates as a nonhuman actor that is imbued with moral significance, which in turn shapes the making of science and technology.

73. Cultural critic Jon Dovey (2000) describes intersections of education and entertainment as "edutainment."
74. Miles 2004, 41.
75. For a more comprehensive discussion of feminist bioethics, see Shildrick 1997 and 2005. See Haraway 1991.
76. Shildrick 2005.
77. Bishop 2011.

NOTES TO CHAPTER 7
1. Fistula Foundation 2012; Roush et al. 2012.
2. Mary Burke (2010) considers the medicalization of transsexualism alongside the politicization of trans communities to demonstrate the ways in which medicalized transgender subjectivities make way for transgender rights movements.
3. Frank 2004, 19.
4. Wolff 1959, 276.
5. Kristeva 1982.
6. Changing Faces 2009.
7. Goffman 1955,152.
8. Frank 2004, 28.
9. Facial Surgery Research Foundation 2007.
10. Ferguson 2007.
11. Scoliosis describes the curvature of the spine.
12. Schweik 2009, 290.
13. See Eco 2007 for a genealogy of ugliness throughout time and cultures.
14. Dreger 1999; Hughes et al. 2006; Karkazis 2008; Talley and Casper 2012.
15. In May 2013, a South Carolina adoptive couple filed a lawsuit in conjunction with the Southern Poverty Law Center against the South Carolina Department of Social Services, a hospital, a medical school, and individual hospital employees to contest the postbirth surgical intervention on their adoptive child's intersex condition. While the child in question has already undergone intervention, the legal action could establish a precedent that prevents others diagnosed with disorders of sex development from undergoing early-life normalizing interventions that potentially undermine their bodily integrity and occur without their consent. See Nelson 2013 for more details.
16. See Shapiro 2010 for an elegant analysis of the interplay between biomedical technologies, identity formation, and community development in conjunction with the transformation of sex, gender, and sexuality.
17. Resources are accessible via the Changing Faces website www.changingfaces.org.uk.
18. These organizations can be accessed online at www.aboutfaceusa.org, www.lets-face-it.org.uk, www.aboutfaceusa.org, www.facingforwardinc.org, and http://aboutface.ca.
19. As Tobin Siebers notes in *Disability Aesthetics* (2010), "We all have bodies. This is not a truism. It is not an exercise in the obvious. It is a fact—and a fact of a special kind. It is an incontestable fact. Everything we do, we do as or by means of our body. We cannot get beyond the fact that we are bodies. The body is, simply put, where everything in human culture begins and ends" (136).

NOTES TO THE POSTSCRIPT

1. Sociological research that gives voice to "understudied populations" and marginalized groups is theoretically, methodologically, and politically significant. For exemplars, consider the following recent works. Soma Chaudhuri (2013) explores gender and labor relations on Indian tea plantations, specifically the processes through which women are scapegoated as witches and experience violence as a result of geopolitical transformations. Kristen Schilt's *Just One of the Guys?* (2011) offers a comparative analysis of the employment experiences of trans men before and after transition in order to explore workplace gender inequality. Dan Morrison's (2013) research on deep brain stimulation uses critical qualitative methods to chronicle the patient experience of those with brain implant devices. Lyndi Hewitt (2011) explores the narratives of transnational feminist activists in order to explore how solidarity can be formed across differences in the service of feminist social change. In *Missing Bodies: The Politics of Visibility*, Monica J. Casper and Lisa Jean Moore (2009) take this analytic thread one step further by exploring whose bodies are missing from our cultural register and what consequences are produced by such absences.

2. Berger 2006.

3. The practice of gratitude appears routinely in research on positive psychology as a strategy for increasing happiness. Integrating appreciation is correlated with higher rates of self-esteem and life satisfaction alongside stress reduction and increased coping with trauma (Lyubomirsky 2008).

NOTES TO THE APPENDIX

1. Alexander 1993; Rathje and Murphy 1992.

2. Fosket 2002, 40.

3. Clarke 2005.

4. Hine 2007; Marcus 1998; Rapp 1999.

5. Prior 1997, 77.

6. Wentling et al. 2008 provides an instructive on teaching transgender, but the authors simultaneously demonstrate the ways in which "transgender" routinely functions in tokenizing ways within sociological theories of gender.

7. Haraway 1988.

8. Harding 1991; Hartsock 1983; Hill-Collins 1990; Smith 1989.

9. Rosaldo 1989.

10. Shakespeare 1998.

11. Casper 1998, 19.

12. Longmore 1997.

13. Changing Faces 2009.

14. Garland-Thomson 2009.

15. Siebers (2006) and Morrison and Casper (2012) have noted that suffering is rarely acknowledged in disability studies given the political emphasis the field places on resisting totalizing narratives of defectiveness. Morrison and Casper provide a theoretical framework that puts disability studies and critical trauma studies into conversation with one another in order to think about physical suffering through a constructivist, critical disability politic.

REFERENCES

ABC Television Network. 2006. *Extreme makeover application*. http://abc.go.com/primetime/specials/makeover/application.html.

ABC Television Network. 2007. *Extreme makeover 7/2 series return*. www.abcmedianet.com/assets/pr%5Chtml/061807_09.html.

Ad Hoc Committee of the Harvard Medical School. 1968. Of the Harvard Medical School to examine the definition of brain death: A definition of irreversible coma. *Jama* 205: 337–40.

Africa News. 2007. Kenya: Volunteers put smiles on the faces of children with cleft lips. *Africa News*, August 29.

Agich, George J. and Maria Siemionow. 2004. Facing the ethical questions in facial transplantation. *American Journal of Bioethics* 4: 25–27.

Alexander, Judd H. 1993. *In defense of garbage*. Westport, CT: Praegar.

Althusser, Louis. 1971. *Lenin and philosophy and other essays*. London: Monthly Review Press.

American Journal of Bioethics. 2004. *What is the mission of AJOB?* www.bioethics.net/information.php?infoCat=faq&infoId=9.

American Society of Plastic Surgeons. 2010. *2010 Report of the 2009 Statistics National Clearinghouse of Plastic Surgery Statistics*. www.plasticsurgery.org/Documents/Media/statistics/2009-US-cosmeticreconstructiveplasticsurgeryminimally-invasive-statistics.pdf.

Andrejevic, Mark. 2003. *Reality TV: The work of being watched*. Lanham, MD: Rowman & Littlefield.

Angermeyer, Matthias and Herbert Matschinger. 1994. Lay beliefs about schizophrenic disorder: The results of a population study in Germany. *Acta Psychiatrica Scandinavica* 89: 39–45.

Ankeny, Rachel A. and Ian Kerridge. 2004. On not taking objective risk assessments at face value. *American Journal of Bioethics* 4: 35–37.

Argus, Cape. 2007. South Africa: Cape duo's journey of a "thousandsmiles" brings smiles to the innocent. *Africa News*, February 3.

Aronson, Naomi. 1984. Science as a claims-making activity: Implications for social problems research. In *Studies of the sociology of social problems*, edited by J. Schneider and J. I. Kituse, 1–30. Norwood, NJ: Ablex.

Auger, Jeannette A. 2000. *Social perspectives on death and dying*. Halifax, NS: Fernwood Publishing.

Baker, Dave B. 2007. *Extreme makeover for pets: When your dog just can't take life without a set of $1,800 balls*. Dig & Scratch. www.digandscratch.com/?page_id=12.

Barden, R. Christopher, Martin E. Ford, A. Gayle Jensen, Marcy Rogers-Salyer, and Kenneth E. Salyer. 1989. Effects of craniofacial deformity in infancy on the quality of mother–infant interactions. *Child Development* 60: 819–24.

Bargiela-Chiappini, Francesca. 2003. Face and politeness: New (insights) for old (concepts). *Journal of Pragmatics* 35: 1453–69.

Barnes, Colin. 1998. The social model of disability: A sociological phenomenon ignored by sociologists. In *The disability reader: Social science perspectives*, edited by Tom Shakespeare, 65–78. London: Cassell.

Bartky, Sandra Lee. 2003. Foucault, femininity, and the modernization of patriarchal power. In *The politics of women's bodies*, edited by Rose Weitz, 25–45. Oxford: Oxford University Press.

Baylis, Francoise. 2004. A face is not just like a hand: Pace Barker. *American Journal of Bioethics* 4: 30–32.

Becking, Alfred G., D. Bram Tuinzing, J. Joris Hage and Louis J.G. Gooren. 2007. Transgender feminization of the facial skeleton. *Clinics in Plastic Surgery* 34:557–64.

Berger, Emily K. 2006. Legal rights of the poor and minority to have families: Judges as family planers, the vilification of the poor, and destruction of the black family. *Rutgers Race and Law Review* 8: 259–90.

Berger, John. 1972. *Ways of seeing*. London: Penguin.

Bernard, Ariane and Smith, Craig S. 2006. Woman makes first appearance after face transplant. *New York Times*, February 6.

Birnbaum, Jeffrey H. 2005. Lobbyists can boast of their share of good deeds. *Washington Post*, December 26.

Bishop, Jeffrey 2011. *The anticipatory corpse: Medicine, power, and the care of the dying*. Notre Dame, IN: University of Notre Dame Press.

Black, Daniel. 2001. What is a face. *Body and Society* 17: 1–25.

Bleier, Ruth. 1986. *Feminist approaches to science*. Elmsford, NY: Pergamon Press.

Blum, Virginia L. 2003. *Flesh wounds: The culture of cosmetic surgery*. Berkeley: University of California Press.

Blumer, Herbert. 1969. *Symbolic interactionism: Perspective and method*. Berkeley: University of California Press.

Bolpur, Sabyasachi Roy. 2006. Operation brings back smile through Operation Smile. *The Statesman*, November 4.

Bordo, Susan. 1993. *Unbearable weight: Feminism, western culture, and the body*. Berkeley: University of California Press.

Bordo, Susan. 2000. *The male body: A new look at men in public and private*. New York: Farrar, Straus, and Giroux.

Boswell, Holly. 1995. *The tyranny of passing*. www.lannierose.com/words/tyranny.htm.

Bourdieu, Pierre. 1978. Sport and social class. *Social Science Information* 17: 819–40.

Bourdieu, Pierre. 1984. *Distinction. A social critique of the judgment of taste*. London: Routledge.

Bourdieu, Pierre. 1986. The forms of capital. In *Handbook of theory and research for the sociology of education*, edited by John G. Richardson, 241–58. New York: Greenwood.

Bowen, Jon. 1999. Gaining face. *Salon*. www.salon.com/health/feature/1999/05/19/face_transplants/index.html.

Boyd, Emily M. 2007. *Altering bodies, transforming selves: Emotion and gender on makeover*. Unpublished dissertation. Florida State University.

Braidotti, Rosi. 1996. Signs of wonder and traces of doubt: On teratology and embodied differences. In *Between monsters, goddesses and cyborgs: Feminist confrontations with science, medicine and cyberspace*, edited by Nina Lykke and Rosi Braidotti, 135–52. London: Zed Books.

Brown, Penelope and Steven C. Levinson. 1987. *Politeness: Some universals in language usage*. Cambridge: Cambridge University Press.

Browne, Harry. 2013. *The frontman: Bono (In the name of power) (Counterblasts)*. Brooklyn: Verso.

Brumberg, Joan Jacobs. 1998. *The body project: An intimate history of American girls*. New York: Vintage.

Burke, Mary C. 2010. *Transforming gender: Medicine, body politics, and the transgender rights movement*. Unpublished dissertation. University of Connecticut.

Burns, Tom. 1991. *Erving Goffman*. New York: Routledge.

Business World. 2007. Agency helps Operation Smile light up children's lives. *Business World*, August 3.

Butler, Peter E. M., Alex Clarke, and Richard E. Ashcroft. 2004. Face transplantation: When and for whom? *American Journal of Bioethics* 4: 16–17.

Cahill, Spencer and Robin Eggleston. 1995. Reconsidering the stigma of physical disability: Wheelchair use and public findness. *Sociological Quarterly* 36: 681–98.

Callahan, Christine. 2004. Facial disfigurement and sense of self in head and neck cancer. *Social Work in Health Care* 40: 73–87.

Canguilhem, Georges. 1991. *The normal and the pathological*. Cambridge, MA: Zone Books.

Caplan, Arthur. 2004. Facing ourselves. *American Journal of Bioethics* 4: 18–20.

Casper, Monica. 1998. *Making of the unborn patient: A social anatomy of fetal surgery*. New Brunswick, NJ: Rutgers University Press.

Casper, Monica J. 2014. A ruin of elephants: Trans-species love, labor, and loss. *Oppositional Conversations*. www.oppositionalconversations.org.

Casper, Monica J. and Lisa Jean Moore. 2009. *Missing bodies: The politics of visibility*. New York: NYU Press.

Catlin, Roger. 2007. On TV, being gay is so passe, now transsexuals are in. *Harford Courant*, November 11.

Causey, Kelly A. and Candan Duran-Aydintug. 1997. Tendency to stigmatize lesbian mothers in custody cases. *Journal of Divorce and Remarriage* 28: 171–82.

Centers for Disease Control and Prevention. 2012. *Facts about cleft lip and cleft palate*.www.cdc.gov/ncbddd/birthdefects/cleftlip.html.

Centers for Disease Control and Prevention. 2013. *Middle East respiratory syndrome (MERS)*. www.cdc.gov/coronavirus/mers/index.html.

Chambers, Tod. 2004. How to do things with AJOB: The case of facial transplantation. *American Journal of Bioethics* 4: 20–21.

Champion, Daily. 2006. Nigeria: Lagos embarks on free corrective surgery. *Africa News*, June 13.

Changing Faces. 2009. *Living with disfigurement: Managing the challenge*. www.changingfaces.org.uk/downloads/Living%20with%20a%20Disfigurment%20Managing%20the%20challenge%20(web).pdf.

Changing Faces. 2012. What happened to that boy, mummy? www.changingfaces.org.uk/show/feature/Children-FE-campaign-handling-reactions.

Chaudhuri, Soma. 2013. *Witches, tea plantations, and lives of migrant laborers in India: Tempest in a teapot*. Lanham, MD: Lexington.

Clark, David L. and Catherine Myser. 1996. Being humaned: Medical documentaries and the hyperrealization of conjoined twins. In *Freakery: Cultural spectacles of the extraordinary body*, edited by Rosemarie Garland Thomson, 338–55. New York: NYU Press.

Clark, Kenneth B., and Mamie K. Clark. 1939. The development of consciousness of self and the emergence of racial identification in Negro preschool children. *Journal of Social Psychology* 10: 591–99.

Clarke, Adele E. 2005. *Situational analysis: Grounded theory after the postmodern turn*. Thousand Oaks, CA: Sage.

Clarke, Adele E., Janet K. Shim, Laura Mamo, Jennifer Ruth Fosket, and Jennifer R. Fishman. 2010a. Biomedicalization: A theoretical and substantive introductions. In *Biomedicalization: Technoscience, health, and illness in the US*, edited by Clarke et al., 1–46. Durham, NC: Duke University Press.

Clarke, Adele E., Jennifer Fishman, Jennifer Fosket, Laura Mamo and Janet Shim. 2003. Biomedicalization: Technoscientific transformations of health, illness, and U.S. biomedicine. *American Sociological Review* 68: 161–94.

Clarke, Adele E. and Joan H. Fujimura. 1992. What tools? Which jobs? Why right? In *The right tools for the job: At work in twentieth century life sciences*, edited by Adele E. Clarke and Joan H. Fujimura, 3–44. Princeton, NJ: Princeton University Press.

Clarke, Adele E., Laura Mamo, Jennifer Ruth Fosket, Jennifer R. Fishman, and Janet K. Shim, eds. 2010b. *Biomedicalization: Technoscience, health, and illness in the US*. Durham, NC: Duke University Press.

Cole, Teju. 2012. The white savior industrial complex. *Atlantic Monthly*, March 25.

Coleman, Marilyn, Lawrence H. Ganong, and Susan M. Cable. 1996. Perceptions of stepparents: An examination of the incomplete institutionalization and social stigma hypotheses. *Journal of Divorce and Remarriage* 26: 25–48.

Condren, Bernadette. 2007. A world of difference in a smile. *Courier Mail*, October 27.

Connell, Raewyn. 2009. ACCOUNTABLE CONDUCT: Doing gender in transsexual and political retrospect. *Gender and Society* 23: 104–11.

Connell, Raewyn. 2012. Transsexual women and feminist thought: Toward new understanding and new politics. *Signs* 37: 857–81.

Conway, Lynn. 2000. Lynn's facial feminization. http://ai.eecs.umich.edu/~mirror/FFS/LynnsFFS.html.

Cooley, Charles. 1902. *Human nature and the social order*. New York: Scribner.

Corrigan, Patrick W. and David L. Penn. 1999. Lessons from social psychology on discrediting psychiatric stigma. *American Psychologist* 54: 765–76.

Corvino, Deborah Calav. 2004. *Amending the abject body: Aesthetic makeovers in medicine and culture*. Albany: State University of New York Press.

Crawley, Melissa. 2006. *Mr. Sorkin goes to Washington: Shaping the president on television's the West Wing*. Jefferson, NC: McFarland.

Daily Star. 2006. Mariah is just smiles better. *Daily Star*, May 22.

Daston, Lorraine and Katharine Park. 1998. *Wonders and the order of nature: 1150 1750*. New York: Zone Books.

Davis, Kathy R. 1998. Bankruptcy: A moral dilemma for women debtors. *Law and Psychological Review* 22: 235–49.

Davis, Kathy R. 2003 Surgical passing: Or why Michael Jackson's nose makes "us" uneasy. *Feminist Theory* 4: 73–92.

Davis, Kiri. 2005. A girl like me. http://www.mediathatmattersfest.org/films/a_girl_like_me.

Davis, Lennard J. 1995. *Enforcing normalcy: Disability, deafness, and the body*. Brooklyn: Verso.

Davis, Lennard J. 1997. *The disability studies reader*. New York: Routledge.

De Arellano, Annette B. Ramirez. 2007. Patients without borders: The emergence of medical tourism. *International Journal of Health Services* 37: 193–98.

Deery, June. 2006. Interior design: Commodifying self and place in *Extreme Makeover, Extreme Makeover: Home Edition*, and *The Swan*. In *The great American makeover: Television, history, nation*, edited by Dana Heller, 159–74. New York: Palgrave MacMillan.

Deustch, Helen and Felicity Nussbaum. 2000. *"Defects": Engendering the modern body*. Ann Arbor: University of Michigan Press.

DeVries, Raymond and Janardan Subedi, eds. 1998. *Bioethics and society: Constructing the ethical enterprise*. Upper Saddle River, NJ: Prentice Hall.

Dixon, Michael J., Mary L. Marazita, Terri H. Beaty, and Jeffrey C. Murray. 2011. Cleft lip and palate: Understanding genetic and environmental influences. *Nature Reviews Genetics* 12: 167–78.

Dohnt, Haley K. and Marika Tiggeman. 2006. Body image concerns in young girls: The role of peers and media prior to adolescence. *Journal of Youth and Adolescence* 35: 141–51.

Doke, Linda. 2007. Direct selling means personal investment. *Sunday Times*, August 19.

Dorr, Donal. 2000. *Mission in today's world*. Maryknoll, NY: Orbis Books.

Dovey, Jon. 2000. *Freakshow: First person media and factual television*. Sterling, VA: Pluto Press.

Dreger, Alice Domurat, ed. 1999. *Intersex in the age of ethics*. Hagerstown, MD: University Publishing Group.

Dudley, Rachel. 2012. Toward an understanding of the "medical plantation" as a cultural location of disability. *Disability Studies Quarterly* 32. http://dsqsds.org/index.

Dull, Diane and Candace West. 2002. Accounting for cosmetic surgery: The accomplishment of gender. In *Doing Gender, Doing Difference: Inequality, Power, and Institutional Change*, edited by Sarah Fenstermaker and Candace West, 141–68. New York: Routledge.

Durkheim, Emile. 1965. *The elementary forms of the religious life*. New York: The Free Press.

Eco, Umberto, ed. 2007. *On ugliness*. New York: Rizzoli.

Ekman, Paul. 1992. Facial expressions of emotion: New findings, new questions. *Psychological Science* 3: 34–38.

Ekman, Paul and Wallace V. Friesen. 2003. *Unmasking the face*. Los Altos, CA: Malor Books.

Elber, Lynn. 2002. "Makeover" shows ugly side of perfection. *Associated Press*, December 9.

Elahi, Mohammed Mehboob, Ian T. Jackson, Omar Elahi, Ayesha H. Khan, Fatima Mubarak, Gul Bano Tariq, and Amit Mitra. 2004. Epidemiology of cleft lip and cleft palate in Pakistan. *Plastic and Reconstructive Surgery* 113: 1548–55.

Elliott, Anthony. 2008. *Making the cut: How cosmetic surgery is transforming our lives*. London: Reaktion Books.

Etcoff, Nancy. 1999. *Survival of the prettiest: The science of beauty*. New York: Doubleday.

Evanier, Mark. 2010. Bottom of the barrel. *POV Online*. www.newsfromme.com/archives/2010_02_10.html#018488.

Evans, Mary and Ellie Lee. 2002. *Real bodies: A sociological introduction*. London: Palgrave Macmillan.

Express Tribune. 2012. Saving Face's Rukhsana gets a house, still vows action against Obaid-Chinoy. http://tribune.com.pk/story/412465/saving-faces-rukhsana-gets-a-house-still-vows-action-against-obaid-chinoy/.

Facial Surgery Research Foundation. 2007. *The saving faces art exhibition*. www.savingfaces.co.uk/index.php?option=com_content&task=view&id=15&Itemid=36.

Farmer, Paul. 1996. On suffering and structural violence: A view from below. *Daedalus* 125: 261–83.

Farmer, Paul E., Bruce Nizeye, Sara Stulac, and Salmaan Keshavjee. 2006. Structural violence and clinical medicine. *PLoS Medicine* 3: e449.

Fausto-Sterling, Anne. 1992. *Myths of gender: Biological theories about women and men*. New York: Basic Books.

Featherstone, Mike, ed. 2000. *Body modification*. London: Sage.

Ferguson, Laura. 2007. Toward a new aesthetic of the body. New York University School of Medicine. http://medhum.med.nyu.edu/blog/?p=63.

Fife, Betsy L. and Eric R. Wright. 2000. The dimensionality of stigma: A comparison of its impact on the self of persons with HIV/AIDS and cancer. *Journal of Health and Social Behavior* 41: 50–67.

Fistula Foundation. 2012. *What is fistula?* www.fistulafoundation.org/index.html.

Fosket, Jennifer Ruth. 2002. *Breast cancer risk and the politics of prevention: Analysis of clinical trial.* Unpublished dissertation. University of California, San Francisco.

Foucault, Michel. 1973. *The birth of the clinic: An archaeology of medical perception.* New York: Pantheon.

Foucault, Michel. 1988. Technologies of the self: A seminar with Michel Foucault. Amherst: University of Massachusetts Press.

Foucault, Michel. 1990. *The history of sexuality: An introduction.* New York: Vintage.

Foucault, Michel. 1999. *Birth of the clinic.* New York: Routledge.

Fox, Renee C. and Judith P. Swazey. 1974. *The courage to fail: A social view of organ transplants and dialysis.* Chicago: University of Chicago Press.

Franco-Diyco, Nanette. 2006. Marketing: A reason to smile. *Business World,* December 8.

Frank, Arthur W. 2004. Emily's scars: Surgical shapings, technoluxe, and bioethics. *The Hastings Center Report* 34: 18–29.

Garber, Marjorie. 1997. *Vested interests: Cross-dressing and cultural anxiety.* New York: Routledge.

Gardner, Carol Brooks and William P. Gronfein. 2006. Body armour: Managing disability and the precariousness of the territories of the self. In *Body/embodiment: Symbolic interaction and the sociology of the body,* edited by Dennis Waskul and Phillip Vannini, 83–94. Burlington, VT: Ashgate.

Garland-Thomson, Rosemarie. 1994. Redrawing the boundaries of feminist disability studies. *Feminist Studies* 20: 583–97.

Garland-Thomson, Rosemarie, ed. 1997. *Freakery: Cultural spectacles of the extraordinary body.* New York: NYU Press.

Garland-Thomson, Rosemarie. 2002. Integrating disability, transforming feminist theory. *National Women's Studies Association Journal* 14: 1–32.

Garland-Thomson, Rosemarie. 2005. Feminist disability studies. *Signs* 30: 1557–87.

Garland-Thomson, Rosemarie. 2006. Ways of staring. *Journal of Visual Culture* 5: 173–92.

Garland-Thomson, Rosemarie. 2009. *Staring: How we look.* Oxford: Oxford University Press.

Gates Foundation. 2013. What we do: Polio strategy overview. www.gatesfoundation.org/What-We-Do/Global-Development/Polio.

Gilman, Sander L. 2001. *Making the body beautiful: A cultural history of aesthetic surgery.* Princeton, NJ: Princeton University Press.

Gimlin, Debra. 2010. Imagining the other in cosmetic surgery. *Body & Society* 16: 57–76.

Ginsberg, Elaine K. 1996. *Passing and the fictions of identity.* Durham, NC: Duke University Press.

Glaister, Dan. 2005. U.S. doctors prepare for first human face transplant. *The Guardian,* September 19.

Goering, Sara. 2004. Facing the consequences of facial transplantation: Individual choices, social effect. *American Journal of Bioethics* 4: 37–39.

Goffman, Erving. 1955. On face-work: An analysis of ritual elements in social interaction. *Psychiatry: Journal for the study of interpersonal processes* 4: 7–13.

Goffman, Erving. 1963. *Stigma: Notes on the management of spoiled identity.* Englewood Cliffs, NJ: Prentice-Hall. Goffman, Erving. 1967. *Interaction ritual.* New York: Pantheon.

Gould, Steven Jay. 1981. *The mismeasure of man.* New York: W.W. Norton.

Grealy, Lucy. 1994. *Autobiography of a face*. New York: Houghton Mifflin.

Greco, Joann. 2012. The psychology of ruin porn. *Atlantic Monthly*, January 6. www.theatlanticcities.com/design/2012/01/psychology-ruin-porn/886/.

Gusfield, Joseph R. 1989. Constructing the ownership of social problems: Fun and profit in the welfare state. *Social Problems* 36: 431–41.

Haiken, Elizabeth. 2000. The making of the modern face. *Social Research*. www.newschool.edu/centers/socres/vol67/issue671.htm.

Halloran, Richard. 2006. U.S. Navy doctors deliver mercy at sea: Hospital ship's crew treats poor in Southeast Asia. *Washington Times*, July 31.

Hanlon, Michael. 2005. The surgery of science fiction. *Daily Mail*, December 1.

Haraway, Donna. 1988. Situated knowledges: The science question in feminism and the privilege of partial perspective. *Feminist Studies* 14: 575–99.

Haraway, Donna. 1991. *Simians, cyborgs and women: The reinvention of nature*. New York: Routledge.

Harding, Sandra. 1991. *Whose science? Whose knowledge?: Thinking from women's lives*. Ithaca, NY: Cornell University Press.

Harrison, Jack, Jaime Grant, and Jody L. Herman. 2012. A gender not listed here: Genderqueers, gender rebels, and otherwise in the national transgender discrimination survey. The Williams Institute. http://escholarship.org/uc/uclalaw_williams_rw.

Harry Benjamin International Gender Dysphoria Association (HBIGDA). 2001. *HBIGDA standards of care*. www.wpath.org/publications_standards.cfm.

Hartsock, Nancy. 1983. *Money, sex, and power: Toward a feminist historical materialism*. Boston: Northeastern University Press.

Heisler, Troy. Diane Vincent, Annie Bergeron. 2003. Evaluative metadiscursive comments and face-work in conversational discourse. *Journal of Pragmatics* 35: 1613–31.

Hewitt, Lyndi. 2011. Framing across differences, building solidarities: Lessons from women's rights activism in transnational spaces. *Interface* 3: 65–99.

Higgs, Dellareese M. 2008. *Behind the smile: Negotiating and transforming the tourism imposed identity of Bahamian women*. Unpublished dissertation. Bowling Green State University.

Hill-Collins, Patricia. 1990. *Black feminist thought: Knowledge, consciousness, and the politics of empowerment*. Boston: Unwin Hyman.

Hinchliffe, Mark. 2007. Kia's extreme makeover. *Courier Mail*, March 31.

Hine, Christine. 2007. Multi-sited ethnography as a middle range methodology for contemporary STS. *Science, Technology, and Human Values* 32: 652–71.

Hogle, Linda F. 1999. *Recovering the nation's body*. New Brunswick, NJ: Rutgers University Press.

Holmes, Su and Deborah Jermyn. 2004. *Understanding reality television*. New York: Routledge.

Holtgraves, Thomas. 1992. The linguistic realization of face management: Implications for language production and comprehension, person perception, and cross-cultural communication. *Social Psychology Quarterly* 55: 141–59.

Hornblum, Allen M. 1997. They were cheap and available: Prisoners as research subjects in twentieth century America. *BMJ: British Medical Journal* 315: 1437–41.

Hsu, Hsuan L., and Martha Lincoln. 2007. Biopower, bodies . . . the exhibition, and the spectacle of public health. *Discourse* 29: 15–34.

Huff, Richard M. 2006. *Reality television*. Westport, CT: Praeger.

Hughes, Ieuan A., Chris Houk, S. Faisal Ahmed, and Peter A. Lee. 2006. Consensus statement on management of intersex disorders. *Journal of Pediatric Urology* 2: 148–62.

Hughes, Michael. 1998. *The social consequences of facial disfigurement*. London: Ashgate.

Huxtable Richard and Julie Woodley. 2005. Gaining face or losing face? Framing the debate on face transplants. *Bioethics* 19: 505–22.

Incite! Women of Color Against Violence, ed. 2007. *The revolution will not be funded: Beyond the non-profit industrial complex*. Cambridge, MA: South End Press.

Ines, Maria Lobato, Walter José Koff, Carlo Manenti, Débora da Fonseca Seger, Jaquelinev Salvador, Maria da Graça Borges Fortes, Analídia Rodolpho Petry, Esalba Silveira, and Alexandre Annes Henriques. 2006. Follow-up of sex reassignment surgery in transsexuals: A Brazilian cohort. *Archives of Sexual Behavior* 35: 711–15.

Ingraham, Chrys. 1994. The heterosexual imaginary: Feminist sociology and theories of gender. *Sociological Theory* 12: 203–19.

Intersex Society of North America. 2006. Why is ISNA using "DSD"? www.isna.org/node/1066.

Irish Times. 2007. That certain smile. *Irish Times*, January 10.

James, Andrea. 2006. Letter to HBIGDA. www.tsroadmap.com/physical/face/ffs-hbigda2.pdf.

James, Caryn. 2002. It's all in the mix: A plastic surgery reality show. *New York Times*, December 11.

Jefferson, Margo. 1994. The scars of disease, external and internal. *New York Times*, September 28.

Kalish, Richard A. 1966. A continuum of subjectively perceived death. *The Gerontologist* 6: 73–76.

Karkazis, Katrina. 2008. *Fixing sex: Intersex, medical authority, and lived experience*. Durham, NC: Duke University Press.

Kaw, Eugenia 1998. Medicalization of racial features: Asian American women and cosmetic surgery. In *The politics of women's bodies: Sexuality, appearance, and behavior*, edited by Rose Weitz, 167–83. New York: Oxford University Press.

Kessler, Suzanne. 1998. *Lessons from the intersexed*. New Brunswick, NJ: Rutgers University Press.

Kessler, Suzzanne. 1990. The medical construction of gender: Case management of intersexed infants. *Signs* 16: 3–26.

Kessler, Suzanne J. and Wendy McKenna. 1978. *Gender: An ethnomethodological approach*. Chicago: University of Chicago Press.

Kemp, Theresa. 2004. *Future face: Image, identity, innovation*. London: Profile.

Kent, Gerry. 2000. Understanding the experiences of people with disfigurements: An integration of four models of social and psychological functioning. *Psychology, Health, & Medicine* 5: 117–29.

Kristeva, Julia. 1982. *Powers of horror: An essay on abjection*. New York: Columbia University Press.

Kuhse, Helga and Peter Singer, eds. 2006. *Bioethics: An anthology*. Malden, MA: Blackwell.

Kundera, Milan. 1984. *The unbearable lightness of being*. New York: Harper Perennial.

Kusa, Zuzana. 2005. Representations of virtues: Examples of presidential billboards. *Slovak Sociology Review* 4: 323–50.

Lacey, Gary, Vicki Peel, and Betty Weiler. 2012. Disseminating the voice of the other: A case study of philanthropic tourism. *Annals of Tourism Research* 39: 1199–220.

LaFerla, Ruth and Natasha Singer. 2005. The face of the future. *New York Times*, December 15.

Landsdown, Richard, Nichola Rumsey, Eileen Bradbury, Tony Carr, and James Partridge. 1997. *Visibly different: Coping with disfigurement*. London: Butterwordth-Heinemann.

Lane, Brad Houston and Jessica W. Giles. 2009. Being "made up": Semiotics, pedagogy, and identity in America's Next Top Model. In *Handbook on social change*, edited by Brooke H. Stroud and Scott E. Corbin, 221–34. Hauppaugge, NY: Nova Publishing.

Lane, Harlan. 1997. Constructions of deafness. In *The disability studies reader*, edited by Lennard J. Davis, 153–71. New York: Routledge.

Langlois, Judith H., Lisa Kalakanis, Adam J. Rubenstein, Andrea Larson, Monica Hallam, and Monica Smoot. 2000. Maxims or myths of beauty: A meta-analytic and theoretical review. *Psychological Bulletin* 126: 390–423.

Laqueur, Thomas Walter. 1990. *Making sex: Body and gender from the Greeks to Freud*. Cambridge, MA: Harvard University Press.

Latour, Bruno. 1987. *Science in action: How to follow scientists and engineers through society*. Cambridge, MA: Harvard University Press.

Latour, Bruno. 2004. How to talk about the body?: The normative dimension of science studies. *Body & Society* 10: 205–29.

Lawton, Julia. 2002. *The dying process: Patients' experiences of palliative care*. London: Routledge.

Lehmann-Haupt, Christopher. 2002. Lucy Grealy, 39, who wrote a memoir on a disfigurement. *New York Times*, December 21.

Levinas, Emmanuel. 1985. *Ethics and infinity: Conversations with Philippe Nemo*. Pittsburgh: Duquesne University Press.

Lewis, Jacqueline. 1998. Learning to strip: The socialization experiences of exotic dancers. *The Canadian Journal of Human Sexuality* 7: 51–66.

Link, Bruce G. and Jo C. Phelen. 2001. Conceptualizing stigma. *Annual Review of Sociology* 27: 363–85.

Lock, Margaret. 2001. *Twice dead: Organ transplantation and the reinvention of death*. Berkeley: University of California Press.

Longmore, Paul K. 1997. Conspicuous contribution and American cultural dilemmas: Telethon rituals of cleansing and renewal. In *The body and physical difference: Discourses of disability*, edited by David T. Mitchell and Sharon L. Snyder, 134–60. Ann Arbor: University of Michigan Press.

Look to the Stars. 2007. *Jessica Simpson*. www.looktothestars.org/celebrity/96-jessica-simpson.

Lorber, Judith. 1993. Believing is seeing: Biology as ideology. *Gender and Society* 7: 568–91.

Los Angeles Times. 2006. Smile spread around the wide world. April 23.

Luscombe, Richard. 2003. Silicone victims: A body to die for. *Observer Miami*, May 25.

Lyubomirsky, Sonja. 2008. *The how of happiness: A new approach to getting the life you want*. New York: Penguin.

Macartney, Jane. 2006. China performs face transplant. *The Times* [London], April 14.

MacCannell, Dean. 1989. Faking it: Comment on face-work in pornography. *American Journal of Semiotics* 6: 153–74.

Macgregor, Frances Cooke. 1953. *Facial deformities and plastic surgery*. Springfield, IL: Thomas.

Macgregor, Frances Cooke. 1974. *Transformation and identity: The face and plastic surgery*. New York: Quadrangle.

Macgregor, Frances Cooke. 1990. Facial disfigurement: Problems and management of social interaction and implications for mental health. *Aesthetic Plastic Surgery* 14: 249–57.

Manning, Phillip. 1992. *Erving Goffman and modern sociology*. Redwood City, CA: Stanford University Press.

Marcus, George. 1998. *Ethnography through thick and thin*. Princeton, NJ: Princeton University Press.

Marcus, Ruth. 2007. Mitt Romney's extreme makeover. *Washington Post*, February 21.

Martin, Emily. 1995. *Flexible bodies: The role of immunity in American culture from the days of Polio to the age of AIDS.* Boston: Beacon.

Martin, Emily. 1999. *The woman in the body: Cultural analysis of reproduction.* Boston: Beacon.

Martinez-Jimenez, Santiago, Jorge Carrillo, Aura L. Rivera and Santiago E. Rossi. 2006. Illicit cosmetic silicone injections carry lethal consequences. *Medical News Today*, December 1.

Maschke, Karen J. and Eric Trump. 2004. Facial transplantation research: A need for additional deliberation. *American Journal of Bioethics* 4: 33–35.

Mason, Michael. 2005. Face transplantation takes leave of science fiction. *New York Times*, July 27.

McGee, Micki. 2005. *Self help, inc.: Makeover culture in American life.* Oxford: Oxford University Press.

McLaughlin, Sabrina. 2003. Face to face. *Current Science.* September 12.

McQueen, K. A. Kelly, Frederick M. Burkle, Eaman T. Al-Gobory, and Christopher C. Anderson. 2007. Maintaining baseline, corrective surgical care during asymmetrical warfare: A case study of a humanitarian mission in the safe zone of a neighboring country. *Prehospital and Disaster Medicine* 22: 3–7.

Mead, George Herbert. 1934. *Mind, self, and society.* Chicago: University of Chicago Press.

Merkin, Rebecca S. 2006a. Power distance and facework strategies. *Journal of Intercultural Communication Research* 35: 139–60.

Merkin, Rebecca S. 2006b. Uncertainty avoidance and facework: A test of the Hofstede model. *International Journal of Intercultural Relations* 30: 213–28.

Miles, Steven H. 2004. Medical ethicists, human curiosities, and the new media midway. *American Journal of Bioethics* 4: 39–43.

Mojtabai, A.G. 1994. I was too ugly to go to school. *New York Times*, September 24.

Montgomery, Robert L. 1999. *Introduction to the sociology of missions.* Westport, CT: Praeger.

Morreim, Haavi. 2004. About face: Downplaying the role of the press in facial transplantation research. *American Journal of Bioethics* 4: 27–29.

Morrison, Daniel. 2013. *Social worlds and narrative analysis of patient experiences with brain implant technologies.* Unpublished dissertation. Vanderbilt University.

Morrison, Daniel R. and Monica J. Casper. 2012. Intersections of disability studies and critical trauma studies: A provocation. *Disability Studies Quarterly* 32. http://dsq-sds.org/index.

Murray, Laura Rena. 2011. The high price of looking like a woman. *New York Times*, August 11.

Myers, Greg. 2003. Risk and face: A review of the six studies. *Health, Risk, & Society.* 5: 215–20.

National Public Radio. 2012. Documentary follows Pakistan's acid attack victims. www.npr.org/2012/02/21/147180165/documentary-follows-pakistans-acid-attack-victims.

Neill, Steven. 1966. *Colonialism and Christian missions.* New York: McGraw-Hill.

Nelson, Steven. 2013. Parents of intersex child sue over "unnecessary" surgery. *U.S. News & World Report*, May 14.

New York Times. 2002. Frances Cooke Macgregor. *New York Times*, May 12.

Oldenburg, Ann. 2003. "Makeover" is making waves. *USA Today*, May 13.

On the Media. 2012. Tweeting graphic videos from Syria. www.onthemedia.org/2012/feb/10/tweeting-graphic-videos-syria/.

Opala, Joseph and Francois Boillot. 1996. Leprosy among the Limba: Illness and healing in the context of world view. *Social Science and Medicine* 42: 3–19.

Operation Smile. 2006. Operation Smile int'l youth ambassador Jessica Simpson, Operation Smile CEO and founder Dr. Bill Magee Jr. and Rep. Trent Franks (R-AZ) to meet with members of Congress. www.operationsmile.org/docs/pr20060316.pdf.

Operation Smile. 2007a. Our history. www.operationsmile.org/aboutus/history/.

Operation Smile. 2007b. 2006 annual report. www.operationsmile.org/aboutus/history/.

Operation Smile. 2010. 2010 annual impact report. www.operationsmile.org/news_events/publications/2010-annual-report.html.

Operation Smile. 2013. Operation Smile FAQ. www.operationsmile.org/faq/.

Osterweil, Neil. 2006. Face transplant recipient's habit could jeopardize recovery. *MedPage Today*, January 19.

Oudshoorn, Nelly. 1994. *Beyond the natural body: An archaeology of sex hormones.* Thousand Oaks, CA: Sage.

Ousterhout, Douglas K. 1987. Feminization of the forehead: Contour changing to improve female aesthetics. *Plastic and Reconstructive Surgery* 79: 701–11.

Ousterhout, Douglas K. 1994. Feminization of the transsexual. Self-published pamphlet.

Ousterhout, Douglas K. 2011. Dr. Paul Tessier and facial skeletal masculinization. *Annals of Plastic Surgery* 67: S10–S15.

Page, Robert M. 1984. *Stigma.* London: Routledge.

Palmer, Gareth. 2004. "The new you": Class and transformation in lifestyle television. In *Understanding Reality Television*, edited by Sue Holmes and Deborah Jermyn, 173–90. New York: Routledge.

Partridge, James. 1990. *Changing faces: The challenge of facial disfigurement.* London: Penguin Group.

Patchett, Ann. 2004. *Truth and beauty: A friendship.* New York: Harper Collins.

Peiss, Kathy. 2011. *Hope in a jar: The making of America's beauty culture.* Philadelphia: University of Pennsylvania Press.

Peterson, Maxine E. and Robert Dickey. 1995 Surgical sex reassignment: A comparative Survey of International Centers. *Archives of Sexual Behavior* 24: 135–56.

Petit, Francois, Antoine Paraskevas, and Laurent Lantieri. 2004. A surgeon's perspective on the ethics of face transplantation. *American Journal of Bioethics* 4: 14–16.

Petrozzello, Donna. 2002. Reality TV is getting a face lift with ABC's "Extreme Makeover." *New York Daily News*, August 12.

Phelan, Jo C., Bruce G. Link, Ann Stueve, Bernice A. Pescosolido. 2000. Public conceptions of mental illness in 1950 and 1996: What is mental illness and is it to be feared? *Journal of Health and Social Behavior* 41: 188–207.

Pitts-Taylor, Victoria. 2007. *Surgery junkies: Wellness and pathology in cosmetic culture.* New Brunswick, NJ: Rutgers University Press.

Powell, Tia. 2006. Face transplant: Real and imagined ethical challenges. *Journal of Law, Medicine, and Ethics.* Spring: 111–15.

Prior, Lindsey. 1997. Following Foucault's footsteps: Text and context in qualitative research. In *Qualitative research: Theory, method, and practice*, edited by David Silverman, 63–79. Thousand Oaks, CA: Sage.

Product Red. 2007. Product (red) manifesto. www.joinred.com/manifesto/.

Quill, Timothy E. 2005. Terri Shiavo: A tragedy compounded. *New England Journal of Medicine* 352: 1630–33.

Rapp, Rayna. 1999. *Testing women, testing the fetus: The social impact of amniocentesis in everyday life.* London: Routledge.

Rathje, William L. and Cullen Murphy. 1993. *Rubbish: The archaeology of garbage.* New York: Perennial.

Ravard, Jean-Francois and Henri-Jacques Stiker. 2001. Inclusion/exclusion: An analysis of historical and cultural meanings. In *Handbook of Disability Studies*, edited by Gary L. Albrecht,
Katherine D. Seelman, and Michael Bury, 490–514. Thousand Oaks, CA: Sage.

Raymond, Janice. 1979. *The transsexual empire*. New York: Columbia University Press.

RCS Working Party. 2003. *Facial transplantation: Working party report*. Royal College of Surgeons.
www.rcseng.ac.uk/rcseng/content/publications/docs/facial_transplantation.html.

Robertson, John A. 2004. Face transplants: Enriching the debate. *American Journal of Bioethics* 4:
32–33.

Rosaldo, Renato. 1989. *Truth and culture: The remaking of social analysis*. Boston: Beacon.

Rose, Nickolas 2007. *The politics of life itself*. Princeton, NJ: Princeton University Press.

Rosengarten, Marsha. 2005. The measure of HIV as a matter of bioethics. In *Ethics of the Body*,
edited by Margrit Shildrick and Roxanne Mykitiuk, 71–90. Cambridge, MA: MIT Press.

Roth, Alex. 2005. Silicone endangers transgender group. *Union Tribune*, July 3.

Roush, Karen, Ann Kurth, M. Katherine Hutchinson, and Nancy Van Devanter. 2012. Obstetric
fistula: What about gender power?. *Health Care for Women International* 33: 787–98.

Rumsey, Nicola. 2004. Psychological aspects of face transplantation: Read the small print carefully. *American Journal of Bioethics* 4: 22–25.

Rumsey, Nichola and Diana Harcourt. 2004. Body image and disfigurement: Issues and interventions. *Body Image* 1: 83–97.

Russell, James A. 1994. Is there universal recognition of emotion from facial expression? A review
of the cross cultural studies. *Psychological Bulletin* 115: 102–41.

Schilt, Kristen. 2011. *Just one of the guys? Transgender men and the persistence of gender inequality*.
Chicago: University of Chicago Press.

Schippers, Mimi. 2007. Recovering the feminine other: Masculinity, femininity, and gender hegemony. *Theory and Society* 36: 85–102.

Schweik, Susan M. 2009. *The ugly laws: Disability in public*. New York: NYU Press.

Serano, Julia. 2007. Whipping girl: A transsexual woman on sexism and the scapegoating of femininity. Berkeley, CA: Seal Press.

Shabot, Sara Cohen. 2006. Grotesque bodies: A response to disembodied cyborgs. *Journal of
Gender Studies* 15: 223–35.

Shahid, Aliyah. 2011. Roger Ebert before and after. *Daily News*. www.nydailynews.com/entertain-
ment/roger-ebert-famed-film-critic-debuts-face-prosthetic-masking-cancer-ravaged-jaw-
article-1.152787.

Shakespeare, Tom, ed. 1998. *The disability reader: Social science perspectives*. London: Cassell.

Shapiro, Eve. 2010. *Gender xircuits: Bodies and identities in a technological age*. New York:
Routledge.

Sharp, Lesley A. 2006. *Strange harvest: Organ transplants, denatured bodies, and the transformed
self*. Berkeley: University of California Press.

Shaw, Gary, C. R. Wasserman, C. D. O'Malley, M. M. Tolarova, and E. J. Lammer. 1995. Risks of
orofacial clefts in children born to women using multivitamins containing folic acid pericon-
ceptionally. *The Lancet* 346: 393–96.

Sheldon K. and L. Caldwell. 1994. Urinary incontinence in women: Implications for therapeutic
recreation. *Therapeutic Recreation Journal* 28: 203–12.

Shildrick, Margrit. 1997. *Leaky bodies and boundaries: Feminism, postmodernism, and (bio)ethics*.
London: Routledge.

Shildrick, Margrit. 2002. *Embodying the monster: Encounters with the vulnerable self.* Thousand Oaks, CA: Sage.

Shildrick, Margrit. 2005. Beyond the body of bioethics: Challenging the conventions. In *Ethics of the body: Postconventional challenges*, edited by Margrit Shildrick and Roxanne Mykitiuk, 1–28. Cambridge: MIT Press.

Shilling, Chris. 2003. *The body and social theory.* Thousand Oaks, CA: Sage.

Shilling, Chris. 2004. Physical capital and situated action: A new direction for corporeal sociology. *British Journal of Sociology of Education* 25: 473–87.

Shilling, Chris. 2007. *Embodying sociology: Retrospect, progress and prospects.* Boston: Blackwell.

Shim, Janet. 2010. The stratified biomedicalization of heart disease: Expert and lay perspectives on racial and class inequality. In *Biomedicalization: Technoscience, health, and illness in the US*, edited by Adele E. Clarke, Laura Mamo, Jennifer Ruth Fosket, Jennifer R. Fishman, and Janet K. Shim, 218–41. Durham, NC: Duke University Press.

Siebers, Tobin. 2006. Disability in theory: From social constructionism to the new realism of the body. In *The Disability studies reader* 2nd ed., edited by Lennard J. Davis, 173–83. New York: Routledge.

Siebers, Tobin. 2010. *Disability aesthetics.* Ann Arbor: University of Michigan Press.

Siemionow, Maria. 2009. *Face to face: My quest to perform the first full face transplant.*   New York: Kaplan.

Simmons, William Paul and Monica J. Casper. 2012. Culpability, social triage, and structural violence in the aftermath of Katrina. *Perspectives on Politics* 10: 675–86.

Smiley, David. 2009. Transgender "pumping party" felon Donnie Hendrix back in a sting. *Miami Herald.* http://miamiherald.typepad.com/gaysouthflorida/2009/07/pumping-party-felon back-in-a-silicone-sting.html.

Smith, Craig. 1999. *Goffman and social organizations: Studies in a sociological legacy.* London: Routledge.

Smith, Dorothy. 1989. *The everyday world as problematic: A feminist sociology.* Evanston, IL: Northwestern University Press.

Spelman, Elizabeth V. 2002. *Repair: The impulse to restore in a fragile world.* Boston: Beacon.

Stevenage, Sarah V. and Yolanda McKay 1999. Model applicants: The effect of facial appearance on recruitment decisions. *British Journal of Psychology* 90: 221–34.

Stevens, Maurice. 2009. From the past imperfect: Toward a critical trauma theory. *Letters.* www.vanderbilt.edu/rpw_center/Letters/ls09a.htm.

Strong, Carson. 2004. Should we be putting a good face on facial transplantation? *American Journal of Bioethics* 4: 13–14.

Sudnow, David. 1967. *Passing on: The social organization of dying.* Englewood Cliffs, NJ: Prentice-Hall.

Sullivan, Deborah A. 2004. *Cosmetic surgery: The cutting edge of medicine.* New Brunswick, NJ: Rutgers University Press.

Sweeting, Helen and Mary Gilhooly. 1991. Doctor, am I dead? A review of social death in modern societies. *OMEGA—Journal of Death and Dying* 24: 251–69.

Sweeting, Helen and Mary Gilhooly. 1997. Dementia and the phenomenon of social death. *Sociology of Health & Illness* 19: 93–117.

Synott, Anthony. 1989. Truth and goodness, mirrors and masks—part I. A sociology of beauty and the face. *The British Journal of Sociology* 40: 607–36.

Synott, Anthony. 1990. Truth and goodness, mirrors and masks—part II. A sociology of beauty and the face. *The British Journal of Sociology* 41: 55–76.

Synott, Anthony. 2008. Ugliness: visibility and the invisible prejudice. *Glimpses* 1.1: 5–8.

Tait, Sue. 2007. Television and the domestication of cosmetic surgery. *Feminist Media Studies* 7: 119–35.

Talley, Heather Laine. 2011. Not a pretty girl: Facial feminization and the theory of facial sex difference. In *Gendering difference: Studies in contemporary science and sedicine*, edited by Jill Fischer, 189–204. New Brunswick, NJ: Rutgers University Press.

Talley, Heather Laine. 2012. Getting work done: Cosmetic surgery as commodity, as constraint, as choice. In *Routledge international handbook of the body*, edited by Bryan Turner, 335–46. New York: Routledge.

Talley, Heather Laine and Monica J. Casper. 2010. Oprah goes to Africa: Philanthropic consumption and political (dis)engagement. In *Stories of O*, edited by Kimberly Springer and Trystan Cotton, 99–114. Oxford: The University of Mississippi Press.

Talley, Heather Laine and Monica J. Casper. 2012. Intersex and aging: A (cautionary) research agenda. In *Gay, lesbian, bisexual, and transgender aging: Challenges in research, practice, and policy*, edited by Tarynn M. Witten and A. Evan Eyler, 270–89. Baltimore, MD: Johns Hopkins University Press.

Tarchetti, Iginio Ugo. 1869. *Fosca*. Milan: Ugo Mursia Editore, cited in Umberto Eco, ed. 2007. *On ugliness*. New York: Rizzoli..

Taussig, Michael. 2012. *Beauty and the beast*. Chicago: University of Chicago Press.

Telegraph, The. 2012. Too graphic for the Internet: Shocking footage of children caught up in Syria violence. *The Telegraph*, February 6. www.telegraph.co.uk/news/worldnews/middleeast/syria/9063761/Syria-Twitter-debate-on-graphic-footage-of-children-caught-up-in-violence.html.

Templeton, Sarah Kate. 2007. Fury at TV face surgery show. *Sunday Times*, June 3.

Thomas, Abraham, Vijay Obed, Anil Muraka, Gopal Malhotra. 1998. Total face and scalp replantation: Case report. *Plastic and Reconstructive Surgery* 102: 2085–87.

Thompson, Robert. 2003. Finding happiness between commercials. *Chronicle of Higher Education*, October 17.

Timmermans, Stefan. 1998. Social death as self-fulfilling prophecy: Duavid Sudnow's "passing on" revisited. *Sociological Quarterly* 39: 453–72.

Timmermans, Stefan. 1999. When death isn't dead: Implicit social rationing during resuscitative efforts. *Sociological Inquiry* 69: 51–75.

Trevino, A. Javier. 2003. *Goffman's legacy*. Lanham, MD: Rowman & Littlefield.

Turner, Bryan S. 1996. *The body and society: Explorations in social theory*. Thousand Oaks, CA: Sage.

Turner, Bryan S. 2001. Disability and the sociology of the body. In *Handbook of disability studies*, edited by Gary L. Albrecht, Katherine D. Seelman, and Michael Bury, 252–66. Thousand Oaks, CA: Sage.

UN Refugee Agency. 2013. *Angelina Jolie*. www.unhcr.org/pages/49c3646c56.html.

Wald, Rebecca L. and John F. Knutson. 2000. Childhood disciplinary experiences reported by adults with crano-facial anamolies. *Child Abuse & Neglect* 24: 1623–27.

Wallusis, Jerald. 1998. *The new insecurity: The end of the standard job and family*. Albany: Statue University of New York Press.

Walsgrove, Derek. 1987. Policing yourself: Social closure and the internalization of stigma. In *The manufacture of disadvantage: Stigma and social closure*, edited by Gloria Lee and Ray Loveridge, 45–57. Philadelphia: Open University Press.

Waskul, Dennis D. and Phillip Vannini. 2006. Introduction: The body in symbolic interaction. In *Body/embodiment: Symbolic interaction and the sociology of the body*, edited by Dennis Waskul and Phillip Vannini, 1-18. Burlington, VT: Ashgate.

Wasserman, Gail A. and Rhianon Allen. 1985. Maternal withdrawal from handicapped toddlers. *Journal of Child Psychology & Psychiatry & Allied Disciplines* 26: 381–87.

Watts, Amber. 2009. Melancholy, merit, and merchandise: The postwar audience participation show. In *Reality TV: Remaking television culture*, 2nd ed., edited by Susan Murray and Laurie Ouellette, 301–20. New York: NYU Press.

Weber, Brenda. 2005. Beauty, desire, and anxiety: The economy of sameness in ABC's *Extreme Makeover. Genders.* www.genders.org/g41/g41_weber.html.

Weber, Max. 1978. *Economy and society.* Berkeley: University of California Press.

Wentling, Tre, Elroi Windsor, Kristen Schilt, and Betsy Lucal. 2008. Teaching transgender. *Teaching Sociology* 36: 49–57.

West, Candace. 1996. Goffman in feminist perspective. *Sociological Perspectives* 39: 353–69.

West, Candace and Don H. Zimmerman. 1987. Doing gender. *Gender and Society* 1:125–51.

Whitelaw, Andrew. 1986. Death as an option in neonatal intensive care. *The Lancet* 328:328–31.

Wiggins, Osborne P., John H. Barker, Serge Martinez, Marieke Vossen, Claudio Maldonado, Frederico V. Grossi, Cedric G. Francois, Michael Cunningham, Gustavo Perez-Abadia, Moshe Kon, and Joseph C. Banis. 2004. On the ethics of facial transplantation research. *American Journal of Bioethics* 4: 1–12.

Windsor, Elroi J. 2011. *Regulating healthy gender: Surgical body modification among transgender and cisgender consumers.* Unpublished dissertation. Georgia State University.

Wolff, Kurt H. 1959. *Georg Simmel, 1858–1918: A collection of essays, with translations and a bibliography.* Columbus: Ohio State University Press.

World Health Organization (WHO). 2001. *Global registry and database on craniofacial anomalies.* www.who.int/genomics/anomalies/en/CFA-RegistryMeeting-2001.pdf.

World Health Organization. 2006. *Facts about health in the African region of WHO.* www.who.int/mediacentre/factsheets/fs314/en/index.html.

World Professional Association for Transgender Health (WPATH). 2011. Standards of care (SOC) for the health of transsexual, transgender, and gender nonconforming people, 7th version. Minneapolis, MN: World Professional Association for Transgender Health.

Wyllie, Robert. W. 1970. Divination and face work. *British Journal of Sociology* 21: 52–62.

Zdichavsky, Marty, Jon W. Jones, E. Tuncay Ustuner, Xiaoping Ren, Jean Edelstein, Claudio Maldonado, Warren Breidenbach, Scott A. Gruber, Mukunda Ray and John H. Barker. 1999. Scoring of skin rejection in a swine composite tissue allograft model. *Journal of Surgical Research* 85: 1–8.

Zia, Taiba. 2013. Acid violence in pakistan. *UCLA Center for the Study of Women.* http://escholarship.org/uc/item/65v958z1.

Zussman, Robert. 1992. *Intensive care: Medical ethics and the medical profession.* Chicago: University of Chicago Press.

ABOUT THE AUTHOR

Heather Laine Talley is Assistant Professor of Sociology at Western Carolina University. More about her writing and work can be found at www.heatherlainetalley.com.